Rebel Yell 2
*More Stories of Contemporary
Southern Gay Men*

HARRINGTON PARK PRESS
Southern Tier Editions
Gay Men's Fiction
Jay Quinn, Executive Editor

Love, the Magician by Brian Bouldrey

Distortion by Stephen Beachy

The City Kid by Paul Reidinger

Rebel Yell: Stories by Contemporary Southern Gay Authors edited by Jay Quinn

Metes and Bounds by Jay Quinn

The Limits of Pleasure by Daniel M. Jaffe

The Big Book of Misunderstanding by Jim Gladstone

This Thing Called Courage: South Boston Stories by J. G. Hayes

Rebel Yell 2: More Stories of Contemporary Southern Gay Men edited by Jay Quinn

Rebel Yell 2
More Stories of Contemporary Southern Gay Men

Jay Quinn
Editor

Southern Tier Editions
Harrington Park Press®
An Imprint of The Haworth Press, Inc.
New York • London • Oxford

Published by

Southern Tier Editions, Harrington Park Press®, an imprint of The Haworth Press, Inc., 10 Alice Street, Binghamton, NY 13904-1580.

PUBLISHER'S NOTE
This is a work of fiction. Names, characters, places, and incidents either are the products of the author's imagination or are used fictitiously, and any resemblance to actual persons, living or dead, business establishments, events, or locales is entirely coincidental.

Cover design by Marylouise E. Doyle.

Library of Congress Cataloging-in-Publication Data

Rebel yell 2 : more stories of contemporary southern gay men / edited by Jay Quinn.
    p. cm.
    ISBN 1-56023-158-0 (hard) — ISBN 1-56023-159-9 (soft)
    1. Gay men's writings, American. 2. Southern States—Social life and customs—Fiction. 3. Short stories, American—Southern States. 4. American fiction—Southern States. 5. American fiction—20th century. 6. Gay men—Fiction. I. Title: Rebel yell two. II. Quinn, Jay.

PS647.G39 R434 2002
813'.0108920642'097509045—dc21
                                                                                        2002024221

CONTENTS

Preface

Southerners have been criticized for their cultural reluctance to pragmatically dismiss the past to adapt the great American cult of the now and the new. That criticism has inspired pithy responses from Southern writers well before me. However, my response to that specific criticism by non-Southerners is my contention that who we were, who we are, and what we're going to be are inextricably the same. I prefer to quote New Orleans' Anne Rice who wrote, "We don't really change; we just become more of what we are."

I find proof of this nearly every day. I get home and *immediately take off my shoes and socks* exactly as I was trained to do at six years old. I let the dogs out because *it's my responsibility*. I take off my watch, my shirt, then my pants *so I can't mess them up*. I empty my pants' pockets of change, keys, and wallet and *put them where I can find them in the morning*. Forty-three years old and I still hear and keep the routine drilled into me by a series of women's authoritative voices: Grandmama's, Mama's, Dorothy's, and Johncie's.

I put on my after-work clothes that I can *mess up*. Winter times, it's some shorts and a T-shirt. Summer times, I wear my boxers or get in a bathing suit. Molted out of the man's work-a-day uniform, I'm like me, when I was a boy, only now and not so long ago.

I grab some dog cookies and *go outside*. I trained my dogs on my own. They eagerly trot up and sit, tails going like forty miles a minute before I give them their cookies. Watching these big red dogs chew greedily and look up at me gratefully makes me think of Tank. He was a black Lab I had when I lived up on the Outer Banks. He didn't get his dog cookie until after our dusk walk on the beach. Now, these twin dogs turn their long Dobie heads in an eerie synchrony then gallop off in unison to see what's up.

Summer times, I sit on the edge of the pool and stare up at the softening sky. Winter times, I put my feet up on the table and tilt back to regard the same scene, softened further by the middle-aged macular degeneration that handsomely blurs everything in the impressionistic pinkish light of dusk. I remember sharper sunsets seen from a kitchen window in Raleigh and from the deck of my house in Avalon Beach.

I remember a long gone man that I loved coming home bronzed, salty, and hardened by a day banging nails under a relentless sun. I remember my daddy coming home from work, smelling like his office, air-conditioning, cigarette smoke, and the lingering scent of Old Spice.

Summer or winter, spring or fall, this is my private time of day. Soon, my partner will be home, smelling like his office, air-conditioning, cigarette smoke, and the lingering scent of Cool Water. But now, I can relax into the aimlessness of thought that is really a sort of net mending. In this *zazen* state, I'm knitting together my day and the chain of days from boy to man that makes me singular in my ordinariness.

My grandmama used to say you can't get beyond your raising. Taken in tandem consideration, Anne Rice's concept and my grandmama's admonition frame the structure of this anthology. Who we were as young'uns is part and parcel of who we are as men. Childhood's ass-whippings, hugs, and late evening, summertime drives to Dairy Queen, with all the car windows rolled down and cicadas singing over harshly taught rules of identity *and knowing your place* make a true Southern man.

Regardless of geographic happenstance, what man, gay or straight, doesn't recall in achingly clear detail his first realization of selfhood in the sweaty tumble of boys being boys, or the sweaty tumble out of sticky dreams, hungry for that first touch of another's beckoning skin?

Old dogs, old hurts, old cars, old sneakers and bathing suits and bits of string and condoms and pissing matches and single silent stars return to benchmark a man's every experience through the boy's wide wondering eyes. Our memories that guide us now are the idiosyncratic collection of things found in the jeans pockets of a seven-year-old, or a twelve-year-old's scabbed-over grudges, or the hard demands in a seventeen-year-old's shorts.

Rebel Yell 2 is a collection of stories that plot the shifting sequence of events, significant to boy and man. In this framework, built here with a telling twang that is specifically male, Southern, and gay, you might just find an answer to why Southerners reference their histories incessantly, especially their personal ones. Eudora Welty put it very well when she observed, "The events in our lives happen in a sequence in time, but in their significance to ourselves they find their own order . . ."

Jay Quinn

Acknowledgments

I would like to thank everyone at The Haworth Press without whose faith and support this companion volume to *Rebel Yell* could not have come about.

Also, I must thank Anita Landis, Greg Herren, Paul Willis, David Rosen, Richard Labonte, Jim Grimsley, Paul Russell, and Joe Hayes. Your good words and company are a gift.

And to my Jeff and the big red dogs running all over the house, this one's for you.

1   Miles Away

Martin Wilson

Harvey was the one who told Michael about the public bathrooms at the mall. He and Harvey were not friends, nor did they even speak very much. But Harvey—who Michael's friends imitated by talking with exaggerated lisps or in a high-pitched voices and by limping their wrists, and who last year had tried, unsuccessfully, to start a one-member gay and lesbian student group at school—would certainly be the authority on things Michael wanted to know about. It was true that Harvey was a bit flamboyant: He wore pastel shirts and crisp black jeans, his hair was dyed a completely and proudly artificial magenta, and a he wore a tiny rainbow earring in his left ear. But Michael's friends' sissyish imitations of Harvey weren't exactly accurate, because Harvey's voice was not high nor the least bit feminine, but instead hoarse and scratchy, and his demeanor exhibited defensive toughness, meanness even, not sugary sweet girlishness or giddiness. He seemed like a boy who knew things.

So on a soggy and gray Thursday morning—early, before most of the other students would arrive—Michael found himself with Harvey in the school parking lot. The day before at his locker, Michael had asked Harvey to meet him there, and Harvey had agreed, provided that Michael buy him a pack of cigarettes, which he had done the night before at the Circle K near his parents' house. Now Harvey sat on the hood of Michael's car, smoking one of these cigarettes, looking ever so composed. Michael stood facing him uneasily, with his hands in his pockets, his sneakers shifting about on the cracked asphalt. He kept looking around, hoping no one would see the two of them. Michael realized they should have met somewhere more secluded, even off school grounds, but it was too late for that.

"That's where a lot of guys go, to the mall. If that's what you're looking for," Harvey said. Michael didn't like the smug way Harvey stared at him, especially with the cigarette dangling between his thin lips.

"Well," Michael said. "I'm not really looking—"

"Listen, I don't care one way or the other. I'm just saying—that's where you go."

"In the bathrooms, I mean, do you, they . . . do it there?" Michael asked.

Harvey let out a sharp and quick laugh and said, "Yeah, usually. There are other ways to meet men. But the mall is the best place."

"I don't know. It sounds weird," Michael said. He saw some cars pulling in the lot and was eager to get Harvey off his car and into the school. Being seen with "Fagboy" would conjure all kinds of questions Michael didn't want to have to answer.

"No one's holding a gun to your head. Do it or don't." With that, Harvey dropped his cigarette on the ground, hopped off the car, and moved close to Michael, *too* close. "It's your life," he said. Michael backed away, smelling the stench of smoke mixed with cherry cough drops on Harvey's breath.

"Yeah, well thanks for the info."

Harvey nodded his head at Michael and gave him another smirk. "I must admit, I'm surprised. I thought I could pick them out of a crowd. But you? I'd have never guessed."

"Guessed what?"

"Oh, come off it. I'll keep your secret, don't worry."

"What secret?" he said, knowing he sounded ridiculous and stupid, since he'd just asked Harvey, point blank, about where he could find men.

"Okay, whatever," Harvey said, smirking again. "All I can say is, have fun." And then he walked away with his confident and defiant strut, probably giddy with this newfound knowledge.

Michael got back in his car and felt his heart pounding, and by the time it slowed, his friend Tad had driven up, gotten out of his Jeep, and knocked on Michael's window. Michael got out and joined Tad, who was just then peeling and eating a banana.

"You look kind of spaced out," Tad said.

"I'm fine. Just trying to wake up." He tried not to look as Tad stuffed the banana in his mouth. It conjured up too much, namely cock sucking. He'd seen this movie where the two teenage girls practice blow jobs on bananas, so he'd tried that too, sitting in his room sucking on one till he gagged so much that tears tore down his face as if he were really crying.

"I went over to Tina's last night," Tad said. Tina was his girlfriend. Michael knew for a fact she sucked Tad's dick every weekend—Tad had told him. Michael's own girlfriend, Kelly, who had not yet sucked his own dick, was friends with Tina, and sometimes everything felt claustrophobic, the four of them always hanging out together, like some small club where there were no secrets allowed, nor any new members.

"She wants us all to go to the beach together for Spring Break, stay at her aunt's condo," Tad continued.

"That sounds cool," Michael said, trying to feign interest.

"Yeah, we'd each have our own bedrooms." Tad winked and smiled.

"Yeah, cool."

"Michael?"

"Huh?"

"I swear, you're spaced out this morning. You sure you're all right?"

"Oh, yeah. Sorry. Listen, I should get going, go to my locker. I'll see you at lunch, okay?" And without waiting for a response, Michael rushed inside and headed straight for his locker. Once there, fiddling with his lock, he saw Harvey down the hall, staring at him and leaning against a locker, wearing a look of knowingness. Michael finally got his lock to click open and turned to look at the books inside. He pretended to rummage around for something, anything to avoid having to look at Harvey. When he finally shut his locker and stared in Harvey's direction, Harvey was gone. The relief Michael felt was a quick comfort, because he knew the nerves and panic would come back eventually. He also knew that he'd started something today he couldn't stop.

Later that afternoon after school, Michael went to the mall with Kelly because she said she had some shopping to do. "You really want to go with me?" she asked in the car, surprised because Michael usually hated these excursions.

"Sure," he said.

"Fine with me," she said, kissing him quickly on the lips before fastening her seat belt. Kelly, tall and brunette, intimidated Michael's friends—in fact, she scared many of the boys at his school. It was not because she was so pretty, which she was in an earthy and vibrant way (as opposed to fragile or manufactured beauty), but because she was always willing to say anything, especially things most people would keep inside. She'd tell her friends that their hair looked bad, or that their shirts were the wrong color, or that their boyfriends were assholes and not worthy—things they didn't always want to hear, even if they were truths. In addition to this brutal and blunt honesty, she rarely smiled. When she did smile, it didn't look quite right; her smiles looked more like forced face contortions rather than natural expressions of pleasure. Some might have called her a bitch, but not to her face. Because of all this, she'd never been the most popular girl with the boys, but among the girls she was meekly respected and never found herself messed with. How had Michael dealt with her for the past year? Very delicately, and expertly. She needed a boy to boss, a boy who mostly listened. He needed a girl to keep any questions at bay. Until now, the arrangement—and Kelly didn't know it was an arrangement—had gone smoothly.

At the mall, they walked through the wide galleries hand in hand. Michael hated this form of advertisement. Michael saw it as Kelly's way of expressing her ownership of him. She had given him a beeper for his sixteenth birthday, almost a year earlier, and he clipped it to his back pocket whenever he went out on his errands. His friends called him pussy-whipped, but never around Kelly. When his mother saw the beeper, she worried that he was selling crack cocaine on the west side of town. When he voiced complaints to Kelly about wearing it, she asked him, "What if I have an emergency? What if I beeped you and you didn't have it on? This could be life and death."

"Come with me to Parisians," she said. "I need to get some new mascara."

"You don't wear mascara, do you?"

"Of course I do. I just don't wear too much of it like Tina does."

"Why don't I walk around a little while you get your makeup?"

"You don't want to go with me." It was a statement, not a question.

"Do I have to?"

"Yes."

Michael usually caved in to her every whim, because it was easier than arguing. But today he grew a spine. "No, I'll just walk around the mall while you get your makeup. I want to go a few places anyway."

"Well, you're the one who wanted to come with me in the first place, but fine, do what you want," she said. Then she withdrew her hand from his and walked away, leaving Michael standing under a skylight. She walked fast, as she always did when she was angry.

The mall had been renovated and added on to recently, and lately it was always crowded. Many of the new stores were not open yet, their entrances boarded up with painted murals announcing the opening dates. Everything—the floors, the walls, the columns—was done up in white and forest-green marble, bathed in the light that seeped in from the new glass roof. Michael sat on an iron bench next to some decorative planters and watched the people walk by him carrying their noisy bags. Occasionally he caught snippets of their conversation and wished he hadn't, because these people were either too happy or in grumpy, tired moods. When he saw men walk by, he would scrutinize their faces, and if they happened to look his way, he would search their eyes for something, some signal. He didn't know what he was looking for, and he wasn't sure he would know it if he saw it.

He bought a scoop of butterscotch ice cream and ate it as he walked around, looking in store after store. Then he realized that he hadn't told Kelly when he would meet up with her. Well, she could always beep him. He fingered the beeper, took it off and jiggled it in his hands like a toy, waiting for it to go off.

He didn't dare go to the bathrooms, not today. Not with Kelly around—though the thought had crossed his mind. Instead, he lurked in the area, peeping in the pet store and checking out the stereos in Radio Shack, both stores that were across from the mall bathrooms. To get to the actual bathrooms, you had to go through some heavy gray doors and then down a long white hallway; it was as if they were hidden rooms that only those in the know could find. In the stores, Michael didn't focus much on the merchandise, but instead on the people who walked by on their way to the bathrooms.

Michael had been in those bathrooms once, many years back, before all the mall renovations. He'd vomited in there because he'd eaten three corn dogs from the Saucy Dog in one rapid sitting. He'd bent over one of the toilets that was streaked with loose hairs and

caked with urine and puked, and afterward he washed his face in the
sink. Back then he had no idea about the bathroom's reputation. And
still, part of him wondered if Harvey had been telling the truth. He
wondered if anything ever really happened there. How could it? It all
seemed so lurid and dangerous, almost too exciting and forbidden for
this cheesy mall, this unexciting town.

The beeper went off, jolting him. He switched it off with annoy-
ance and made his way to Parisians, where he found Kelly, her hands
full of small bags, her face wearing a scowl. Without saying much, he
drove Kelly home, to a neighborhood not far from his own, over the
river and down a busy road that was shaded on each side by pine trees
invaded by kudzu. Kelly was like kudzu, he thought—creeping all
over him, suffocating him, hiding whoever he really was.

"Do you want to have dinner with us?" Kelly asked when he pulled
up to her house.

Considering her silence, the invitation surprised him. He said,
"No, my mom's expecting me."

She looked at him, as if trying to figure it all out. "You never want
to be with me anymore," she said.

Michael sighed. "I just went to the mall with you."

"Big fucking deal. Plus, you weren't even with me half the time.
You went sneaking off somewhere. Well, if you don't want to be with
me . . . oh, fuck it." She got out and slammed the car door too hard and
dashed to her front door.

"I don't," he said to himself. He drove off and this time yelled, "I
don't!" It scared him, this sudden flash of rage. It scared him so much
that he found a cheery pop song on the radio and sang that all the way
home, forcing himself to smile, making himself pretend that nothing
really had to change.

At home in his bedroom, Michael kept pictures and clippings of
men in a manila folder, which he tucked under the cushion of the old,
army-green easy chair that sat in the corner by his window. He would
lock his door and take out the photos and look at them one by one. It
was a pathetic, mostly tame assortment of pictures of handsome,
well-built men: pages from the Sears catalog, featuring the square-
jawed men modeling underwear, with their hairy chests and innocent
bulges, men often draped by a beautiful, wifely female; pictures of

the sexiest actors torn from glossy movie magazines; and one page from a *Hustler* that he swiped from Tad's stash, a scene showing a woman sucking a man, both of their eyes closed in rapture, a picture he'd wanted only so he could gaze at the guy's dick, which looked both freakish and fantastic, veiny and full and potent.

He sat in his room looking at them, and it was easy for him to get an erection, even though he wanted a variety of naked pictures; at the convenience store near school, he always saw the *Playgirl* magazines peeping out on the top rack, both calling his name and mocking him in their nearness. That night, just as he was unzipping, looking at a picture of a shirtless Antonio Sabato Jr. that he'd torn from his mother's *People,* the phone rang. He let it ring a few times before picking up. He had his own line now—one of his Christmas presents—because his parents had grown tired of his nightly two-hour chats with Kelly. He thought it might be Kelly, finally over her pouting spell. Or he thought it could have been some of his other friends—he secretly hoped it was Tad. But it was Harvey.

"Oh, hey," Michael said, surprised and slightly disappointed when he recognized the scratchy voice. He wondered how Harvey had found his number, but then realized that it was listed like anyone else's.

"Did you go yet?" Harvey asked. He was eating something chewy—Michael could hear unpleasant smacking noises.

"To the mall?"

"No, to Timbuktu. Yes, the mall."

"Listen," Michael began. "Just because . . . well, that talk we had today, that was between me and you, right?"

"Are you scared I'm going to tell your secret?"

"No," he lied. "It's just, it's just that I don't know if I'm going to go there. I don't know if I want to." Michael slapped shut his folder of pictures, as if the men in the pictures were staring at him accusingly.

"Well, if you go, Saturday morning's big," Harvey said. "All the men are off from work. And all the boys are out of school."

"Have you ever gone there?"

"A few times."

"What did you do there?"

"I performed a monologue from *Hamlet*—what do you *think* I did? I sucked some man off and he sucked me off and stuff. Duh."

"Oh," Michael said, suddenly feeling queasy, a mixture of jealousy and distaste mixing in his belly, as he pictured Harvey and some older man doing that. Kelly refused to do that for him, but Tad told him that Tina did it all the time and that is was awesome, that it was like having the life sucked out of you but in a good way.

"Oh? Is that all you have to say?"

"I just don't think I want to go there. That's all."

"Suit yourself." Harvey hung up.

Michael sat there with the receiver on his ear until it started barking busy signals. He hung up the line and placed the folder under the cushion again, its snug hiding place. He crawled under his covers and rubbed his dick against the soft sheets until he came, making a sticky puddle that he didn't bother to clean up.

On Saturday Kelly came over to his house, uninvited and unexpected. Michael was reading his mother's *Vanity Fair* out by the pool, his feet dipped in the water. She came out the back door and sat down next to him, took off her sneakers and plunged her feet in, swishing the water around in whirlish circles.

"The water's cold," she said. Her voice was quiet, and Michael knew something was worrying her. He knew she had come over to argue or to make up, to have some kind of talk.

"After a few minutes you get used to it." He set down the magazine.

"Tina called me," she said. "She said Tad said you were acting funny lately. He thought something was wrong. I told her I thought so too. Then she asked if we had a fight."

"What'd you tell her?"

"I told her we did. I told her I don't know what's wrong with you, but I know something is." She reached and touched Michael's hand, which he kept rigid, unresponsive. She withdrew.

"Nothing's wrong," he said.

"*Something* is. Is it that you don't like me anymore?" She took her feet out of the water and tucked her knees against her chest.

Michael just stared into the water. He thought that if he just ignored her, she would go away. It was easier than trying to make up something.

"You're not going to tell me?"

"I like you. It's not that. It's just . . . "

"What?"

"We're just in high school for Christ's sake," he said. "What do you want from me?"

Kelly leaned back on the concrete, sticking her feet back in the water. It seemed to Michael an odd, light-hearted gesture. Someone watching from a distance would have seen a scene of playfulness and youthful joy.

"What do I want?" she asked, perching up again. She stared at him for a minute and then brought her mouth next to Michael's ear and whispered, "You know, Mike, it's not like I can't do any better. Dan Hathaway has been hinting that he wants to ask me out for weeks. He says you don't deserve me." Her voice was rigid and controlled, not her usual tone of defiance and emotion.

"Dan?" he said, jerking his head away from the nearness of her mouth. Dan Hathaway was a football player who was trying to sleep his way through every available and unavailable girl. He was broad-shouldered, blue-eyed, and buzz-cut blond, with deep dimples, a walking poster for Uncle Sam. "Maybe he's right; maybe I don't deserve you. Maybe you should start seeing Dan. Maybe you two should fuck." When he said that, he felt guilty for not having even a *twinge* of jealousy. He even had a hopeful flutter in his stomach— Dan Hathaway could take her off his hands and everything and everyone would be happy, for a while anyway.

"Okay, maybe we *will* go out. I mean, you obviously don't want me." Her voice cracked musically, but she coughed and firmed up her jaw. Then she stood up and Michael thought she would leave, but she stayed there, hovering above him.

"One last time, before I go: What's wrong? Can't you at least tell me why you don't want to be with me?" The tone of pleading concern in her voice was new to him. It almost made him want to tell her. Tell her that *she* wasn't the problem at all. But he just couldn't, not right then. He had never been with a man before, had never even kissed a guy—he'd lived, so far, in a fantasy world, where it was all easy and natural and amazingly satisfying. He dreamed once that he was lying in bed with Tad, their bodies entwined, their lips raw from kissing, and just as Tad was about to whisper something to him, he woke up. And then there were other dreams, about the golden-boy lifeguard at the club, about Mr. James, the barrel-chested driver's ed teacher, about the movie stars. Every time he woke and realized that none of the dreams were true, he could barely pull himself out of bed, knowing he had to pass another day without a chance of fulfillment. Would Kelly understand that? How could she?

"I don't know what's wrong with me," he finally told her. He could see Kelly's reflection swaying in the pool water. "I'm sorry."

Behind him, he heard her say, "Okay, fine. But don't call me anymore. We're officially over." Then she left, with no tears, no protestations, just angry surrender.

Feeling free of burden and weight, on Sunday Michael tried the mall bathrooms. Before he went, he drank some of the bourbon from his father's liquor cabinet, taking the equivalent, he guessed, of four shots; afterward he felt, if not bold, loosened up a bit, nervous but not terrified. The mall was crowded, filled with too many families, many still wearing their Sunday church attire—their poses and faces of piety and togetherness made him, for a moment, almost want to chicken out. But he got over that soon enough—nothing could stop him today.

He found his way to the hallway that led to the bathrooms, but he walked slower and slower down the hall. A woman came out of the ladies' room just as he passed the door, startling him as if he'd been caught at something. He fiddled with his hair and then pushed open the bathroom door.

At first he was shocked by its contrasting darkness and brightness: The doors to the stalls were the same dark green faux marble of the rest of the mall, while the floors and walls were tiled in a white as pure as perfect teeth in toothpaste commercials. The faucets were silvery and too brightly polished. He'd expected a dirty place, not this gleaming cleanliness. He'd expected sticky floors and dull colors, paper towels littered on the floor, stalls with holes in them, spotted mirrors. Michael almost left, so thrown out of whack was he by this immaculate purity, but then he saw feet under a stall. He purposely entered one a few doors down.

He pulled down and his pants and sat on the cold, and clean, plastic seat—he'd at least appear to be there for the usual reason. In the silence he wished he'd had the nerve to ask Harvey about how things happened in here. His buzz from the bourbon wasn't strong enough anymore, and now his heart thudded, his breaths were short. He heard the squeak of a toilet paper dispenser and then the whoosh of a toilet flush, the clump of the man's shoes on the tile, a sink turning on, the door opening and then closing again.

He reminded himself that people actually just used the bathroom here, innocent pisses and shits. And so he sat and waited. The walls of the stalls, like everything else in this bathroom, were spotless; there was no lewd writing on the stall walls yet, and if there had been, some determined janitor had scrubbed it away. Michael wished he had brought a thick, black marker, maybe to make a date. He wondered if anyone ever answered the things like "meet me 4/23/98 at 6:00 sharp for a blow job" or "for a good time call Joe Blow." It was possible. Then he heard more men enter the bathroom, more sounds of flushing, trickling piss, groaning shits and the accompanying farts, and running water. Was there some signal he should have been giving? A tap of the foot? A cough? A whistle? Did he need to send a fucking invitation? How the hell did Harvey do it, Harvey with his colored hair, his stupid clothes?

Finally, when he knew he was alone, he left his stall and washed his hands at the sink. A man came in wearing a yellow tank top with a stencil of a smiley face on it; his hair was cut to the scalp and he had a tattoo of a rose on his left bicep, which Michael noticed was shapely, buff. He looked at Michael and nodded his head and then entered a stall. It wasn't much of a look, but he *did look*. Was that a sign? Or was this just a friendly straight man? How did a gay man look? Michael certainly didn't think of himself as looking gay—he wasn't "obvious," like Harvey or even the caterer his mother was using for his graduation party, a thirtyish man who had a high voice and wore a bow-tie and who smiled at Michael more than a normal man would have.

Michael continued to wash his hands. In the mirror he saw the man's feet in the stall pumping up and down, his jeans down around his ankles. He stood there waiting for something to occur to him, but then another man entered the room—an older man in a suit—and so he quickly left. His heart still thudded, and when he got to the main part of the mall again he sat down at a table in the food court. He sat there for a while and watched people eating, even watched for the man in the tank top, but he never walked by, so Michael finally went home.

At school the next few days Michael kept to himself, steering clear of the spots where he knew he'd run into Kelly or his friends—by the vending machines during break, on the bleachers by the tennis courts, in the parking lot. Of course, avoiding them completely was impossible, especially Tad, who hunted him down trying to get the scoop on the break up. Michael did the best he could to just shrug off the questions and walk away. During lunch hour Michael would sit in the library, essentially hiding.

On Wednesday he sat at one of the long wooden study tables, trying to read his Advanced Chemistry text. Harvey came in the library, strutting and looking satisfied, as if about to explode in joy. He sat down next to him, but Michael acted as if he didn't notice him. Harvey gently nudged his knee into Michael's thigh.

"I hear you and Kelly are breaking up."

After pausing and peering at Harvey with disdain, he said, "We're broken."

"Interesting. So does she know about you? Did you tell her?"

Michael closed his book and faced Harvey, taking him in as if it were the first time he'd seen him. His eyes, which Michael had never much noticed before, were blue and lazy-looking, the eyes of someone either stoned or relaxed, and were easily the most striking feature on his long, thin face; his hair, which needed to be cut, was still its magenta color, though his natural brown poked through in places, like vigilant weeds; and his skin was tan, like he had recently gotten some sun. His figure was slight, possibly bony, but his hands were large and strong-looking. Michael wouldn't call Harvey handsome, but he had some level of attraction to him. He might be considered, in a weird way, cute—if you liked odd guys. He tried to picture Harvey making out with the muscular guy from the mall bathroom, the two trading tongues in a stall, the man pushing weak Harvey down to his knees . . .

"Well? Did you?" Harvey said.

"What? I mean, what do you think? Of course I didn't tell her."

"I bet she suspects."

"No way," Michael said.

"I spotted you a mile away." Harvey gave him one of those boastful looks.

"What are you doing in here anyway?" Michael asked.

"I just wanted to talk to you." Harvey rolled his eyes and then squinted them at Michael. "Get testy, why don't you? Fine, I'll leave you alone." He pushed back his chair and started to walk away.

"Wait. I'm sorry."

Harvey paused, half-standing, and looked down at Michael.

"I mean, listen . . . do you want to hang out after school?" Michael asked. "Maybe?"

Harvey sat down again. "I guess," Harvey tried to say as if he were interested, but not *too* interested.

"We can't go to my house," Michael said. He could never explain this to his mother or father, because they knew all of his friends, and to introduce a new one, especially Harvey, would only draw questions.

"That's okay. You can come over to mine if you want. I'll write down my address." Harvey tore off a corner of one of the pages of Michael's text book and scribbled down his address. "It's off Fifteenth a few blocks."

Michael stared down at the table. "I'll be over after school, say around four."

Harvey nodded and walked off, looking back only once to offer a tentative smile, as if he did not believe Michael to be serious. He looked vulnerable then, not his usual smirky and defiant self—Michael had melted him.

He went home and showered, scrubbing in spots he'd never scrubbed much before—his dick, his balls, even his butt—making sure he was clean and perfect, making sure he smelled nice. Before driving to Harvey's house, Michael poured some more of his father's bourbon into a flask and stuck it in the back pocket of his jeans.

Harvey and his parents lived in a quiet neighborhood on the other side of the river, close to the University, where all the houses were wooden with surrounding expansive porches. The neighborhood was filled with formidable pine and messy persimmon trees that shaded everything, and Harvey's house rested next to a small, man-made lake. The house was painted light yellow, the yard was weedy and strewn with pine needles, and an old maroon Volvo was parked in the single garage, over which hung a basketball hoop without a net. Nothing spectacular about any of it, but reassuring.

Michael parked in the pebbled driveway and before he could knock, Harvey yanked open the clunky front door. Harvey had changed into jeans, a white shirt, and a navy-blue sweater vest, and his hair was wetly combed, making it look dark purple and black. "Come on in," he said, sounding nervous, as if he were welcoming in some crazy stranger.

The house smelled of furniture polish and every room was filled with bookcases and furniture covered in plastic: a house of readers and neat freaks, cramped but clean. Harvey led him into the kitchen, which had an unobstructed view of the small lake, which Michael thought looked like a big black puddle. "My parents aren't home, so the house is kind of a mess."

But it wasn't. The counters had been wiped clean and no dirty dishes sat in the sink. This was just nervous chatter, something to fill the air. Michael just nodded, relieved they didn't have to deal with the parents. "What do they do?" he asked.

"They're both English professors at the university. They're at some James Joyce conference in Orlando all week." Harvey shrugged his shoulders and pulled out two tumblers from one of the cabinets. "Exciting, huh?"

"Yeah." Michael attempted a weak laugh. "So that's why you do so good in English."

"I guess."

"So they're really out of town? They just left you here?"

Harvey nodded, placing the glasses on a little wicker table. "They always leave me alone, but I like it. I like being alone. So you want something to drink?"

"I have a flask of bourbon." Michael took it out. Harvey seemed almost shocked to see it.

"I don't like that stuff," Harvey said. "All we have is milk, orange juice, and some wine."

"I'll drink my bourbon, if that's okay."

"Sure."

They both sat down at the table and drank—Harvey a glass of juice, from which he barely sipped, and Michael straight from the flask. It burned his throat and made his eyes water. "Do you ever swim in that lake?"

"No, it's kind of nasty, filled with frogs and snakes."

Again, Michael noted the difference in Harvey. Here he was a little nervous, less antagonistic, his tough exterior guard let down. He also seemed a little dull. He was an awkward host, eager to please but not certain how to do so. He almost seemed like a completely different person. Michael could barely even imagine *this* Harvey holding a cigarette, much less smoking one—hell, much less having sex in a mall bathroom.

"Can I see your room?" Michael asked. Now *he* felt like the bold one, the cocky one.

"It's nothing special."

Michael capped his flask and set it on the table. He was impatient with the small talk. "Then what do you want to do?"

Harvey took a long sip, as if thinking his answer out carefully. "I know you don't want to be here, so you can leave if you want."

"Who said I didn't want to be here?"

"I can just tell. You're too scared to be with me sober, so you're getting drunk."

"I'm not scared. Not at all."

Harvey got up from the table and dumped his glass in the sink. He turned to face Michael. "You have friends. You had a girlfriend even. Why would you hang out with me?"

"You know why." Michael stood up and stared at Harvey, but Harvey wouldn't look back. "Look at me." Nothing. "Should I leave?" Still nothing—it was like Harvey was in some shocked trance. "Okay, I'll just leave." When Harvey didn't say anything, Michael walked to the front door and let himself out. But instead of getting in his car and leaving, he sat down on the porch steps and put his head between his legs. He couldn't go, he couldn't. After a few minutes, Harvey came outside and sat next to him. Michael felt his heart lighten. Harvey was smoking one of the cigarettes Michael had given him.

"Three months until we graduate," Harvey said.

Michael took the cigarette from Harvey, took a drag, and then passed it back. His left leg brushed against Harvey's jeans. "And then three more months before college," he said.

"You're leaving town, aren't you?"

Michael nodded. He was going up north, to Wesleyan, a private school in Connecticut, where his father had gone. He hoped Connecticut was very different from Alabama; he suspected it would be—it *had* to be.

"I have to stay here. My parents get a tuition break for me, since they're on faculty. Plus, I didn't get any scholarships anywhere, so I'm stuck here."

"It's not so bad here."

Harvey laughed at this and handed Michael the cigarette. "Easy for you to say; you get to leave."

Michael, with his free hand, squeezed Harvey's knee caps—it was sharp and bony and wonderful. He looked up, wanting to see Harvey's eyes, how he reacted to such a gesture, but Harvey was looking away.

Harvey said, "Not out here."

"Let's go inside," Michael said.

"Okay."

Michael called his parents to say he would be home late. "I'm studying at a friend's house," he told his mother.

"Kelly called," she said. "She called your line and then ours. She said it was really urgent."

"Oh, okay. Anyway, I'll be home later."

"How much later, Michael?"

"I'm not sure. After dinner maybe. Listen, I have to go," he replied and then hung up the phone.

Upstairs Harvey had tried to make his room dark, but enough of the fading sunlight crept through the blinds so that Michael could see pretty clearly. The room, unlike the rest of the house, was messy, cluttered with movie magazines and CDs and half-eaten packages of crackers. The walls were covered with a few posters of pop singers, a few picture frames lay on his dresser, and his small desk was covered with books and papers and a laptop computer.

"Nice room," he said.

"It's okay. Sorry for the mess."

Michael had always been nervous with Kelly in the moments before they messed around—nervous because he never felt sure about what he was doing, never secure about what she wanted or would allow him to do—and afterward, he always felt such relief that it was over. Now he felt calmer, excited, as if he were about to open a big present.

"Well," Michael said. He smiled.

"Well," Harvey said, still visibly tense.

Michael lay down on the bed—a lumpy full-size, with the sheets all bunched up—situating himself on his hip in a brashly seductive pose. Without being invited Harvey lay next to him, clumsily. Michael began touching Harvey's flat little chest, then massaging it. Harvey closed his eyes. Then Michael positioned himself, as smoothly as he could, on top of Harvey, who breathed heavily, his eyes still clamped shut.

"I'm not crushing you, am I?" Michael asked.

"I'm okay," Harvey whispered.

Michael kissed him, first on the cheek, then on the nose, and finally the lips. At first Harvey seemed to have no idea what Michael wanted to do with his tongue, but after a few minutes he opened up and let Michael plunge in, even nibbled Michael's tongue as it circled his mouth, which tasted of orange juice. The kiss, wet but hard, lasted until they needed to breathe. After that, they both fumbled with their clothes, interrupting the moment by pausing for buttons and zippers, peeling themselves like kids who couldn't wait to get out of their uncomfortable Sunday clothes.

Michael took in Harvey's nakedness—his skinny waist, his bony hips, his bouncing and funny-looking dick. His own dick, which he saw Harvey staring at unabashedly, flopped about like a dog jumping on a leash, eager to break free. "You like it," he said, and for the first time that afternoon, Harvey laughed. Then Michael gently pushed Harvey down on the bed and moved on top of him, enjoying the feel of Harvey's warm and slightly sweaty skin against his. They were both smooth, almost hairless, and Michael pressed his erection onto Harvey's, grinding the two together. And he kissed him, hard, and sucked on his neck. He moved his mouth from Harvey's chin to his chest, to his stomach, and with one of his hands grabbed Harvey's dick, holding it. Harvey was silent then, not even groaning, and when Michael looked at him he saw that he had a satisfied, almost goofy look on his face. He spit in his palm and rolled his hand up and down Harvey's erection, and then licked it, getting it slicker. "I want you to come all over yourself," Michael said. He felt like a pro. He felt, for the first time, sexy.

Harvey just nodded and groaned, and after a few minutes, before Michael's arm could get tired, Harvey began making gasps, clenching his hands into the bedspread, and then came in fast, long spurts onto his flat stomach, and on Michael's hand, warm and thick.

"Oh, Jesus," Harvey said.

Michael straddled Harvey, moving up his groin above Harvey's chest. "Now suck mine, okay?"

"Okay." And he did, propping himself forward on the pillow, taking it slowly and only half-way at first, choking a bit, but then finding a way to fit it in his mouth, a bit to the side so that it bumped the inside of his cheek, then swallowing the whole thing, up and down, only every now and then a little toothy, which both hurt and felt great, all at once. Michael rubbed the back of Harvey's head, the absurd purple hair, and it was not long before he had to pull his dick out and shoot against the head board and dribble the rest onto Harvey's shoulder. "Jesus," he said. Then they both laughed.

They didn't clean up, but just lay on the bed next to each other, smiling at each other, laughing some more. Michael pulled Harvey against him and shut his eyes.

"That was—" Harvey began.

"Shhh. Let's just be quiet for a while. Let's rest."

They let an hour pass. It was now dark outside; the only light came from the red numbers of Harvey's digital alarm clock. On the bed, both lying on their backs, propped up by pillows, they finally covered themselves with the bedspread—even though they were hot and sweaty—and passed back and forth a glass of ice water Harvey had gone to get.

Michael just closed his eyes and enjoyed the feel of Harvey next to him. He didn't think about Kelly or his friends or his parents, or about the next few months, or the coming year, when he would be miles away from home, from anyone who knew him here, including Harvey. He'd blocked all of that out of his mind. For the first time in months, he felt light and relaxed. It was as if he was already miles away from his old life.

"I never went to the mall," Harvey said, breaking the silence. He turned on his side and perched his head of sweaty hair on Michael's shoulder.

"I figured as much," Michael said.

"You did?"

"Yep. I knew it was bullshit." He smiled and pecked Harvey on the forehead—it felt like such a natural gesture.

Harvey said, "I read in the paper once that they raided the bathrooms there and caught a few men. That's how I knew about it."

"I'm glad you didn't go."

"Me too," Harvey said.

Michael opened his eyes and noticed the clock. "Hey, it's nine o'clock." He knew it was late enough for his parents to be worried—especially lately, when everyone thought he'd fallen off the deep end. But he didn't want to leave. And though he tried not to, he thought about being at school the next day. Eventually he would have to face Kelly, Tad, the others. One look at the clock had knocked him out of his little post-sex clear-headed moment: School. And now there would be Harvey to deal with.

"Hey, I don't want you to be angry with me if I ignore you at school," he said.

Harvey was silent; Michael could only hear the wheeze of his breathing.

"I mean, you know how it is. We really only have a few more months to go. We should lay low, you know?"

"I understand," Harvey said, though Michael could hear the hurt in his voice. But he couldn't help it—it was the way it had to be, for now.

"That doesn't mean we can't do this again."

"I understand," Harvey said again. He nudged his chin against Michael's cheek and rubbed it while kissing him awkwardly near the eye. His lips were dry.

Without looking at him, Michael took one of Harvey's hands and began rubbing it, squeezing his palm with his thumb. "I should go soon." But instead of making a move to leave, he pulled Harvey in tighter and kissed him, knowing and welcoming where this would lead.

ꕥ 2   A Late and Summer Storm

Eugene M. McAvoy

From the top floor of the Norfolk Southern building, behind the safety of windows reinforced with masking tape, you survey the sky. To the southeast, the afternoon darkens into a seamless palette of gray. To the north, clouds spin like the blades of pinwheels inexorably to the west. Rain skewers the afternoon, and your chrome and glass enclosure sways erratically in the wind.

Secretaries and the crop of new hires stare with eyes all pupils at the sky, then at a clock hovering at 2:28. Securing and resecuring plastic bags around their darkened computer terminals, they await word from their supervisors that they may leave, that they may return to their homes to ride out the storm. As though to calm them, to reassure them that there is something, anything they can do to battle nature, the company has piped in radio reports from the National Weather Service, regularly providing coordinates on this latest storm—some man's name that starts with an F. Already you have forgotten.

Phones alight with calls from anxious wives to report downed power lines, uprooted trees, and flooded underpasses. Voices, hushed and unconvincing, respond with promises that all will be okay. Yet this is just the beginning; the storm still approaches. The worst, you know, if it is to come, is still to come.

You remain silent, stoic, leafing absently through a stack of messages beside the phone. Maintenance reports from Roanoke require revision. You have been added to the Labor Day call list. Your doctor has canceled tomorrow's appointment because of the storm. You remain unmoved.

Hurricanes, you know, at least their threat, are normal this time of year. From June through November, a season longer than even the resorts in Virginia Beach offer tourists, meteorologists repeatedly warn of yet another hurricane that might make landfall here, or perhaps on the Outer Banks, or maybe as far away as Cape May. Like an impudent child, burrowed behind a string of islands jutting to the southeast, the Tidewater turns her face to the Atlantic and dares the storms to come. And as summer presses its palm upon the wetlands, the storms do come, disappointing in their lack of ferocity.

For years, these warnings have proven false, wolf cries from the networks, as the cyclones carve their swaths to the south or west, decay into little more than tropical depressions, or worst of all, simply turn their backs upon the bay and head out to sea, leaving the fist of land you call home unscathed. After a lifetime of unfulfilled expectations, you are inured to these storms, but still surprised, awed even, when the wind slashes an evening turned green by thunderheads, joyous in your hope, that one, true storm will crash into the coast, tear your home from its foundation, and send you sputtering and sprawling into a rising, then receding surf.

But this is no different. You can tell. This storm, like so many others before, will linger just offshore, unmoving, neither gaining nor losing strength. It will simply hang on, caught between two stagnant fronts, until it vanishes in its own mist, nagging, eroding beaches replenished by the Corps of Engineers only two years ago, flooding low-lying streets with its black and brackish promise. Long after your co-workers have left to board up their windows and sandbag their doors, to raid the grocery stores of bottled water, batteries, and Spam, you stand at the window, staring into the dusk.

Awash in your thoughts, the jetsam of memory that gathers as surely as the storms this time of year, you turn from the window and loosen your tie. Time to enter the fray. Time to head home.

* * *

By the time you arrive at the bungalow crouching beneath a crown of oaks and pines, Karen, your wife of six hundred days, is focused on preparing for the storm. The television is tuned to the Weather Channel; the battery-powered radio dialed to the National Weather Service. A voice hoarse and inhuman with static offers the same information in its interminable loop, to seek shelter when authorities advise. A human voice interrupts; emergency services have been activated in Virginia Beach; residents in coastal neighborhoods should seek shelter immediately; the Norfolk City Council is meeting to evaluate conditions.

On the dining room table, a dozen candles lay beside a suitcase stuffed with clothes and a stack of maps, all routes to the west highlighted in brilliant orange. Still shrink-wrapped and crisp, four rolls of masking tape lean against a box of fireplace matches. Karen, in jeans and a sleeveless smock, her hair pony-tailed at the crown, smiles nervously when you enter.

"Whatever happens," she says, pointing to the table, "we're ready."

Without speaking, you nod and walk into the bedroom. Hanging your suit on plastic hangers spaced evenly across the wooden bar, you rifle through the closet, sift through drawers for a change of clothes that promises comfort. Better, you think, to shed your skin.

* * *

Over dinner, the winds grow stronger, and lightning begins in the east. In brief flashes, captured, it seems, for seconds longer by the canopy of clouds, you watch the pine trees lean away from the wind, then circle and totter as the wind abruptly changes direction. The oaks, like shrubs beneath the pines, sag under the weight of rain, then flutter in the breeze, lifting and settling on eddies of wind. Their branches creak arthritically toward the house, toward the roof, and you can almost feel their weight upon you, forcing you and the house deeper and deeper into the saturated soil. Beside you, Karen watches too; in the harsh glare of lamplight, you can make out her silhouette in the window.

"The pines are going to snap," you tell her.

She shakes her head. "No, they're bending. They'll make it again," she says, "just like always."

"I've told you they don't bend," you reply too quickly, almost harshly. "They lean. This time they're going to snap."

Fabric rustles as she moves closer. The air around you settles like smoke, becomes thick and heavy as she places her hand over yours. "Could you tape the windows when you're done? I'll make a fire."

You glance at the place where your hands touch, then stiffen and turn back toward the window. "It's too hot for a fire," you say. "And if the glass is going to shatter, it's going to shatter. A Band-Aid won't stop it." After a beat of your pulse, perhaps two, you slide your hand away and hear Karen's land softly on the table.

Outside, a bolt of lightning bisects the sky, and you brace yourself for thunder.

Karen peers questioningly at her hand, as though unaware or not believing it is empty. Then she pulls it back, and for a moment it is as though she never touched you.

"You won't even try," she says, "will you? Just won't take the chance." She rises from the table and with an empty plate in each hand retreats to the fluorescence of the kitchen. In the space she has left behind her, the sound of breaking plates arrives with the thunder.

*   *   *

The Prozac, not the lightning of the summer storm, keeps you awake—a side effect the psychiatrist says is expected. Excitability. Agitation. All normal. So at 3:04 a.m., you lie alone in the king-sized bed, eyes open wide and muscles tense, while Karen still putters in the kitchen. She is quiet, but above the bass of occasional thunder, you hear her. You consider calling out to her, telling her you're awake, apologizing, asking her to talk, but you can think of nothing to say. Instead, you ignore the rattle of cups and the drone of the dishwasher; you ignore an urge that struggles toward consciousness, and you count. You count flecks of glitter embedded in the sculptured ceiling, the seconds between a flash of lightning and the arrival of thunder, the lies you have told your wife, your therapist, yourself.

A drink would help you sleep, a tall glass of bourbon, amber, over ice, like your father used to serve to the neighborhood men who gathered each Sunday to watch the Redskins, packing themselves shoulder to sweating shoulder into the den. Even a beer, bitter and heady, could chase the night away, but you cannot drink. Antabuse assures it. The psychiatrist forbids it. You have answered too many of her questions—questions that anyone else would answer the same—with the response that confirms her diagnosis. Emphasizing the word with an arched eyebrow and the jab of a yellow pencil she usually keeps tucked behind her ear, she says you are an alcoholic and hints at worse. And because you can no longer explain your dreams, because you can't understand the moods, the sudden desire to escape, to assume a new identity, to die rather than to be you, you believe her. You accept her diagnosis. You accept her medications.

And the medications keep you awake.

As the miniature mirrors pressed into the ceiling glare back, you try to remember why you are alone in this bed you know better than yourself, counting. You try to understand why the scent, the sight of your wife drives you away. You try to remember why you saw this doctor in the first place, what possessed you three months ago, standing at the top of a building overlooking the city, to refer yourself to a specialist. Was the pressure of a day like all the others finally too much? Not enough? Did you think of jumping? Did you think of falling?

You remember, once during a summer now lost in shade, jumping from a rickety bridge over Bennett's Creek into the lazing water below. In the span of your descent, your stomach lurched into your chest, and your breast heaved, empty and open to the sunlight around you. For a split second, you felt weightless, soaring, a part of something at once trivial and important. Before plunging into the water shimmering faintly green below, you sensed a knowing. No more. No less. Just a knowing.

You wonder now if this is the reason you jumped, if this is the reason that three months ago you dialed the seven numbers printed innocuously, almost politely, under Employee Assistance. Yet when you approach the reason, you jerk upright in bed and shove your thoughts back toward the darkness of memory. You pray to remain a man. You return to the numbing task of counting.

Yet the numbers do not calm you, cannot distract you. They simply pass like an overheard conversation into the wind. The numbers climb. Darkness spreads through the room, into your body, and into your brain, quenching a final spark dangling at the end of an excited dendrite. And you sleep.

* * *

At 4:37 you are startled awake. Shadows on the wall fade to black and assure you that only lightning woke you. You count. One–one thousand. Two–one thousand. Three–one thousand. The thunder from three miles away rattles the glass in the window at your head. Beside you, naked flesh presses against your thigh; Karen has come to bed. Her slow, measured breaths tell you that she sleeps. You inch to your side of the mattress, until your skin touches the cool, wooden rail at the bed's extreme, and blink away your dream, the same dream you have had for the past three months.

You are on a corner, under a street lamp; it is night. A policeman drapes a gray, woolen blanket over the chalk-lined body of a young man. He lies face down on the sidewalk, head turned toward the street, arms outstretched. By a force you refuse to name, you are drawn to him, to that body void of life. You lie beside him, your fingers tracing the chalk line that surrounds but never touches his flesh. Your warmth radiates toward his side, and the blanket between you melts away.

For a moment you see his face, a face you are sure is yours. Lifeless blue eyes stare into the night; brown hair still damp clings to bluing skin. You stroke his cheek with the back of your hand. It is cold. You shiver. And under your touch his body vanishes. The night grows dark.

Shaking off the dream, you catch your breath, rub your burning eyes. Your fingers play upon the clammy surface of your cheek, then dig into your skin until blood seeps to the surface. Outside the window, rain pelts relentlessly against the roof. You picture the droplets of water cascading down asbestos shingles, collecting in gutters that run along the roof's edge, gutters clogged with pinecones and needles, oak leaves, debris. The water flows in sheets over the rim of the gutters. It batters the earth, compresses the soil below, and the sound alone assures you that the garden you planted only months ago is already washed away. You imagine the morning glories and goldenrods releasing their fragile grasps on the soil and floating on muddy water toward a grate. For several seconds they swirl like your thoughts above a drain. Then, with a burp, entrapped air bursts to the surface; the drain clears, and the petals disappear, sucked below the street by the torrent of the late summer storm.

Conscious of the games your mind enjoys, you remind yourself not to imagine. For eight years you have forced yourself not to merge memory with dream, to keep the two separate, not to confuse them. But as you lie in bed, darkness pressing softly against you, you realize how miserably you have failed. You are unsure now, and have been for months, just what portion of your memories is true and what portion is false, what ratio of truth there is in these visions that come on the corpse of night.

Is it memory or dream that two friends rose early one summer morning to watch the sun rise over the Chesapeake Bay? Is it memory or dream that only one returned? Is it fact or fiction that the two of you rowed upstream to fish and finally to rest on a knoll and watch a storm roll in from the Atlantic? Like mud in a pan, or sand in a sieve, you shake the memories right and left, forward and back, trying to find a gem, one precious stone to sustain you—even if the stone is disdain.

Your friend was quiet that morning. Before the sun crested on the horizon, you pushed the boat into water thigh deep and aimed it past the finger of Willoughby Spit to the northwest. Rowing more slowly, breathing more softly than you had ever known, he cut a wide berth around the naval base as you navigated the skiff at the edges of the channel. Already, sailors gathered on the deck of a destroyer preparing to get underway. With the Elizabeth and Nansemond rivers emptying into the James before you and the James flowing into the bay behind, you were struck in that moment with envy for these men, for their journey, months of sun and sea, clean and tangible, the thrilling comfort of interdependence, of shared need, of an ocean unsullied by land.

Drifting on the vortex at this confluence, you told your friend, as though it were a secret, of the confusion you always felt at this point on the river. You tried to explain the incongruity of belonging and not belonging in a place quickened by entire fleets that arrived and departed as surely as the seasons, a place slowed by the ebb and flow of tides more regular than the sun. When he responded with only a shrug, you remained silent for the rest of the trek, southeast past Lambert's Point and Port Norfolk, east past Town Point, between railroad trestles raised against the sky and beneath the Campostella Bridge, already a shadow in the waxing light.

Your friend's shoulders and chest grew damp, then drenched with sweat. Veins in his forearms danced beneath his skin as he dipped the oars into the water and heaved them against river and lock in a powerful arc toward him. Beneath rolling skin, the veins hibernated when he raised the oars from the water and drove forward, as though reaching toward you, preparing for another stroke. His breath, deep and even, sought the frontiers of his chest and abdomen, and strained against the faded fabric of his T-shirt. Impassively and silently, he rowed, relinquishing the oars to you only long enough to sip from a Mason jar of water, or to dry his face with a soiled towel. When he took back the oars and returned to rowing, you resumed your role as navigator, squinted past the reef of his face, and pointed the skiff directly into the sun.

Hours later, only as you rowed north, up Broad Creek where the houses thinned and stands of birch grew to the water's edge, shielding you from the prying eyes of morning, did your friend finally speak. "I know what you mean," he said from out of nowhere. "I feel like I don't belong in my skin."

The sun stood high and moisture thickened the air when you finally stowed the skiff in scrub on the creek bank and hiked—only a few feet above sea level—to the rise that had been your hideaway for as long as you could remember. From its crest, obscured only by office buildings and apartment complexes that grew taller and more numerous from the marshlands with each passing year, you could see land and the ribbons of water that were its bane and blessing for miles around. And though you could not see the ocean, not the reality of it, you believed you could smell its salty freshness above the loamy scent of decay in the clearing.

The two of you sat that morning, facing east and staring into the sun. Though the morning chill had not yet lifted, the heat from your friend's body penetrated the distance between you and drove the chill from the air. Mist rose in soft clouds from his skin. Surrounded by damp earth and stagnant water, you could smell the warmth of him, more clearly than even the sea, a dry scent of dust and salt and sand, comforting and hopeful. As the day opened before you and became animated with its promise, so too did your friend.

You are surprised now, alarmed you would say if you spoke of it, that you cannot recall his words precisely. They seem more important now, eight years after their fact, than they seemed when you sat in their midst. Surely he spoke about family and women and the future and money. The same old things. And, perhaps because you had heard it all before, because his story was expected, that is why you don't remember.

But you are shattered, still, by what you do recall with diamond-perfect clarity. The sun shone directly in your eyes, and you shielded them with your right hand cupped like a visor at your brow. Behind you, wan, yellow light filtered like an afterthought through the canopy of birch. Beside you, your friend spoke softly and smiled the half-smile it would take you years to recognize as the smile of distance and heartbreak and defeat. When he turned directly toward you, his voice low but insistent, one tear, only one, sought a furrow down his face.

"You're like my shadow, he said. "That part of me I need to get away from, but don't want to get away from." He laughed, then, a hollow laugh, low and hopeless. And in that moment, as inappropriate as it may have been, for the first and only time in your life, you felt as pure and as bright as mercury, as dangerous as shards of quicksilver bobbing on the sea. You pulled your hand away from your eyes, and sought in momentary brilliance the shoulder of your friend. Quickly and tightly you gripped, his tendons tense and angry beneath the combined flesh of shoulder and finger.

"I love you," you said. Or think you said. You are unsure now of the truth.

But this you know is true. In the time it took to pull your hand away or for him to pull away from your hand, he was gone.

This, you also know, is false, but the memory persists. He stepped back and stumbled, fell into the earth, into the water, into the darkness of time. Like the coyote on a Saturday morning cartoon, he shrank as he fell farther and farther away, disappearing at last into a cloud of dust.

The memory, you know, makes no sense. It follows no pattern of logic you can recognize, but still you tell yourself that he simply and quietly fell. Between then and now, except for nights when rain batters the roof and lightning lights the sky, he has simply and graciously vanished.

In his absence, you moved as far away as you dared. You moved back. You saw what little was left of the world to see. You saw nothing. You completed college, got a job, made a normal life for yourself. And when thirty pulled closer than twenty, knowing that life with anyone was better than life alone, you found a wife and made her a friend. In time, you learned to love her, and that love now seems, or should seem you tell yourself, more a part of you than the salt air, a stand of birch, and the thin line between memory and dream.

You stare into the darkness. Karen begins to snore, then stirs, and settles back into regular, rhythmic breathing. Your hand like a stranger's strays down your body. It brushes the wiry hair on your chest, then drifts further to softer but thicker hair. You twirl it around your fingers and cup your testicles in your palm. You hold them for a minute. No response—another side effect the psychiatrist, with the hint of a smile, claims is normal. You release your hold and pull your hand to your face to sniff the scent of sweat and soap that lingers on your fingers. It is a masculine scent, and you are reassured.

Karen kicks in her sleep.

You turn to the wall and shut your eyes.

* * *

Karen is already awake, standing in the kitchen, when you pull yourself out of bed. From the corner of your eye, you see her watching as you walk into the bathroom. In the living room, the television screen glows with the image of pregnant, gray clouds windmilling about a locus of blue, the void at the center of the storm. Though you cannot hear the forecast, a track of red arrows shows that the storm has moved to the east. The winds have abated.

You peer into the mirror above the bathroom sink, and finger a scab on your cheek. Your head pounds behind the temples with what three months ago may have been a hangover. But you remember last night. You did not drink; you dreamed. The dream alone hammers in your head.

Karen continues to stare as you rifle through the medicine chest, find the plastic vial of aspirin, and with trembling fingers remove the cap. She looks away when you retrieve only cotton.

When you walk into the kitchen, she steps aside.

"Do you want to talk?"

You pour a cup of coffee, stir in three tablespoons of sugar, and look at her. Over the blue satin nightgown you gave her for your first anniversary, she wears a terry-cloth robe that reaches to the floor. Her light red hair, strawberry blonde she calls it, is brushed away from her face. Her eyes are red and swollen. She looks tired, angry, sad.

Your words come out dry. "About what?"

"Forget it," she says. She stalks into the living room and throws herself onto deep velvet cushions. With her knees pulled to her chest, she wraps her arms around her legs and rests her chin in the crook of her elbow.

The thick air in the kitchen presses against you, but you force your-self to remain still. You open a window above the sink and sip your coffee. Though it is already past one, the sky is dark. The rain contin-ues lightly.

Your appointment with the therapist, had it not been canceled be-cause of the weather, would have fallen on a perfect day, dark and cold and threatening, a perfect day to tell your stories, to tell the lies that keep you a man. And though you feel drawn to a truth that eludes you on brighter days, you know that you would not tell her what she wants to hear. Not the truth. Not today.

Instead, she would talk, telling you, as she has told you each week for three months, that you must be honest, you must tell her every-thing. You would nod and say you understand. She would explain again in the nonsensical jargon of her misunderstanding that you can-not run *away from* anything any longer, that you have already done that. Alcohol has done that. She would tell you that you need to run *toward* something, that all you have to do is decide what it is you want to run to.

Again, you would nod, tell her she is right, tell her you're just not sure. You would not tell her that there is no longer a choice. You would, as has become your ritual, simply pay her receptionist thirty-five dollars, make an appointment for the following week, and drive, even in the rain and wind, to the beach.

What you refuse to tell her is that you have already made this jour-ney. Every summer for eight years, you have made the journey. You make the journey every week when you leave her. You are already, have always been, running *toward* something. Toward the bay, the beach. Toward the ocean. To the men whose eyes, when you dare hold their attention, tell you that there is still a choice. No. Not a choice. A chance.

With the wind whispering outside, with your doctor wrapped safely in her suburban assurance, with your wife folding like an ori-gami sculpture into and over herself, you picture your weekly journey toward that thing you dream but continue to deny yourself.

You climb behind the wheel of your '84 Escort, roll up the win-dows despite the heat, and lock the doors. You take the long drive north on Ocean View—an inappropriate name for a road that parallels the bay and not the sea—avoiding the stares of young men darkened by the sun and hardened by the wind. You allow yourself only to glance at them lounging on the trunks of cars, strolling down crowded sidewalks, standing in the cool shadows of seedy motels. And when you have passed them, you stare at their reflections in the rearview mirror.

Though your stomach tightens, though you can't breathe, and sweat pours from your body, though your knuckles turn white on the steering wheel, you make a U-turn at Willoughby Spit, just blocks from where you grew up, and whispering, "God help me," drive back down the road for a second, third, and fourth pass.

From the living room, Karen calls. "Do you want a divorce?"

Her question pulls you back from your reverie, back from daydreams of the beach, from the shirtless and silent men. You wonder what she knows. Certainly no more than you. You finish your coffee and pour another, the spout of the coffeepot rattling against the cup.

"Is there another woman? Are you seeing someone else?"

You squint out the window, at the contrast of green grass against a steel gray sky, and carefully sip your coffee. Though she has said nothing funny, you smile.

She pushes herself from the cushions and walks toward you. "Are you going to say anything?"

Nothing.

"I want you to tell me what's going on," she prods.

Nothing.

Her hands drop to her sides. Her fingers knead empty air.

"Just tell me if you want a divorce."

You look closely at her face, pale but flushed. You sip your coffee and count the freckles across her nose. If you touch her, stroke the bridge of her nose with your thumb, this would end. She would cry and hold you and tell you that she loves you. You can end her pain and anger, but you look away.

Your voice sounds hollow in the cramped, humid kitchen. You avoid the word *we*. "I don't see that the marriage has any future."

She stares. She breathes. She looks away. "Why not?" she asks. So much effort for two simple words.

You tell yourself that what she doesn't know won't hurt her, that this is less painful than the alternative. "Because I don't love you anymore," you say. You lie. You realize, even while the words tumble out, that you want to say *can't,* that you want to say I *can't* love you anymore. And though you know even this is a lie, you sense that somewhere in the words, at the heart of the words, there is a shred of truth.

Her face loses what little color it has, and for a minute you think she will cry, that tears will spring to her eyes and overflow onto her cheeks. Instead, she mouths words that catch in her throat and remain on her lips, the light, fragile lines around her mouth twitching.

Your heart beats rapidly. Sweat rolls from under your arms and down your ribs. It soaks into the waistband of your pants.

She straightens. Her hands ball into fists, and something in her neck, the muscles straining against cartilage and bone, the veins protruding almost masculine from under her skin, reminds you of the woman who told you after your first date that she would marry you, the woman who would not take no for an answer. The woman you fell in love with. Her.

"Then one of us has to leave."

Her anger stirs you. Her strength, the strength you wish you had, thrills you, fills you with resolve.

Not knowing how to make it right, but knowing you must make it right, you try to think of words to calm her, but the lies catch in your throat, mix with the bile and the truth, and you cannot tell one from the other. You cannot make her understand that you want to stay, that you are afraid to stay, afraid that staying will drive her away or make you disappear entirely into those small lines around her lips. She can never understand what the drinking has done, what its absence continues to do. It has changed you and saved you and kills you, and the only way to stay alive is to become what it forces you to be, what you were meant to be, what you have always been.

You tell yourself to fight for her, to do what any decent man would do, to reach for her, hold her. But you are still, still clutching your cup of coffee, now cold.

"No one has to leave," you tell her, "yet. I can . . . we can make this work. I can love you."

She steps toward you. Only inches between you, closer than you have been in months, you feel her breath hot against your face. "I wish you'd never quit drinking. At least then you could lie to yourself." Then, almost as an afterthought, she adds, "Can't you at least lie to me?"

She shakes her head, and her eyes glisten. As you stand, ready to touch her, ready to tell her what you know she wants to hear, she begins to shrink. Before your eyes, her shoulders fall; her head bends toward the floor, and the muscles in her neck relax, leaving only smooth, feminine flesh. For a moment you are struck by her shrinking. You remember, for only a fraction of a second, Lily Tomlin and a mindless movie you saw years before. Then you notice her growing even smaller, her diminution punctuating your normal life about to end, first a question mark, then a comma, finally a period. In the blink of an eye, she is nothing more than a cloud of dust, forever out of reach.

You set your cup softly on the counter, grab your keys and wallet from beside the door. You walk into the rain.

* * *

A week later, the storm passed out to sea, the arrangements made, the night crisp and clear, you visit. Karen gives you a silver frame with the words *To my wonderful husband* engraved in script across the bottom. She laughs, dry and brittle, when she places it in your hands. A present, she explains, that she was saving for your anniversary. She bought it four months early. She nods when you tell her you have nothing for her.

Then she shrugs and says it's okay. She turns back toward you smiling a vacant, practiced smile. She looks at her hands and asks you to remove her wedding ring.

"You're the one who put it on. You should take it off."

You too stare at her hands, remember the first time you held them, the warmth, the comfort, the care they promised. But you do not protest. You slide the ring from her finger.

Then you remove your own and notice the band of white, naked skin where the ring has covered your flesh for six hundred and seven days. You place both rings in her palm. She clutches them in her fist, leans across the sofa and kisses you softly on the lips. Still holding the rings, she strokes your cheek with the back of her fist.

Leaving for the last time, you place the car in reverse and back out of the driveway. Moonlight lances through the oaks in the front yard, and as you watch, they seem to open like palms to the stars. You shift the car into first gear, press your right foot on the accelerator, remove your left from the clutch. You roll your window down and slowly drive away, the evening wind cool against your face. Slipping gently into second, you aim the car to the east, to the bay just two blocks away, and beyond that, hopefully, the sea.

ぷ 3 　 One Night When the Moon Was Full

Dale Edgerton

PART I: HARRY

Buck gave his first party since Christmas on a summerlike evening in late May. He had just painted the house again, inside and out; an ostentatious Queen Anne with a wrap-around porch. Gables jutted upward from the roof, balconies from every upstairs bedroom window. A wandering of rooms led to stairways and bays.

The band began playing at twilight, right after I got there, a band of seven young men in cowboy hats. The lead singer played guitar.

Inside, the house was alive with color and music as women in soft summer dresses or shifts that shimmered with rhinestones and spangles filled the main hall. The men in their pastels and dinner jackets were a handsome addition, smelling of cologne, their deep voices rumbling under the higher excited tones of the women.

I wandered outside, but after an hour was thinking of leaving when the big, tall redhead came toward me smiling. He was wearing a white linen suit and flip flops. I knew he was Buck's college roommate, Eric. He wasn't handsome in the classic sense, but there was something gorgeous about him. Sexy with his dark red hair and bearded face, he resembled paintings of satyrs, even dressed in that white linen suit.

"You're Harry, right?" he said, sticking out his hand. "Eric Lansing. Buck tells me you're a dancer."

I was about to answer when he stepped back and looked at me real hard.

"Man," he said, shaking his head, "'scuse me for starin', but your eyes. You wear contacts?"

My eyes again.

"Man," he whispered. *"Beautiful."*

"If that's a line," I said, "it always works."

He seemed to come to himself then. "Sorry," he told me, "but it ain't no line. *Really.* I'm a straight boy. But I'm telling you the God's honest truth. I never seen eyes that green on a human. You got the prettiest eyes I've ever seen, and that includes Cooter Brown back home. Folks used to come from three states just to look at 'em."

"Are you for real?" I asked.

"Oh, yessir. I always tell the truth. Always have, always will. Cross my heart."

"I believe you." I flicked a bug off his jacket, then more daring, brushed my fingers through his chest hair. "Why did you want to know if I was a dancer?"

He was uncomfortable so I moved back a few inches. I guessed he was a straight boy after all. "I'm choreographing a musical this summer. *L'il Abner.* Auditions are Monday and Tuesday, and I need men."

His eyes were brown, and they crinkled up at the corners when he smiled. "Let me rephrase that."

"Audition me now," I said.

"Right now?"

I took him by the hand and pulled him over by the pool where folks were dancing on a raised platform.

He yanked back the other way. "Wait a minute."

"Look," I said, staring up at him. He had to be at least 6'4". "Don't worry. I won't grab your crotch."

He laughed. "What the fuck? Why the hell not? It won't like I ain't danced with men before. But this ain't no gay bar. Not up there." He kicked off his flip-flops and tugged me with him into the wet grass. "I'll lead," he said. Then he pulled me against him, hard. We were chest to chest. "If we're going to do this, we're going to do it right."

"I can follow anybody," I told him.

Everybody standing around stepped back and gave us room as we swung to a slow Texas swing, the bluesy jazz beat of "Blues for Dixie," a song I remembered from one of my father's records, *Bob Wills and His Texas Playboys.*

The lead singer I'd been noticing all evening strummed his guitar and winked at me when Eric Lansing started slowly rocking with me in his arms.

If you've ever seen that ol' Mississippi, the queen of the Delta land, Then you'll understand why I've got the blues for Dixie.

I pressed him in tighter, his eyes burning into mine with the intensity of a tango dancer. It was like we were performing.

"Raw, isn't it?" I said, making my voice growl.

He grinned at me. "You're raw, boy. A real piece of work."

He dipped me down low so my head brushed the ground, then yanked me back up, slamming me into his chest.

I knew I was drunk, or I'd never be doing this. Usually I was shy at parties. "Will you be sorry in the morning?"

"Not a chance, sugar. You're too damn good. One o' the best partner's I ever had."

The music was ending, and I was braced against his leg, leaning hard into his thigh. My hand was on his shoulder, his around my waist. Our audience applauded, slapped us on our backs and patted our shoulders. Now that it was over, the attention embarrassed me. "Thanks for the dance," I said. "You're a good sport."

"Auditions on Monday. Don't you forget."

PART II: ERIC

Me and Buck was roommates in college, North Carolina School of the Arts, he in drama, me in dance. He was tall dark and handsome, and I looked like somebody'd bashed my face in. I'd hated his guts at first; he was so handsome. I thought with him around no girl would look at me. Then I find out he's queer. Never been happier in my life.

Being a male dancer and straight, I always had opportunities with lotsa women. After I graduated, I got in with the Boston Ballet Company and was with them until January when I got fired for busting the director's nose. He was going to fire me anyway.

So I tucked my tail between my legs and came to live with Buck. Here it was four months later, and all I was doing was waiting tables and bouncing at a redneck bar weekends. I still got chances with women, but when they started talking about relationships, I was out the door.

Me and Buck was smoking cigarettes on the balcony outside my bedroom. The party spread below us like a big Hollywood musical. I was kinda worried since I hadn't met any women who'd interested me in awhile. And I'd just danced with a man, and not at a gay bar neither. All these other gay guys asked me to dance, so I hightailed it upstairs to my bedroom hid till Buck found me.

"You'll get lucky tonight, pal," he told me. "You always do."

I shook my head. "Lucky? Last party you had at Christmas I got myself into a big mess with some ol' gal."

I'd woke up with her the next morning, my head pounding like a son-of-a-bitch, and she started talking about what we was gonna do that night and our relationship. I thought to myself I'd sure as shit done it again.

"Fuck," I said. "I'm sitting here saying I don't wanna wind up with no woman tonight. Early on while you're picking out clothes for me to wear tonight I'm telling you you're handsome. And you shoulda heard me down there a few minutes ago, telling that Harry feller how pretty his eyes was. You think maybe I'm queer and don't know it? I mean, you can go gay, can't you?"

"I don't think so. Who said you could?"

"I remember Mama telling me one time that some girl she knew got a divorce because her husband had gone gay."

Buck looked like he was trying to keep from laughing. "Why do you think you're queer, Eric?" he asked. "Did you finally decide I'm the man for you after all these years? Well, sorry, darlin', but I don't feel that way about you anymore."

That remark took a few seconds to sink in. "Anymore? You mean used to. . . . You used to? You liked me? When was that?"

"When we were roommates. Those first few weeks, I wanted to jump your bones bad."

I tossed my cigarette over the balcony into the bushes. "Weeks?" I said. "Is that all? Shoot, I thought I had a longer lasting effect than that."

"You're crazy."

"I was reading that book you got downstairs about nymphomaniacs where it says a lot of Freudians think guys who go after a lot of women—Don Juans, they call 'em—are latent homosexuals who want to prove theirselves to the world by conquering all these women."

"And when was that book written?" Buck said.

"I don't know."

"Nineteen sixty-four."

Confession time. "It's just that no gal never gave me that special take-your-breath-away kind of feeling I thought I'd get. None of 'em had me walking with my feet off the ground."

Buck patted my check. "You're no queer, honey. You've seen too many movies like the rest of us."

"I may be no queer, but I'll tell you this. The guys around here are so goddamn handsome I feel like giving up. What do you feed 'em?"

Buck smiled. "We feed 'em special things, honey. Lots of protein."

I laughed, and looked over the balcony as the band swung into another Bob Wills tune, "Red Wing." That's when I saw her.

She was wearing a lavender dress, flirting with half a dozen ol' boys who crowded around her. A blonde. I'd always been partial to blondes. I whistled softly between my teeth.

"Who is that?" I said.

Buck squeezed my shoulder. "That is Evangeline McRoyal. Genny, we call her. Just graduated from Ole Miss. Keep your weather eye open with that one, son, and you might be okay. That girl's left a trail of ruined men from Georgia to Maine. God only knows what she did to those boys in Mississippi.

"Part of that wreckage is right down there," he said, pointing where Evangeline stood under a tree with those boys. "Look at 'em, still sniffing around. Obsessed or possessed, or stupid as hell. Hanging on to her every word. Trying to speak every time she takes a breath. Good dogs.

"She's dangerous, boy," he whispered, his lips to my ear. "Delilah. A siren. Those pretty songs lure sailors, honey."

"Oh, come on," I said. "You're going a little overboard, ain'tcha?"

He nodded, said, "Maybe," then scratched his chin. He pulled at his mustache. "Maybe not. See that fellow there? Lee Grisham. The one over there in the snappy blue blazer. Smart, well liked. Gorgeous. Looks like a movie star, don't he? Used to go with her in high school. When she broke off with him, he kind of snapped. Started going over to her house when she was out on dates, walking the floor, gnashing his teeth. Crying buckets. Her mother would give him a dose of nerve medicine then take some herself.

"He started calling her in the middle of the night. Not threatening her exactly, not at first. Being a pest was all. Then he started showing up everywhere she went, following her on dates, following her in his car, in the halls at school. His parents finally had to send him off somewhere. Boys' school they said. But when he came back, he was like a zombie for a while. Drugged out, you know? Prescriptions. Everything legal. He talked about feelings a lot. That I'm okay-you're okay crap. Goes to Duke now. Going to be a psychiatrist."

"Naw," I said.

"Oh yeah. Make a good one, too, I'll bet. Every one of 'em I ever knew was crazier'n hell."

Buck turned back to the party, looked down at the group. "See the big one," he said. "The one big as a bear? Mean like one, too. Mean as a snake. James Morgan Grant, son of John T., the state senator. Few Christmases ago he got all lickered up, got him a thirty-eight and drove himself over to the Civic Center night of the Holly Ball. Said he was gonna shoot himself, and Genny, and whoever tried to get in his way.

"Somebody had sense enough to call the police. Lou Percassi came down. You met him yet? Lou the Screw. Was an MP in the Army. From New Jersey originally. Voice sounds like he eats asphalt. Anyway, Lou walks in the ballroom wearing a trench coat, just like Columbo. Strolls over to James Morgan and says, 'Gimme the gun, you stupid shit.'

"James Morgan hands it right over. You don't mess with Lou when he's riled. The two of 'em leave together, and the ball goes on like nothing had happened. Nothing except Genny's reputation shoots up a couple or more notches. The most sought-after girl in town. Crowned Holly Queen that night. A big deal around here.

"And James Morgan, he slept it off in jail. Next week he went on up to Richmond and got married as planned. Most people at the ball that night had an invitation to that wedding, including me. Big wedding. Episcopal. Must've been seven hundred people there. Didn't last though, so he came on back home and married a local girl. That's her over there staring daggers at Genny.

"James Morgan is the youngest mayor we've ever had here. And I'll bet you that boy'll be governor of this state one day. You remember I said that when it happens."

He pointed out Angier Watson, a sports writer for the paper, one of my drinking buddies. He had on a three-piece seersucker, but still looked right seedy. Needed a haircut, bad. Angier must've been around thirty-four or thirty-five and had already left wife number three. Buck said Genny'd turned him down about twenty-five times and he'd probably ask her again tonight.

"TROUBLE," he said.

But I was young and stupid and didn't give a shit. Buck and me, two buddies from college, one gay and one straight. A leading man and a rube. And this rube was smelling that trouble and ready to jump in with both feet. Ready to fall, hard, either in love, or off of the world.

PART III: HARRY

The band was taking a break, and the lead singer was standing next to me at the bar. He was tall, lanky, and blond. I kind of figured he might be gay, the way he'd watched me dance with Eric Lansing. I hoped so, though I wasn't one of those characters who wished every good-looking man was gay. After all, we do need some straight ones on our side. But his voice had gotten to me. When he'd been singing, I could feel the notes like they were coming out of me, up from my solar plexus, pouring out of my throat like honey. It was the same feeling I'd had when I'd played the clarinet in high school. The tones I got out of that thing seemed to come from my soul.

And he had on that white cowboy hat. I always did like a cowboy.

"I like your music," I said.

"Thank you." He smiled and took off his hat, pushing blond hair from his face. "I 'preciate that."

His hand was rough when he took mine, a man who worked with his hands. "Ricky Lester. RJ."

I noticed his long, thick fingers. He had pretty teeth shining underneath a dark blond mustache, a tiny gap between the two front ones.

"Harry Dare," I said. "Where're you guys from?"

"Alabama. Tuscaloosa."

I laughed. "Roll Tide!"

His eyes were deep brown. When they looked into mine, my gaydar went off.

"You have a great voice," I said. "Where did you train?"

"Church choir."

"Really?" I said.

We stood there, looking at each other, heating up, until he finally took in a deep breath and let it out. "We're done here at midnight," he said. "I was wondering if maybe you might. . . . Now I might be outta line, here. Was that your boyfriend you was dancing with?"

He had noticed me! The smile he gave me was one nobody had ever given me before. It took my breath, much like music.

"No. He's not my boyfriend."

"Wanna go get some coffee after I'm through here?" he asked.

Footsteps rustled the grass, then someone came through the bushes. "Ricky Joe, they need you back over there, son."

It was the drummer. Dark hair, goatee. He smelled sweet, like marijuana. A longneck bottle was in his hand.

"Well, hey," he said. "Who's this?" His smile was almost obscene. I liked it.

"Come on, Sid," Ricky said. "We got to go."

"I'm out the first two numbers." He leaned closer to me. "Catch you later, RJ."

I thought I saw a look of hurt pass through Ricky's brown eyes before he turned and left us by the bushes.

The drummer moved even closer, his smell very strong. "You are some kind of cute," he said.

"And you are hot to trot."

"My middle name," he whispered, his breath warm on my face. "Whatcha doing later on?"

"I think I have a date with Ricky."

"Really?" he said, pushing his hat up higher. "Then I reckon I'd better do this while I can."

He pulled me to him.

I'd always been able to get almost any man I wanted. Thing about it was, I didn't want to have sex with all of them. I wanted them pay to attention to me, like I was special, even if it were only for a night. All I really wanted was for them to kiss me. I liked to kiss. Even when I'd dated girls, I'd enjoyed that part of it, though men were better. Men were rougher kissers. They held you tight. I liked feeling their muscles and the hardness of their backs.

Sid began swaying with the music, his mouth against mine, tongue in my mouth as he danced me deeper into the shadows. Men always thought they could maul me during a dance. Just what I gave off to make them think that, I didn't know. But Sid couldn't keep his hands off me. Most of the time, like now, I didn't mind it. But it was this kind of behavior that led me to the bedroom. I figured once we'd been kissing this way, and got hot enough, we might as well go the whole way. It was flattering that someone wanted me sexually. And this Sid was one hot taco. I kissed him back, hard, running my hands inside his shirt and down the front of his pants where I found his erection beneath the denim.

"Oh yeah, honey," he whispered. "I'm ready for you."

I felt a hand on my shoulder. "Let's go, Sid," Ricky said. "You're on after this one."

"Hell, no," Sid said. "I'm staying here. The party's just getting started."

"Move your butt."

Ricky looked right in my face, then sauntered off. He had a great ass in those blue jeans.

"See you later, honey," Sid said. He had a great ass, too. But he didn't ask my name.

PART IV: ERIC

The men were still around her as she stood under the colored lanterns by the pool. Her gauzy lavender dress almost see-through, her legs the long smooth ones of a show girl. I stayed in the shadows sipping my beer, watching as a handful of young studs in light summer suits surrounded her. They were begging to dance with her as they sweated in the heat.

"We just got here," I heard her say as she took a tall glass from one of the men. A second lit her cigarette. She smiled at him when she gave her glass to a third and placed her hand on the arm of a fourth. "I'll be here awhile," she said, "so don't worry me, hear?"

There was something about the way she teased those boys that made her seem a part of them, a woman who was comfortable in the company of men, a woman who'd been a tomboy. When she tossed her head and smiled, there was the devil in her face and eyes. She'd have knocked my socks off if I'd been wearing any.

Then the band swung into "Blue Moon," and one of the guys led her to the dance floor. The sad, mellow tones of the crooning saxophone filled up inside me, inside my chest, inside my throat as I watched her. Her movements were sharp and practiced, graceful and sexy. I can smell a trained dancer at twenty paces.

I was breathing the music, or the music became my breath since this girl had taken mine away. That's when I stepped out into the light and strolled through the dancers, real slow like, taking my time.

She was humming with the saxophone, pure and clear, her perfume smelling like the bite of a lemon. A lemon with sugar. Tart, juicy, and sweet. Made my mouth water.

I could have reached out and touched her then, but my hands were sweaty and shaking. And as I stood there, smelling that smell, the words of the song came back to me. Rogers and Hart. A song written for Jean Harlow in the 1930s.

As I stood there, smelling that smell, the words of the song came back to me. Rogers and Hart.

A song written for Jean Harlow in the 1930s.

> *And then there suddenly appeared before me*
> *The only one my arms will ever hold.*

I was singing out loud, singing to her. And when she looked at me and smiled, the dimples danced at the corners of her mouth, tiny dimples like the ones Shirley Temple had used to placate the nation.

"Do I know you?" she said.

I shrugged and touched the brim of my hat. "Maybe," I said, thinking I sounded real cool. "Who wants to know?"

Her face was so beautiful my hands started shaking again.

"I do," she said, her eyes playing with me.

I set my beer on a table behind me and tapped her partner's shoulder. "'Scuse me, bud, but this is my dance."

Her body melted against me, a perfect fit into mine. "Sing some more," she said. "I love it when men sing to me."

My hand slid down to the small of her back, touching her warm bare skin. "I bet it happens all the time," I said.

"Almost every night."

She put her head against my shoulder, like she knew me, and started humming again. Even her hair smelled like lemons.

"Blue moon," I whispered, dancing with my feet off the ground, singing some more.

She looked up at me. Her eyes were blue gray. And with the moonlight shining in them, they seemed streaked with silver stars. "Who are you?" I asked, my heart lost somewhere in those eyes.

The music had ended, but I was still holding onto her hand. "I'm Genny," she said. "And who are you?" Her fingers were dimpled, too, the nails oval, polished clear.

"Eric Lansing," I said, knowing the name would mean something to her since she'd been talking to folks around here who liked to gossip. "And you're Genny. I've heard a lot about you."

She squeezed my hand. "I'm sure you have," she said.

I took out my cigarettes, offering her one. When I lit it for her, I held the flame longer than I had to. I hadn't relaxed yet, couldn't think of a smart thing to say, was grateful when Buck rescued us, told us to meet us around on the front porch. He was getting a drink.

Evangeline sat in the porch swing and tucked one leg under the other. Buck won't too long getting there, thank God. I was still tongue-tied as shit. He draped his jacket over a rocking chair. His bow tie was already untied, his shirt opened halfway down his chest. Looked like those guys on the covers of romance novels. Ones with their shirts ripped half off, a lock of black hair over one eye while carrying some hot-looking virgin up the stairs against her will.

"How's it looking back there, son?" he asked me. "Everyone behaving? Everyone having a good time?"

He was slurring his words and kind of glassy-eyed. No big surprise since he'd been boozing since mid-afternoon. Slow, but enough to keep a good buzz on. I hoped he didn't get too drunk. He got sloppy and mean-mouthed sometimes. I hated when I had to collar him, throw him in a cold shower. And I sure as hell didn't want to have to slap him upside his head again. I mean, I was his best friend, and I was living under his roof.

"Looks like," I said. I leaned back against the baluster rail and slid my foot out of the flip-flop to scratch my ankle with my big toe. Wind chimes sang with the crickets as the wind rustled the trees above us. The smell of roses wafted from the neighbor lady's garden next door. The music and voices from the party sounded far away now, like a door had shut them off in a room.

Genny got up off the swing brushing the wrinkles out of her dress as she came toward me, slow and sexy, the high heels making her chest stick out and up. I felt the old schlong coming to life. "Could I have another one of your cigarettes?" she said. Her voice alone could have brought it to attention.

Buck saw me sweating. Looked like it was all he could do to keep from busting out laughing. He gave me a wink, put his foot on the rocker and pumped himself back and forth in the swing. "Eric's choreographing *L'il Abner,*" he said. "You ought to consider it."

"I'd consider Stupefyin' Jones." She took the cigarette I offered her and let me light it for her.

Buck stopped swinging. "Stupefyin' who?"

"Stupefyin' Jones," I said. "She's the gal that paralyzes men with her beauty."

Buck laughed. "That's a part you were born to play, Genny."

She smiled. "Oh, isn't it just."

Her arm was brushing mine, her lemon perfume making me crazy. I was either going to have to grab her like the guys on the book covers, or go in the house and take care of myself. I didn't want to be another guy in her line of ruined men, but I had to risk that. I'd never backed off from nothing, jumped in feet first not giving a damn. Things didn't always work out the way I wanted, but still . . .

A long time ago I told myself I was never going to be like my daddy. He never took a chance. I won't never gonna look back and say, "Damn! If only I'd done that."

She looked up and smiled. Her eyes, starred by candlelight, challenged me.

Sailor to the siren.

I was ready to take her on.

PART V: HARRY

I was still at the party when the band played their last set. Buck was leaning against a tree watching the band, the smoke from his cigarette curling around his head. "Hey, baby," he said. "You having a good time?"

"Yes, I am. A very good time."

As always, I got goose bumps when Buck put his arm around me. But I'd known him so long I figured if anything was going to happen between us, it already would have. He should have seduced me when I'd been innocent, a long time ago. But he was so handsome, like a blue-eyed young Hemingway. His bottom teeth were crooked, and I thought that was sexy, too.

"Dance?" he said, flicking his cigarette into the grass. He still had on his jacket, but his shirt was opened almost all the way.

"Sure." I took his hand. He smelled of cigarettes, bourbon, and sweat.

It was a slow dance, and Buck held me as close as Eric was holding my cousin Genny.

RJ was singing, hitting notes I could feel down to my toes. He watched me while he sang, looking so sad I felt guilty. I wondered if he'd still want to go out after the party. I shouldn't have let that Sid do those things to me, but it had been fun.

> *I'll be loving you, always,*
> *With a love that's true, always.*

"What are you doing?" Buck asked. He looked over his shoulder. "You flirting with some other guy while you're dancing with me?" he teased. "Well, fuck. I like that."

"He's cute," I said. "And I like the way he sings. He wanted to take me out for coffee after the party, but I screwed that up good."

Buck glanced at him again then turned back to me. "He's yours," he said. "I can tell."

I laughed at that. "How would you know?" I said. "You have worse luck with men than I do."

He pinched me on the butt, and spun me. "Touché, baby. But if it's Ricky you're worried about, don't. Ricky's very forgiving, no matter what you've done."

"I dunno about that. He caught me making out with the drummer."

"The drummer?" Buck said, glancing over at the band. "Stay away from him," he told me. "He's no good. But Ricky, Ricky's a good fellow. I got a sixth sense when someone's good for someone. It's just that sixth sense don't work for me. So if you want that singer up there, you go for it."

"He's kind of redneck."

Buck laughed. "And the drummer ain't?" His electric blue eyes were so close to my own, his lips nearly touching mine. "We're all kind of redneck, honey. My mama may have come from money, but my daddy idn't nothing but pure-T Smoky Mountain white trash. I say go for it. You never know. And if nothing comes of it, well, at least you've had yourself a helluva good time."

The band took another break, and I thought maybe Ricky would come over. But he took his guitar and started up the hill. I had to run to catch him, calling out his name. He finally stopped and waited for me, frowning, taking another one of those deep breaths. "I busted a string," he said.

"Huh?"

"I busted a string and I left my extras in the van."

I followed him, watched as he began working on his instrument. His mouth was a tight straight line. "You gonna call him?" he asked, breaking a long uncomfortable silence.

"Am I going to what?"

"You gonna call him? Did y'all make plans? 'Cause he's bad to go after ever'body I'm interested in."

I really felt ashamed now. "Sorry," I said. "I just love to kiss."

Ricky ducked his head.

"I do," I said. "I'm sorry. But I love to kiss men. Give me half a chance and they've got me in a lip lock."

He looked up.

"Come here," I told him, grinning, knowing full well how irresistible I looked now. "I'll show you."

Ricky Joe put down his guitar. He swept off his hat, dropped it to the ground, and took me in his arms. It was just like a cowboy movie. He was a great kisser, too.

"Lemme come home witcha, baby," he said, nibbling on my lower lip. "I got no place to go but home with them other boys. I wanna talk to you."

"About what?" I asked, leaning against him, undoing the top buttons on his shirt.

"Shoot. You know about what."

He tried to kiss me again, but I pulled my head back. "I'm not sure I want to talk. It's late. I'm tired and I need to go to bed. Alone."

"Come on, baby," he said. "You're driving me plum crazy."

"Oh yeah?"

"Yeah," he said, grinning.

"Well, maybe for a cup of coffee."

He sat down in the opened of the van, and restrung his guitar. Every now and then he'd look up and me and wink. He was going to fall in love with me. This type always did. The guys who were struggling with their sexuality, married men and the like.

Eric Lansing was getting ready to take my cousin Genny home in his pickup truck when I came back to the house with RJ. Buck was with them, saying goodbye. "Hey, partner," he called out, "I got a check for you."

"Thanks," RJ said, tucking it in the back pocket of his tight-fitting jeans.

Buck saluted him. "Thank you. You guys are great, as always."

"We got one more set."

"Then go to it, boy."

Genny was half in, half out of the truck, her long legs crossed as she smoked a cigarette. "Are you behaving yourself, cousin?" she asked.

"No," I said. "Are you?"

She glanced at Eric Lansing and smiled. "Of course I am. We're going for a cup of coffee. You want to go?"

"I pass," I told her. "I got something else to do."

"I'll just bet you do."

"Harry's auditioning for *L'il Abner,* too," Eric said.

Genny looked from him to me. "You two know each other?"

"Oh sure," Eric said, crossing his big arms and leaning back against his pickup. "We's old friends, ain't we, sugar?"

I laughed. I was going to like this Eric Lansing. I hated that he would probably become another one of Genny's castoffs. I hoped we could stay friends when that happened.

Buck and RJ were still talking, arranging another stint. Eric winked at me and jerked his head in their direction. "Did you snag him with those eyes?"

RJ took my arm and pulled me over into the darkness. His face was dappled in the full moonlight. "You gonna wait for me?" he said.

"Sure I am, honey."

"I won't be long."

"I'll wait right here."

"Promise?"

"Promise." And I kissed him to seal my word, I guess.

He stepped back held me at arm's length. His guitar was between us, strapped around his neck. He let out a breath and shook his head. "Damn," he finally said. "You got the prettiest green eyes I ever seen."

𝒜 4   Jesse: November 1992

Felice Picano

The first few times, Ray had helped him with the infusolator. But when he'd gotten home today, Jesse had immediately noticed the note telling him that Ray was at J.K.'s due to a "minor" emergency. Whatever that meant. Given J.K.'s dependency upon Ray for the smallest things, that note might signify anything: that J.K. had broken a fingernail or that he'd been beaten nearly to death by a hustler. The note asked if Jesse would be able to do the infusolator by himself? Or maybe not, maybe he'd wait till Ray got home? That ought to be shortly before dinnertime. Jesse decided he would do it himself. He'd learned how at the hospital, observing the step-by-step demonstrations, before and after they'd installed the Hickman Catheter in his chest, and while awkward, it wasn't difficult. Hook up the medicine and other squishy plastic bags to the intravenous rack. Open each bag with a quick twist of the wrist. Test the point to see if anything came out. Let the tube hang to his chest. Get comfortable with a book or TV remote. Snap open the stopper on the infusolator. Use the peroxide and cotton balls to cleanse the area, particularly the skin around the plastic opening a few inches above his heart. Insert the needlelike tip from the hanging tube into the infusolator. Watch it trickle into him, drop by drop, hour after hour. Think "positive, life-enhancing" thoughts. Replace it with each of the two other tube tips, cleansing chest and plastic before and after. Remove when empty. Snap infusolator closed. Rewash.

He'd better get used to doing it himself, no? What if the doctor told him he'd have to do it more than once a day? And at the office too? No, that wouldn't be a good idea, letting people at Casper, Vine see how ill he was, despite how great they'd been about it so far.

From the novel *Onyx.*

Ray had arranged the medical supplies in the lower section of the dining room sideboard. The medical stand with its arms for hanging the plastic bags—the DHPG itself, as well as the electrolyte and sugar solution—he'd placed in the living room corner between the curtained window and a bookcase. A contemporary-looking, snakelike reading lamp had been coiled around one arm of the IV rack to drop to the big, Danish, redwood and caramel-leather reading chair Ray had bought a few months after they moved in together. The idea was to downplay the medical aspect: make it a hip-sitting area. It sort of worked.

He'd always thought of the Danish number as Ray's chair, and usually settled on the sofa or perched in the Bloomies' barrel seat. But when they'd gotten home from that pre-op hospital meeting with doctors, registered nurses, and a social worker, Ray said, "This is the best spot, Jess. I know you don't like this chair, but it can be comfortable." Which was funny because Jesse adored the chair, and every opportunity he had that Ray wasn't there, he'd luxuriate in its firm, sensuous contours, stretching across it, using the arms as supports, a headrest, taking pleasure from leather sticking to his skin—like a jealous boyfriend—in summer or when he sweated from fever.

Even before the surgery, they'd worked out not only how Jesse would receive the three-hour infusions, but what might happen later if he became differently incapacitated. It was an easy decision to convert the upstairs bedroom into a prospective sickroom, and even though it was a flight of stairs up, it was near the kitchen and living room, steps from a full bath. But what if the kids slept overnight, Jesse asked. Where would they go? Ray would empty out the business's storage room next to his office, or reorganize it to leave room to open out the folding bed for the night.

Jesse hadn't been able to convey his real anxiety: It would be the first time he and Ray slept in a different room—not counting a few business trips each had taken—in twelve years. Jesse was uneasy, fearful, although he understood that it had to happen eventually: like most healthy people, even in sleep Ray emitted bacteria, and the more unable Jesse became at fighting off bacterial assault, the more isolated he would have to be. Ray slept so deeply that he didn't know how awake Jesse often was, despite fatigue. He'd jolt awake at 4 a.m. in the big bed—Ray ten feet away—light the tiny reading lamp, or put on the headphones and listen to jazz or classical music and gaze at his lover. Read, sketchily. Listen to musical, dreamily. Think.

Mostly Jesse thought about the past: his and Ray's. And he wondered about the future: Ray's, since he had no future. As for their future together, that seemed little more than an ongoing separation. That's what the sickroom upstairs signified, another, further, physical distancing from Ray.

It had begun at his diagnosis with their no longer able to have unprotected sex. Ray had not come close to complaining, of course, but Jesse felt the millimeters of plastic between them. Whenever Ray fucked him or sucked him off had been a momentous step, first in a series of barriers the disease would construct between them. The pace increased a year ago when shingles appeared on Jesse's waist—the initial excruciatingly painful indicator of the virus's active presence—and lest Ray in any way exacerbate the torture by accidentally brushing against him during sleep, Ray had slept on the folding cot, although it was placed next to their bed.

The shingles had disappeared at last, replaced by a variety of minor, less tormenting ailments, some dermatological, others neuropathic. Ray once more slept on the folding bed. Then Jesse's T-cell count dropped more than a hundred points. Ray and the cot journeyed across the big bedroom. Six months ago, a bronchial infection appeared that Jesse's physician was certain originated from a day-long cold Ray had, an infection he'd quickly thrown off, but which had lingered weeks in Jesse. So their sleep setup became permanent. Due to the virus's progress, the two no longer had sex, no longer slept in the same bed, no longer kissed, or nuzzled, or touched, except mornings and nights when Ray disinfected him.

Meaning that HIV had accomplished what no one else had been able to: Not society, which barely tolerated them together; not Jesse's background, which insisted it was morally and ethically wrong; not even his mother who despised his homosexuality and everything and everyone connected to it with a Fundamentalist Christian zealot's passion, with the hatred of a woman betrayed and robbed. Knowing what HIV had done to them hurt Jesse more than knowing he no longer had a future.

That was an odd sidelight, how with this single procedure, Jesse had realized he was going to die, and how instantly he'd accepted the fact. Naturally, he'd gone through all the steps from denial to acceptance before, in the days after the diagnosis, but now, well, now it was indisputable. Medical intervention had been critical, therefore it couldn't be more authentic, could it? In a way that delivered him from what he'd only now recognized had been a kind of apprehension. Before, everything had existed in a possible future, the way that, as a child, the illustrations in his Jules Verne novels had existed. Now, while it might not be as dramatic as pneumonia—or shingles or a bronchial infection—it meant he had a few months, a year if he dawdled.

Jesse had no intention of dawdling. Not for his sake and not for Ray's. He'd never enjoyed being ill. He still remembered his childhood illnesses: Recurring bouts of tonsillitis, his throat so swollen he couldn't even swallow water, at times could barely breathe; and the dull ache after his tonsils had been removed, and that all the ice cream in the world couldn't assuage. Or the itching, burning, scaling, hideous allergies he'd weathered when he was eight, nine, ten years old. Allergies that had returned lately.

The manifestation that brought everything into focus, to a single point, was so much less of a proclamation than any of those minor illnesses would have been: the only indication of something really wrong being a totally sensationless cloud in his left eye. But while not painful, it announced the insidious virus unchecked, growing every day more powerful, depleting him slowly, as though his life was a savings account and he daily withdrawing without ever being able to redeposit. Becoming lackadaisical had grown easy, not bothering to fight, accepting that he would walk more slowly and think less sharply, allow himself to sleep later every day: a kind of movie star dream of death: an oh-so-languid surrender to diminished capacity.

Jesse believed he'd pretty much fulfilled the nearly perfect arc of his intended life, and it would be, at the very least, unaesthetic to loiter on and allow the lovely curve to be marred by an unsightly trailing off.

He knew the high point of the arch: when he'd been made Copy Chief, following three successful print ad campaigns with industry awards and a substantial pay raise, a new corner office, a vice-presidency on its way. That same month, he and Ray, already living together several years, decided to have a commitment ceremony. They invited both families, although naturally only Ray's had come, Jesse's line represented by a second cousin, Alexa, who happened to live in the city. But Mona and Harve Henriques had driven out from Illinois, along with Ray's two aunts, Jana and Rose. Dressed as bridesmaids were Alexa and Kathy (there with her newest husband and the three-and-a-half-year-old Chris, who'd been their cherubic, somewhat confused, blond ringbearer) while Kai Morito from Jesse's workplace had been usher, with J.K. as best man. All in formal wear—morning suits, ascots, cummerbunds—with flowers and live music and a stout, gray-haired clergywoman from Long Island's North Fork. Four couples and three singles from Casper, Vine drove out too, including a partner. Another dozen came from EMI/Capitol. Running the entire three-ring circus was J.K., who'd contrived their wedding to rival something in *Modern Bride,* taking place at a loaned, ten-bedroom, "equestrian estate" in rural Long Island on an early May Saturday.

Ray and Jesse awakened the next morning with Chris between them. He had crawled out of the apparently noisier and more active bedroom of his mother. As the toddler slumbered, they discussed kids, concluding yes—either their own or their families' children would definitely be part of their lives.

Later that summer they'd rented a monster house on the beach at Fire Island Pines, with J.K. and the newly met Liesl as housemates. It had been wonderful, magical, the best summer ever. By fall, Ray was promoted and they could afford winter vacations; London at Christmas, Cancun in February. Life had been good.

And had continued good, losing glitter here and there, slowly, inexorably as the epidemic grew and began striking people around them, the circle drawing tighter and tighter, finally striking them. Yet, if he were sworn in front of a courtroom, Jesse would have to tell the truth: The past twelve years had delivered so much more than he'd ever expected, had so totally fulfilled his hopes and dreams, that nothing—no illness, no separation, no loss—could take from him the belief that although he'd been undeserving, he'd been wonderfully gifted.

Growing up as basically an only child in a rigorously staid, ultra-Christian, tradition-drenched Southern family in a state capital no bigger than most Northern mill towns, Jesse had been certain that what he'd come to think of as his "daydreaming" would always remain exactly that. An only child, because it was only once he turned thirteen that a second pregnancy happened, surprising no one as much as Adele Vaughan Moody, neé Carstairs, who fumed, who barely spoke to her husband the last four months she carried. By then, Jesse had come to figure out those elements needed for defending himself, and for waging guerrilla war against his mother, who seemed to want only one thing, to ingest him whole. Or was it to become him? To live his life for him? It seemed to vary.

Childhood illness turned out to be an unanticipated weapon in their ongoing skirmishes. Mostly because Adele—while she could become as self-sacrificing and loyal as any woman on earth—feared certain infectious illnesses, especially those that might disfigure her lovely facial features. How many times had she retold the pitiful saga of her cousin, May Dunwoodie, a prepossessing young lady slated to marry a Lee of Virginia, who'd lost all in a toss of the medical dice when she'd contracted scarlatina and been left "disfeatured; socially no better than a Nigrah washerwoman."

Jesse's inexplicable facial rashes, his abruptly swollen lips, his blooming acne—reactions to foods or flowers—threw the fear of facial damage into his mother so intensely she (blissfully!) kept away, not merely while he was actually affected, but often long after, leaving him in the care of Mrs. Green, their plump, sweet-tempered cook and housekeeper, who'd never previously hinted at interest or ability in befriending him, or in defending him from the Scylla of his mother's emotional clutch and the Charybdis of her uncontrollable temper.

During the second year of dermal afflictions, Adele withdrew almost altogether from Jesse, no longer requiring him on local forays or shopping trips downtown where formerly he'd been her escort, package-bearer, pet, and victim. She now went alone, or with a woman friend; she even learned to drive.

Jesse remained at home, idle at first, at loose ends, but then eventually much occupied. In good weather, he'd scavenge the lush thickets and disordered groves of the sizable acreage surrounding the Moody house, down to deeply crevassed Foxglove Creek, across the wide meadows to the hickory wood, wherein still lay the perilous ruins of a long-abandoned, cedar-slatted, Confederate ammunition depot. He wandered as far as the Napier's tobacco farm on the one end (always busy, filled with machinery and people) to the granite quarries on the other, playing solitary as a polecat (since Adele had long declared no boy in town good enough to be befriended) hours at a time, pretending to be both Chingachook and Natty Bumppo, Lieutenant Lightfoot

Harry and Colonel Burnside, Jim Hawkins and Long John Silver, Huck and Jim, Robinson Crusoe and Friday, Ned Tannen and Captain Nemo: his storybook heroes, their beloved co-adventurers, loving companions and sworn enemies, all in one, sometimes mixed together.

In this fashion, he grew tanned and agile, energetic and enduring, audacious and daring. In Adele's words when she bothered to notice him, "nothing better than one of those grease-haired, half-breed Cherokees stumbling by the feed store."

Evenings, stormy days, and freezing weather, the boy remained solitary indoors, often for hours at a time, at Mrs. Green's table, watching her bake and roast and steam, listening to her chitchat and anecdotes and eventually, when he'd come to trust her, relating his dreams for the future.

Unlike Adele Vaughan Moody, neé Carstairs, Mrs. Green (Lylah, he discovered was her first, musical, name) did not dash his wishes, saying, "What foolishness! You'll certainly not go off North to live and kill your poor mother with a heart attack. You'll stay here and work in the law offices of your poppa's partners." Or "You don't know what you're saying, boy! You shall not reside with your best male friend forever. You shall marry a girl of good lineage and raise a family and carry on the Moody name. Who fills your head with such cowboy drivel?"

No, Mrs. Green would instead talk of someone she knew (she never said whom) had gone to a big northern city and uncovered not cheats and ogres, but kind and gallant folk, and how that person had thrived; she even once spoke of her cousin Antoine, whom she'd described as artistic and elegant, and how he'd traveled up to Philadelphia and found himself not a woman—he'd disdained such since he was a child—but a young gentleman of similar tastes, and how they'd moved in together and were the toast of their social set. Suggesting that if Jesse wanted to do the same, there was precedent, even if it were—she had to apologize—colored.

The part of the dream he'd never been able to tell her during those intimate chats—forever permeated in his memory by the fragrance of vanilla and almond extracts, freshly baked biscuits and pies, overripe banana mixed with honeysuckle and jasmine during the spring months, spruce and Georgia pine during the fall—was his dream-companion. Sympathetic as he came to know Mrs. Green to be, he'd never been able to bring himself to confide in her what this companion would be like, because it was so opposite of what he thought she dreamt. His friend wouldn't be elegant, wouldn't dress in fresh starched shirts, with triangles of scented handkerchiefs, wouldn't visit for tea and sip at aperitifs.

His companion would be strong, masterful, manly, unpretty, scarred or crag-faced, someone who'd unthinkingly remove his shirt in public as backwoods workmen did laboring at the old Indian quarries, and like them, he'd be sinewy and rock-bodied, unashamed and natural acting—as ready to shake your hand in friendship as strike you for some offense or scorn you for being a fool.

No question in Jesse's mind but that Daddy Moody didn't fit the mold. Once he almost had. Jesse remembered how when he was four, they taken a summer vacation to the beaches of Georgia and how after playing in surf and sand every day, his daddy would take him by the hand into a roofless bathhouse where, among other boys and men, he'd remove his and Jesse's sand-choked bathing suits and rinse them in the overhead shower while they stood nude and washed themselves with soap and water, the curious boy looking at everyone else. And how his daddy lifted him onto the built-in wood benches between lockers of the changing room and dried him with a towel, while his own huge, slabby body glittered with water droplets among the fine, curling, mats of chocolate colored hair. Day after day for two weeks, they shared the ritual, and it had given the little boy ample opportunity to observe not only his father's body, but also that of other men and boys. Even then his daddy's belly had been round, his elbows, knees, and back tending toward fat. The child had asked if he'd look like him when he grew up, and Daddy Moody had said, "No, son, you favor the Carstairs, not the Moodys. You're refined and fine-boned. You'll grow up slender. Lissome, like your mother."

As predicted, fine-boned and lissome, refined and slender he became by the time he was thirteen, partly due to heredity, partly due to the illnesses which had kept him indoors playing alone in the toy room, sitting in the kitchen; partly from his imagination-filled athletics out of doors; while his daddy swelled from slab to flab, from thick-bodied to larded with pounds of extra flesh. Then it was, wishing more than ever to share his outdoor adventures with some beloved youth his age, that Jesse began to recall those other men and boys he'd seen at the beach that lovely summer, men wiry and muscled, skin so taut shower water sprang off as though burned. The teen Jesse began to witness his own fluids flow hot as he slept, as he washed in the tub, and with those unexplained spasms of his growing body, a concomitant longing, almost an agony, grew in him to be alongside one of those men, to touch him and be touched back, to clasp him around the shoulders, clench him by the waist, grasp and stroke, knead and punch those powerful limbs.

"Preternaturally gifted as a young scholar" was how the high school dean described Jesse when recommending him to colleges, despite his mother's constant criticism of him as "dreamy, lazy, and know-nothing." Possibly because of all the reading he had done on his own, thrown back upon his own resources as he'd so long been, examining in detail the twenty-volume *Encyclopedia America,* the two-volume *Columbia Dictionary,* the giant *Oxford Atlas,* H. G. Wells's *Story of History,* and Bury's *History of Greece,* in fact most of the books on his father's office, some unread, their pages still uncut. So Jesse had been admitted to a small, prestigious, barely Southern, East Coast university, where in the first few weeks, he'd discovered, to his astonishment, that everything so far in his life had not made him the complete loser and fool he'd for years considered himself (that his mother insisted he was) but instead a handsome, poised, self-possessed youth: someone desirable.

Not only desirable to girls—who, like Mrs. Green's cousin, Jesse had never quite gotten the point of. The first well-built young man who'd dropped to his knees and sucked Jesse's cock in the shower room merely confirmed what his slightly older, more sophisticated dormmate, Pryor Fleck, laughingly said, "You damned innocent child! Don't you know that with your rotogravure face and your illustrated-book body, with your thick chestnut hair and your great golden eyes, you are as the god Apollo to this dorm, possibly to the whole damn school! Get all you want, boy. But don't spread too much if you want to keep your reputation."

Jesse had thus peered around more closely, and if at first the slumbering old red brick and black-walnut-shaded campus had appeared to offer a plenitude of young men exactly his type, he'd soon enough come to realize that pretty much all of them possessed one serious failing or another, from stupidity and cupidity to vulgarity and effeminacy. Accosted on one of his near-daily runs, and persuaded into joining the track and field team, Jesse instantly lighted upon its cap-

tain, upperclassman jock Beau Wheeling, who seemed the least de-
fective of lads, and even though Beau was "going steady" with a junior named Nancy Janeck, Jesse had in Pry Hadley's words, "publicly
and privately set his cap" for Beau, and after a few weeks of siege—
both subtle and overt—had maneuvered the craggily handsome strawberry blond into his bed, whereupon Beau demonstrated a remarkable
amatory aptitude, for one so ostensibly heterosexual, in what Pry always referred to as "the Hellenic arts."

Beau remained in Jesse's bed until he graduated, by which point
Jesse had almost mastered several noncurriculum assignments, including critical lessons in the male ego as well as barely squeaking
through a course in what was needed to keep a male-male relationship going. His sophomore year, Jesse's "chosen" was even more
open to public scrutiny: Yancey Eubanks, the popular, devil-may-
care quarterback of the Swamp Foxes, was known to be in love with
grain alcohol, himself, football, money, and Jesse—in that order. By
the end of the year, Jesse had reversed the order and in so doing also
managed to haul the maladroit Foxes to near the top of their league as
well as attract an NFL offer for Yancey to play professionally. Of
course, Jesse thereupon consolidated his fame as a heartbreaker by
very publicly dumping Yancey in the middle of the final home game,
driving off at half-time in the sapphire-blue and white Maserati road-
ster of a Savannah millionaire playboy, "Val" (Valentine) De Spain.

De Spain lasted a summer, and his social connections and largesse
for once even managed to partially shut the ever-critical mouth of
Adele Moody, neé Carstairs. At last, however, the precise nature of
her son's various "friendships" was made clear to her, and the horrified Adele, by this time no longer totally encumbered with the full-
time occupation of ruining the life of her young daughter, turned her
attention back to perform an identical service for her son. She applied
untold pressures upon Jesse. A rather embarrassed Daddy Moody—
who scarcely comprehended what the term *invert* meant, never mind
what it might entail—was forced to threaten the boy that he'd have to
"shape up" or leave college and be thrown upon his own resources.
Jesse's allowance was cut, and what he didn't receive was sent to the
perfidious Pry Hadley, bribed by Adele into spying and reporting.
Even more humiliating, Jesse was coerced to present himself at the
offices of a Freudian psychiatrist who claimed to be able to cure what
Jesse now thought of as his natural sexuality.

Made uncertain by all this of what he'd believed to be his preordained trajectory in life and more than a little chastened by what even Jesse had to admit were three unsuccessful love affairs in a row, he subsided into a decline in his junior year. He took a dorm room of his own, threatened Pry Hadley's life, scorned his former pals in the lesbigay campus club, dropped off the team, ceased attending athletic events, and shunned the gyms and locker rooms where his lithe body was in high demand. Instead he took to skulking about campus, lurking in off-quad coffee houses and beaneries, moping about the library, sulking upon the lawns, dressed in outsized and seldom laundered, all-black garb. He let his hair and beard grow long and uncombed. He took up cigarette and pot smoking. He spoke to no one. Refused to answer questions in or out of class. Walked out in the middle of class exams. Didn't hand in term papers.

Meanwhile, Adele insisted on dragging him away from the college and "temptation" every opportunity she saw—each holiday and long weekend—and while he was home, she pushed Jesse into heterosexual liaisons. She almost no longer cared whom he associated with, so long as it was a female. The tenth time his mother introduced him to a "nice girl" and pressured him to drive her home, Jesse did so, parked, and necked with the willing young lady, and ended up persuading her to perform oral sex on him. Legal prosecution was barely averted. Jesse seemed very near a total breakdown. He advanced into his senior year by a cat's whisker.

That interim summer he remained at home but took up residence in a room over the garage, furnished by the previous owners for a chauffeur, and in which he'd played often as a child. His by now thoroughly alarmed father avoided him, and even the rapacious Adele momentarily ceased her demands. Jesse had hoped to spend time as he had done years before with Mrs. Green. But the cook had grown old, was now half deaf, and seemed unclear about exactly whom Jesse was. His sister, now seven, tried to befriend him. After a bit and mostly because Jesse knew they shared physical and verbal abuse at the same hands, they ended up bonding a little.

He managed to clean himself up enough to complete his final courses and to graduate from college. He cut his hair and shaved his beard, and dressed sufficiently well to occasionally hustle the bar of the best hotel in his college town: The only sex he now pursued was geared toward fattening his savings account, for he sensed he'd soon be on his own. Jesse had scored an impressively profitable john not an hour before what would be his final meeting with the quack psychologist. Ostentatiously counting twenties in front of the shrink, Jesse not only explained where it came from but exactly how—and how often—he had labored to earn it. Consequently, he was physically ejected—guffawing—from the office.

On the street, still laughing, Jesse had run into a classmate who'd long had a crush on him. She was unusually somber, and told Jesse she was about to be interviewed by an advertising agency that had sent its headhunter to the school. Partly to accompany her—she was so nervous, and after all had always been kind to him—and partly as a giggle, Jesse also interviewed. Because of his many literature and social studies classes, the personnel man assumed he'd wish to be a copywriter. They had a great time, he and the interviewer, Jesse on the spot creating ridiculous ad slogans and absurd campaigns for imaginary items of clothing and personal care. They periodically went off in gales of laughter. It had been a great hoot. No wonder Jesse was astounded two weeks later when he received a letter from the ad agency with an offer to join the copy department.

He'd told his father of the offer (assuming he'd then tell Adele) and without bothering to attend his own commencement ceremony, had moved to New York a week later. The job was perfect: He became part of a team on new accounts, a half dozen other young people and two experienced ones. He found a studio apartment near Grammercy Park, and desultorily furnished it. He began spending weekend nights at the city's many gay bars and dance clubs, the bathhouses and sex clubs. It was his first years of college all over again: Jesse discovered that without having done anything specifically about it, he was now more physically desirable than ever, able to land virtually every handsome, muscular guy he chose. He whored around for two years, never meeting anyone he wanted to see more than a few times, but at least if he was a slut, he slutted around more privately than he'd done as a college lowerclassman, if still with that single aim in mind: to find his dream companion.

Just as Jesse was beginning to think he'd once more failed, some friends had taken him to a party at a nearby apartment of a man named J.K. Callaway. They thought Jesse and J.K. would get along great. And while they looked good together, and indeed, had good sex twice, it turned out not to be J.K. but a pal of his, one Ray Henriques, re-encountered on a beach towel on the "tar beach" rooftop of J.K.'s apartment building, who actually was the first man to ask if Jesse was seeing anyone, if Jesse was serious about looking to settle down, if he wanted to be married to another man.

They'd seen each other around for some months before that seren-dipitous rooftop tanning session, at various clubs and bars, and of course they had officially met once before, at J.K.'s party. Jesse had been drawn to Ray's slightly off features—his odd mixture of thick, dark blond hair with too deeply set, soft brown, almost Latin eyes; his prominent, ambiguously ethnic nose; his massive-shouldered, small-hipped body with its constantly active, oversize hands; square elbows and knees. This awkward blending of physical anomalies not only held together, but, suffused by Ray's enormous energy and alertness, strongly attracted. But if Jesse had been attracted, he'd also been of-fended when Ray, passing by, had said "'scuse me, Huck." Sensitive that he still had a noticeable accent, Jesse had taken it as hostile re-mark.

At their rooftop re-encounter months later—relaxed in the warm sun, mollified by joints of grass and tall, icy lemonades—the two of them were alone together for a long while as J.K. dropped downstairs to his flat to take a phone call. Ray corrected the misunderstanding, explaining he had intended anything but offense: Huckleberry Finn was his absolute favorite; in fact, he used to jerk off to the illustration of the Clemens character when he was growing up. Did, Jesse, by chance, have a photo of himself he didn't mind getting semen-smeared?

That evening they left J.K.'s together and ended up in bed, and while Jesse was by now used to men lavishing affection upon him, he'd seldom met anyone like Ray, who demanded so much of the same in return.

"You're awfully pretty, kiddo," Ray muttered into Jesse's ear, after sex, unwilling to let him move an inch away. "But you're awfully spoiled too."

"Here I was thinking you were far too aggressive and vain for me to have anything to do with," Jesse had replied, "Much too demand-ing."

Ray chuckled. "I guess this affair is totally doomed from the begin-ning!"

"Totally fucking doomed." Jesse agreed with a laugh.

Now as he drowsed, twelve years after that declaration, Jesse recalled waking up in the hospital a week ago, the infusolator surgically installed a few hours earlier, feeling his entire chest area around the new thing quite sore, as if someone had punched him there, which was how the doctor had predicted it would hurt. Ray had been watching him sleep, waiting for him to wake up, and when he had, Ray had almost jumped out of the chair at him, asking, "How do you feel, kiddo! Terrible, huh?"

While the DHPG finished dripping into him, and the other stuff began, the phone rang and Jesse let the machine pick up, knowing it was his mother making her nightly call of demands, claims and complaints, alarms, anxieties and manipulations. She'd begun phoning him two and a half years ago, the day Jesse's father died, filled with new apprehensions and the very same old lies, with long-used pleas, exhausted attempts at evoking guilt, and fresh maneuvers at disturbing his life. He'd been forced to deal with her, after all. Jesse had to return home for the funeral, and while there, he was impressed by how small and frail and helpless Adele appeared. Of course that didn't last long. Soon enough she was up to her old tricks again. Even so, Jesse felt that he was now at a considerable advantage over her. His life was so good, he could afford to be gracious and giving, especially to one so unhappy and lacking. Besides which, he was 800 miles away, reachable only by phone. So he listened to every third word she said, and if that included something absolutely demanding response, he usually offered one. But once the phone was hung up, he more or less forgot about her. Meanwhile Adele seemed momentarily placated, if by no means satisfied—she would *never* be satisfied—and so they'd resumed some kind of relationship, in which their roles, if not reversed, were at least altered from how they'd always been, to the point that he believed he could no longer be worked upon by the force of her wiles and passions. For the moment, that is, since implacability was her middle name and she would never cease trying until she'd gotten what she wished. Which was why, more and more as he felt himself weakening and letting go, he sometimes didn't pick up the phone when he knew it was her, didn't take her messages, didn't even listen.

When he awoke, an hour later, the tubes were all empty, and Ray was reaching up to the IV rack, removing them, bending down to disinfect Jesse's chest with the cotton balls and peroxide. He looked terrible: pale, upset. As Jesse watched, a tear rolled down one of Ray's cheeks. Jesse touched it. Ray saw he was awake and Ray tried to talk, tried to tell him about J.K.'s emergency, about visiting J.K. He could barely get the words out, he was so disconcerted.

So Jesse said for them both, "J.K.'s got it too!" Jesse had already known that before today, of course; he had intuited it the last time they'd all been together a few weeks ago. Something about J.K.'s skin tone, his suddenly depleted face when seen at a particular angle—the by now unmistakable signature of the disease. Of course he hadn't said anything at the time. Why bother? It would come in its own time. Now it had come.

"Poor Ray. Nothing but bad news. You deserve better."

"No, no!" Ever kind, ever ready to cheer Jesse up, Ray went on to say, "Not all bad. I met a friend of Liesl's at lunch. He wants me to find music to score a movie he directed. A small movie," he added. "A small, independent film."

"Hey. That does sound like good news."

They talked about that a few minutes. Jesse found himself distracted, cogitating about being a boy again. Now look at me, he wanted to say, a lump in a chair hours at a time, passively receiving what may or may not save my sight, but cannot ever possibly save my life. Why start? It would only upset Ray more.

Ray settled onto an ottoman at Jesse's knees, talking about J.K. and the visit to him; then about Liesl and the man making the film. But Jesse had stopped listening, even as he stroked Ray's thick dark blond hair. He was a boy again, suddenly free from the schoolhouse, flying down the hill and across the two-laned, uneven gravel road, long hair swept by wind, limbs elastic with vigor, charging across the road, into a meadow, his book bag flopping against his legs, his jacket behind him eliciting eerie whooshing noises, as he leapt across small chasms and all but flew over the blue grass, pursuing purple-black "darning needles" and scaring polecats and chipmunks out of their hiding holes, eleven years old, accompanied all about as he glided over the landscape by nothing more substantial than cockleburrs and pine-cones, ivory powder-puffs and golden pollen, all of it and him too, immersed in sunlight, dancing, thoughtless, laden with life, in the sun.

5 That Year's Crop of Kisses

Robin Lippincott

We were eighteen, boys becoming men, Peter, Tom, and me; it was the archetypal golden summer during which such a passage often mirrors the transition between high school and college, but none of us was sure. Like mature tadpoles, or hopeful frogs, we were—not without parental coercion—attempting to shed our tails, grow our own two feet, and hop onto the murky shores of adulthood. During that hot summer all three of us seemed to vacillate between extreme behaviors of the one and the other, and we eventually came to realize such a transformation was indeed a slippery one. It was that delicate awkwardness on which our threesome seemed to float.

Peter, half-Irish and half-Czech, was childlike, full of himself, and he loved, above all else, being loved; Tom, the youngest child of elderly parents, was loving; and I, who always seemed to be in the middle whenever the three of us were together, loved both of them.

This was Central Florida, the early 1970s, where eighteen, for most of us, was much younger than it is today. We had met at a group for progressive young Christians. Serendipitously, all three of us started attending meetings at around the same time, and the fact that we were initiates together made us fast friends. Though obviously searching for *something*—friendship, some affirmation of what we already believed, or belief itself—each of us was there, at least at the start, for a different reason. Being somewhat theatrical, I was drawn by and soon participating in the weekly skits, which were conceived by the leaders of the group. Though these sketches were often highly imaginative, the viewer seldom escaped without getting hit over the head with some sort of wholesome moral message, of which I soon

---

"That Year's Crop of Kisses" was first published under the title "The Season of 'We'" in the short story collection *The Real, True Angel,* by Robin Lippincott, published by Fleur-de-Lis Press, 1996.

grew tired. Ever impressionable, Peter was there under the influence
of other friends, friends he would soon drop. Only Tom was sincere in
the pursuit of his faith. But in the end, those meetings were merely a
springboard for the threesome we would become, and it wasn't long
before we stopped attending. Tom said he was sure enough in his
faith, and Peter and I didn't much care—especially in the face of the
opportunity for the three of us to spend time together.

We were children of middle-class homes, living in three different
suburban neighborhoods with our parents and siblings. But all of
that—our parents, our brothers and sisters, where we lived, our pos-
sessions, our other friends—*everything else* seemed to fade into the
background once we met each other; it was as if we were suddenly,
the three of us together, spotlit.

I can still remember my first impressions of both of them. Peter
looked like an angel—round-faced, rosy-cheeked, with curly black
hair; he was decidedly cherubic. And Tom reminded me of Pinocchio
(no moral analogy intended) with his long, pointed nose between
close-together, green, feral eyes; he had one of the most perfect bodies I have ever seen. I first saw it, all of it, when the three of us were at
the lake we frequented that summer. It was in the middle of the afternoon, hot; sunlight sparkled across the surface of the water. Sitting on
the dock swinging our bare feet and talking, about blind faith I think,
one of us, I don't remember which (though it was probably Peter)
dared the other two to take off all their clothes and jump in. Without
hesitation and without saying a word, Tom stood up and removed his
shirt—his broad shoulders tapered down in a perfect V to his narrow
waist; next he took off his jeans, and then his underwear. His buttocks
were rounded and firm, like an unripe peach, and I admired the way
the sinewy muscles in his legs worked into that solid roundness as he
ran down the length of the dock and jumped, cannonball style, into
the water. First Peter, who still had some of his baby fat but was nev-
ertheless muscular, then I (lanky), followed, and once in the water the
three of us wrestled, laughing, our wet, shining bodies occasionally
rubbing together.

Our bodies, in fact—ripe-to-bursting with youth and sexuality—
were a significant, subconscious part of our relating. Though we were
still innocent and remained so that summer, perhaps more conscious
was the knowledge that we were playing, experimenting, and the
tease of release was powerful. One of the ways we let off steam was

through massage, which we had picked up at the meetings. *Back rubs* sounded less sexual, and we soon came to end most nights together naked from the waist up, wearing only our Levi's, straddling one another and kneading away. How I loved feeling their weight on me, the strength in their hands imprinting itself on my body's memory, kneading me into a kind of self-realization.

Another sip of release came through kissing each other—on the lips, which was something Peter started. All three of us were shocked by it at first, but we enjoyed it and so continued to lip-kiss throughout the summer. Though usually quick pecks, the kisses were occasionally long and hard, if always tongueless—except once, when Peter inserted just the tip of his tongue between my lips. I got drunk on it!

We did everything together—camping, hiking, bicycling; we went to the movies and to a concert or two; we slept on the beach one night—an experience made all the more exciting by the fact that it was against the law. And then there was the huge, open field, off the main road on the way to the beach, about five acres or so. We usually went there at night; it was the one place where we could really let go. We'd race, running as fast as we could, calling out and challenging each other, sometimes stripping off our clothes as we ran, each pushing the other two to run faster and faster through the knee-high grass until our legs couldn't keep up and we would inevitably fall down. We stood in the middle of the field and screamed—obscenities, or anything we wanted—at the top of our lungs; or two of us would take the arms of the other and swing him through the air until he was dizzy. We also played the game Trust, where one of us shut his eyes and fell backwards, relying on the other two to catch him: I usually had a hard time with this.

One of the things that made our threesome possible was that, oddly enough, neither Tom nor Peter was dating—perhaps because they were both more tadpole than frog; and I, though I did not know it then, was dating them. Nor were there the usual homosexual jokes so typical among boys-into-men. In fact, I remember one late night after eating at one of our favorite restaurants, a pancake house along busy highway 17-92, we were standing out in the parking lot saying goodbye, hugging and kissing as usual, when two men in a rust-colored car with a poor exhaust system drove by and yelled, over their ragged muffler, Faggots! Peter and Tom were kissing at that very moment and I was standing beside them. I flinched at the sound of the dreaded word and backed away a few steps. Though I did not know, for sure, that I was gay, I experienced a spark of self-conscious recognition at the accusation: I had been found out. But I remember so well Tom and Peter's response: they looked at each other, then at me, and burst out laughing! Ever-generous and daring, Tom walked over and kissed me on the lips, and we all laughed again, though I felt jealous of their easy dismissal of the epithet that had been hurled at us, alone. Then Tom raised the ante even higher, added yet another chip to the kitty of our romance. Looking me straight in the eyes, he said, I love you. It became, then and there, part of our repertoire.

Breakfast was our favorite meal. Whether late at night after back rubs or a trip to the field, or early morning before a jaunt to the beach or a canoe trip down the Wekiva River, or late morning after a late evening and a good night's sleep, we would meet at one of three places, eat breakfast, and talk for hours. Religion was our main topic of conversation. Tom—a steadfast and thoughtful believer who always impressed me because he actually used his mind and took *nothing* at face value— questioned everything and was continually challenging Peter and me. I had difficulty with the concept of faith, because I saw it as being *always* blind: I had never, not once, I said to Tom, seen proof of God's existence; had he? (Of course he had.) And Peter blew about with the wind on matters of faith, but he was well enough versed in Bible-speak to be able to impress Tom when he wanted to.

As for the other main subject of our discussions, music, we had similar tastes, which tended toward the well-crafted folk song by both male and female singer-songwriters. We analyzed the lyrics for hours, and sometimes we sang. In fact, the only time we ever got drunk together, we were sitting on the dock at the lake singing at the tops of our voices. Peter even stood up to better throw himself into the song, his curly-haired silhouette almost black against the spotlight of the full moon.

But then the light, *their light,* which had come to seem as natural to me as that given off by the sun or the moon, went out. On the fifteenth of August, the day after our drunken songfest by the lake, Tom and Peter told me that, come September, they were going away together for three months to work at a camp in the Rockies owned by the young Christians organization. We were standing in the parking lot of the pancake house again. Tom did all the talking. He winced and said that they had put off telling me—they had known for weeks—because they didn't want to hurt me. Otherwise, he said he couldn't really explain it: it was something they wanted to do. He said he was sorry. Peter just stood there with his head down, nodding; he was gutless.

My cheeks burned. I felt hot. Tears welled in my eyes and my throat constricted. Good Christians! I thought, wishing the two of them were dead. But I couldn't say a word. All of the self-esteem I had gained through my friendship with them seemed to drain out of me and collect in a pool at my feet. I turned away, shielding my face. Tom tried to put his arm around my shoulder, but I shook him off. Somehow, I gathered myself together enough to take off running; I ran as fast and as far as I could, until I was out of breath and could run no further.

Over the next two weeks, despite repeated phone calls from both of them, as well as several surprise visits from Tom, I refused to see or talk to either of them—much to the exasperation of my family. And then Tom and Peter left town.

I think it must have rained for two weeks straight that September, and I broke down. I died and came back a completely different person, my chromosomal furnishings seemingly rearranged. Suddenly, I was dark, introspective. Where I had not been a reader before, now I stayed in my room and devoured books. I read all of J. D. Salinger. And these lines from Carson McCullers's *The Member of the Wedding* spoke to me:

> *They are the we of me.* . . . She was an
> *I* person who had to walk around and
> do things by herself.

But I also read heavier, weightier books—*The Diary of Anne Frank, Dear Theo* (van Gogh's letters to his brother), even Dostoyevsky and Kafka.

I did nothing else that fall—didn't look into applying to colleges; didn't get a job. Instead, I sat in my room and read, or looked out the window at the rain; sometimes I took long walks and got soaked. My parents were worried about me, but fortunately they also had the good sense to leave me more or less alone.

I started keeping a journal and scribbled away in it feverishly. It was there that I worked out the many theories as to why Tom and Peter had done what they had, most of which were a variation on the idea that they knew and were embarrassed about my homosexuality, and that they had simply chosen to put some distance between me and them. In the pages of that journal I began the long, slow process of coming to terms with being gay; and it was there that I continually reminded myself, tried to force myself to look at and accept the hard fact that I was no longer part of a "we."

But splitting off from me seemed to kill *them,* too. Something happened between Tom and Peter that fall which would change their relationship forever, a fact Peter later mentioned rather provocatively, then refused to expound on. My best guess has always been that he told Tom he was in love with him, and that Tom simply couldn't handle it.

I saw them only occasionally after that, when they returned from camp, but it was never the same again. And then I moved away, to go to college in Boston, where I have stayed and made a life for myself, with a lover and a good job. Of course I have thought of Tom and Peter on occasion over the past twenty years, but I rarely got past their names; I wouldn't allow myself to remember much of the context.

It was the smell of rain which first set-off the memories—the smell of rain when the temperature and the humidity were just right and my mind was loose and free enough; not often. But once the memories started, *everything* seemed to connect to that time and place. Hearing Nina Simone sing "This Year's Crop of Kisses," I couldn't help thinking of Tom and Peter, for obvious reasons, I suppose: that year's crop *was* particularly sweet to me. Finally, as if this confluence had been building toward an end (and hadn't it?), there were some hard facts: a friend visiting her parents in Orlando had seen Peter and Tom. Both were married, with kids; she said they seemed almost to vie with each other in expressing their curiosity about me, plying her with questions and telling her to be sure to say hello.

Only this summer have I been able to allow the memories to come washing over me; I must have been ready. Remembering has been harrowing; at times I haven't wanted to return to the present. Not because life is so bad now, but because of the heightened intensity of those youthful experiences. And remembering has also reconnected me with some of the happiest moments of my life, experiences which seem so remote and foreign to me now, of another season. . . .

There was a five-story high parking lot in downtown Orlando we occasionally rode our bikes to. Late at night, when the lot was empty, we would walk or sometimes ride our bikes to the top story, and then coast down the declining ramp five floors, feet on our handlebars, wind in our hair. I suppose we had done it often enough that our enjoyment of it was beginning to pale, so Peter—who else?—decided to raise the stakes this particular August night.

Why don't we try doing it holding hands? he suggested.

It was the sort of exercise in risk and trust that Peter thrived on, and which now best characterizes friendship for me.

Tom shook his head and smiled at him, then at me.

Always eager to fit in and be up to whatever challenge or dare the two of them might present, I agreed. I will if you will, I said to Tom.

It was after midnight and the city had grown quiet. Peter just sat there on his bike looking at the two of us, waiting.

It's crazy, Tom finally said, scratching the back of his head. But I'll do it.

We walked our bikes to the top of the lot and positioned them at the edge of the incline. Tom said, If you feel yourself starting to wobble at all, let go, okay? Peter and I nodded. We mounted our bikes. We were nervous. We grabbed hands—I was in the middle and so had nothing to hold onto the handlebars with. I had to trust Peter and Tom with the steering. I felt their firm grips squeezing my hands, felt their pulses and mine beating together, blending. Now! Tom said.

We lifted our feet off the ground and began moving, slowly at first, but very soon we were coarsing through the air as one. The corners were difficult, but wide, and we made the first one. Tom shifted his grasp along my forearm to my elbow. We wobbled, but none of us let go, nor did we fall. We couldn't look at each other but instead had to stare straight ahead, silent, Tom and Peter steering with their free hand. We were going faster now, but we made the second corner as well. It's all downhill from here, Tom said, and Peter started laughing.

But Tom was right. We sailed on, down, faster, to the bottom level, exhilarated, still holding hands, still we.

6 Emory and Henry

Jeff Mann

It was the year America turned 200, the summer of freedom celebrations and especially grand Fourth of July parties. When I think of 1976, however, what I remember is not so much bicentennial excitement as it is a small college in southwest Virginia. It was there that I began to realize the risks incurred by living honestly and freely, even in America, and it was there that I received my first vivid taste of homophobia.

That spring, a junior at Hinton High School, I had first realized I was gay. Several of my friends in the Ecology Club were lesbians, as was the club's advisor, Jo Davison. Then Davison lent me Patricia Nell Warren's novel *The Front Runner.* I was fascinated by its hero, Billy Sive, a track star, and soon began to understand that the admiration I felt for certain classmates and older men was sexual.

Luckily, I already had a lesbian support group, and my father had raised me on the nonconformist literature of Emerson and Thoreau, so this epiphany was less traumatic than it might have been. Living in the Bible Belt, I understood viscerally the need to keep my sexuality a secret, but I was fairly free of self-hatred and eager to graduate so that I might escape my small town and taste the pleasures of gay life.

College was still over a year away, but meanwhile there was a briefer escape in the offing. Jo Davison was a biology teacher, an excellent one, in whose class I'd excelled, and she encouraged me to apply for a National Science Foundation biology honors program at Emory and Henry College. I was accepted, to my delight.

In early June 1976 my parents drove me the few hours through dramatically mountainous countryside to the college, dropped me off at the boys' dorm, Armbrister House, and soon departed. I sat in the porch swing and watched them drive off, both excited and a little frightened to be on my own for the first time, far from family, friends and home. That evening, after orienting myself with a campus stroll, I met my roommates Jim, from New York, and Kenny, from Narrows, Virginia, then began to unpack.

At an introductory meeting the next morning, all the students met Dr. Jones, a biology teacher at Emory and Henry, who had organized the NSF program and who would teach most of the classes. It would last for six weeks, and twenty students would participate. Along with daily classes in botany, microbiology, forestry, and other branches of the life sciences, Dr. Jones had scheduled trips to many local spots of cultural and biological interest: Abram's Falls, Mount Rogers, Saltville's strip mines, Abingdon's Barter Theater, and a week's worth of study at Lake Norris, Tennessee.

There was just enough spare time for me to feel headily independent. I rose early some mornings to jog around the misty track, thinking of my hero, Billy Sive. I wandered around the picturesque campus, admiring its huge old trees, its stream, its columned brick buildings.

One evening I attended an organ recital in the campus chapel, sitting alone in the balcony, where early mornings and late nights of study caught up with me and I fell asleep on the pew. After meals in the cafeteria, I'd head down to the pond to visit Luther, the ill-tempered white swan, who would dutifully bite my boot when I thrust my foot within range of his vicious beak. One evening, straddling a wall near the pond, feeling a little homesick, I looked down to discover, scratched in the stone, the name of an Ecology Club friend of mine from back home, a girl who'd attended the very same program two summers before. The serendipity was comforting.

Having spent my entire life in Appalachia, I found it very stimulating to meet students from other areas of the country. All five kids from New York were Jewish, and this I found especially interesting. For me, Jews were an exotic breed, since I'd rarely encountered them in small-town West Virginia, and the same intellectual curiosity I applied to my classwork drove me to ask many questions about their culture and religion. One girl in particular I grew fond of, Sue, from Syosset, on Long Island. She had long black hair and a big smile. Around her neck she wore a chi, a Hebrew letter whose significance she was to explain, along with many other details of Jewish history.

Sue and I were quite simpatico. What a luxury it was to spend time with someone so intelligent. One evening we inadvertently caused a thrill of gossip to run through the group. After a long talk in the lounge of the girls' dorm, we stretched out at opposite ends of a couch together, covered by the same blanket, listening to Chicago's "Color My World" by candlelight. Drowsing, we heard a door creak. An eavesdropper, apparently, for soon the word was that Sue and I were dating.

It was no wonder that Sue and I were suspected of a romantic or erotic entanglement, for within the first few weeks of the NSF program, the tide of flirtation waxed high, and soon several of the boys and girls in the group of twenty had coupled off. We were living in a hothouse environment, certainly. Pumped with the hormones of late adolescence to begin with, we were living together, eating together, studying together, going to classes together, traveling together: circumstances conducive to dangerously intense feelings.

I wasn't interested in using Sue as a cover for my homosexuality, however. Instead, fairly early in the six-week program, I'd come out both to her and to Lisa, a pretty, big-breasted girl from Aliquippa, Pennsylvania, whom I was to nickname "Sweetums" for her perpetually sunny personality. The other girls, unaware of my queer inclinations, must have regarded me as possible dating material. I only assume this because Sue reported one day that the girls had all methodically rated the guys and had come to the conclusion that, since I had the hairiest legs, I must also have the biggest "bird." I had just enough adolescent macho pride to be pleased at this report, though I wasn't interested in presenting my bird to any of my female classmates.

In fact, I wasn't all that interested in my male classmates, or very many other boys my age. Instead, my lust focused on older men, on several of the college students who were attending summer school at Emory and Henry. Some evenings after studying, I'd head down to the tennis courts and sit in the bleachers to watch sweaty young men bound about in the humid twilight. At some point in the failing light, lamps would switch on, about which the summer moths would crazily congregate.

Occasionally, a few of the athletes would strip to the waist, and I, feigning interest in the game, would move a little closer to study the fur on their chests and bellies, the stubble on their cheeks, the way the muscles in their backs and shoulders moved. Instead of taking such beautiful flesh into my mouth, my age and shyness consigned me to fantasy, to metaphor: the hard curves of their biceps were river-smoothed stones, their moist body hair was dark orchard grass, mosses, fern fronds, the spring-soft needles of larch.

I had never touched a man before, not in the way I wanted to, and sitting there in the dark, stiff beneath my denim shorts, I would try to imagine how they tasted, how they smelt. I had no idea how to approach them, what to say that might encourage their interest, their consent.

One college student in particular grabbed my interest that summer. He much resembled the way I envisioned Billy Sive from *The Front Runner:* tanned, lithe, with a head of golden-brown curls and long, fine-muscled legs glistening with golden hair. Several of the girls in our NSF group clustered about him when they could, usually after lunch in the cafeteria, and I envied them their femaleness, only because it licensed them to flirt with men so desirable. I had grown up around enough intolerant straight men to guess how he was likely to receive my lusty admiration, so I kept it to myself.

He was strikingly handsome and he knew it, showing off his body as often as possible in skimpy tank tops and tiny running shorts. One especially hot afternoon, when I strolled down to the duck pond to offer my boot to The Savage Swan's snapping beak, my idol was lounging in the shade beneath an oak with another coterie of undergrad girls. He had nothing on but blue nylon swim trunks. At sixteen, out barely four months, I was already a chest man. I walked past with exaggerated slowness, thankful for the way that sunglasses conceal a randy stare, and devoured him with the only sense I could. His nipples were glossy and nut-brown, his tanned torso hairless except for the Trail to Happiness, as I had already learned to call it, that ridge of golden fur that bisected his lean belly and disappeared into the top of his nicely packed nylon shorts.

The next time I saw him, several days later, was in the cafeteria, sitting a few tables down with more admirers. In the first of what has proven to be twenty-five years of wicked techniques designed to spy on men's bodies, I deliberately dropped my fork on the floor then bent beneath the table to fetch it. There they were, a few yards away, those long, delicious runner's legs. For a minute I thought of dropping to the floor myself, crawling through the forest, and running my tongue up his thigh before tugging yet another pair of his revealing shorts down with my teeth.

Needless to say, I thought better of it. Still, as I returned to my lunch, I regretted living in a world where such libidinies occur not at all often, a world where I would not discover how such a man might feel as he stripped us both and then lay on top of me naked.

While I wrestled with my hormones, occasionally finding some solitary relief in the shower, I was also experiencing many novelties, the presence of which makes most youthful years seem effervescent and many adulthoods fall a bit flat. Along with classes in genetics and ecology, we enjoyed regular jaunts off campus. In Saltville, Virginia, we drove about a strip-mined site and learned about the deleterious environmental effects of coal mining. We climbed Mount Rogers, the highest mountain in Virginia, and in the process I discovered how gullible city kids are. They were ridiculously afraid of a herd of cows we passed in a field on our way to the top, and when they pointed to cowpies and asked what they were, I took the opportunity to explain that the French use such soft and fragrant fungi in sauces and salads. I recommended that they do the same upon their return home, though where in downtown Manhattan they might find such ripe produce I do not know.

One day in class Dr. Jones passed out tickets and later that afternoon he and his assistants drove us to Abingdon, Virginia, for a play at the Barter Theater, so called because, during the Depression, when it was founded, the poor used to pay for tickets with homegrown vegetables. After a tour of the quaint town and a glimpse of the elegant Martha Washington Inn, we settled into our seats in the theater. The performance that evening was a series of dramatic readings from *Transformations,* Anne Sexton's sardonic take on the Brothers Grimm, accompanied by Walter Carlos' *Sonic Seasonings.* My first taste of both modern poetry and electronic music. I was entranced. The world was beginning to widen. And I knew, even more vividly than before, that the small town where I grew up could never satisfy me, could never give my mind or my body what they craved.

Another afternoon in late June we all hiked to Abram's Falls. After a good walk along a path through thick woods, a good opportunity to learn some of the native plant species, we came to an overlook. Below, across a shady dell, creek water poured dramatically over a rocky lip, smashing into foam on rocks below.

Several hippie hikers who'd gotten there before us had climbed in behind the waterfall's translucent veil. One of them, in the dim emerald light, stripped off his soaked T-shirt, pulled off his boots, and, clad now only in faded denim shorts, stepped forward into the cascade. Laughing and gasping, he backed out of the pounding water, then in again, his long brown hair plastered to his shoulders, the creek running its clear fingers down his chest and back. He was the image of a forest god, a satyr, and I wanted to join him in his freedom and his ecstasy. A shaggy kid with straggling teenaged beard and thick glasses, I wanted to strip and enter the waterfall, become someone else, someone equally desirable, make love to him on carpets of moss.

A week later, the Big Day came, America's birthday, and we all were invited over to Dr. Jones's house for a cookout. One of the girls, Charlotte, arrived wearing a T-shirt that brazenly announced, "Fuck the Bicentennial." I found this disconcerting, for my mother had long forbade me to use that word in public, much less let it grace an article of clothing. But inspired by this naughty example, several of us, over hot dogs and pop, shared lyrics to vulgar songs when Dr. Jones's back was turned: "Gonna tell you all a story 'bout a man named Jed. / He raped Ellie May and he threw her on the bed . . . "

Afterward, a few of us, on a dare, wandered tentatively through a nearby cemetery in the misty, firefly-haunted dark. When I returned to my dorm room alone, I stretched out on the bed and listened to the radio. The Carpenters sang "I Need to Be in Love." Pulling off my shirt in the summer heat, I stood in the dark before the mirror, running my fingers over a chest still a stranger to hair or gym workouts, wondering when and how I would lose my hated virginity.

I was to discover, like most queer youth, the pains of being gay long before the pleasures, however. Having realized the nature of my sexuality only months before, I took to Emory and Henry's library in the first weeks of the NSF program to track down information on homosexuality. Emboldened by ignorance, youthful optimism, and a blithe disregard for the world's disapproval, I didn't go to any great efforts to conceal my reading material. Surely I would be safe from prejudice on the campus of such a bastion of learning.

One evening as I returned from such a library raid, I ran into Tonia, a tall, pretty classmate with long red hair, a spoiled air, and a sharp sense of humor. "What are you reading?" she asked, eyeing my armful of books. I showed her. She wrinkled her nose, then headed off with a piece of news destined to dwarf any other gossip our group had eagerly tossed about that summer.

It took less than twenty-four hours. After a class on microbes the next afternoon, our group dispersed. Most headed out to relax before dinner, but a few lingered in the hall of the biology building. I was talking to Lisa about the next assignment when another classmate, Steve, wandered up. I hadn't gotten to know him very well, but I had noticed, during an afternoon of water volleyball in the campus pool, that he had a fine body, pale, smooth and lightly muscled, that he thus looked almost as appealing as an adult in his form-fitting swimsuit, and that he was a skilled, almost poetic, diver.

"So, Jeff, I hear you're having a gay old time at the library this summer," Steve said snidely. "What's it like to like boys?" I flushed with shock and stood speechless. Lisa, however, was far from paralyzed. Rustling up some of the odd insults of her Pennsylvanian hometown, she spat, "That's none of your business, is it? And how'd you like to kiss my ass, you hoopie, you numnard, you heeneyhocker?!" Steve instantly retreated before this linguistic barrage, this indignant buxom amazon. He turned tail, scuttling down the stairwell and out the door. It was not the first time, nor the last, that men would cause me pain and women would take my part.

I was too young to know what to expect. Had I known, I might have hidden my library books more carefully, despite all my high-flown nonconformist principles. What I got was not violence, or even the threat of violence—we were all too scholarly and well-brought-up for that—but avoidance, whispers, averted eyes. Never again anything as crudely blunt as Steve's comment. Rather, all the body language that makes one aware of one's status as a pariah.

In the difficult days to follow, Sue and Lisa stood by me, of course, very deliberately sitting with me in the cafeteria and in classes. Katie, from Knoxville, a girl with big glasses and bobbed hair, and Lauren, from Silver Spring, a good-looking athletic girl with long Scandinavian blonde braids, also seemed supportive. Of all the boys, only Travis seemed to care less about the rumors. An awkward, skinny, bookish boy with a big Adam's apple and nerd glasses, he'd grown up in the tiny community of Meadows of Dan, Virginia, where he'd probably endured enough ribbing to make him sympathetic to any outcast's plight.

My greatest nemesis was Ira, an unattractive kid from New York with an annoying accent and a sense of entitlement. He never said anything to me directly, probably because I had a bigger build than he did. However, my female friends reported that, in my absence, he was the most insulting of the crew, a baby homophobe. I thought of infant copperheads, whose venom is virulent and ready for the using as soon as they hatch. I hated Ira. I wanted to break his arms and feed him to Luther, who would hold him under the pond's scummy waters with his beautiful white wings till the bubbling stopped and the pond's surface was smooth again.

My roommates Jim and Kenny were the greatest martyrs in the midst of this mess, for they had to share their room with an apparent monster. They began dressing, both morning and evening, in the bathroom down the hall, rather than allowing me to glimpse their skinny, hollow-chested, adolescent bodies, glimpses which, they must have imagined, would madden me as a matador might a bull. With no other place to sleep, they must have lain in bed staring at the ceiling, only yards from the dozing dragon. Did they think that I might descend on them as soon as they'd drifted off, to suck their blood, their breath?

This unpleasant situation built to a head pretty quickly. One evening, as I stretched out on my bed reading, Travis came by and whispered that there was a meeting about to begin downstairs, a meeting Ira had called, a meeting to which I had not been invited. When Travis hurried out, I lay back, stared at the maple leaves filling the windows, and listened to dorm-room doors slam and footsteps descend the stairs. Travis, Ira, Jim, Kenny, Steve, Jeremy.

A long time passed. I gave up any pretense of reading. Though I didn't really expect violence, it did occur to me that I had never struck anyone before in my life, that it was a long drop from my windowsill to the ground. I was too young, too ignorant of history, to realize how ironic it was that Ira, a Jew, was spearheading this persecution. He would have popped me into a concentration camp in a heartbeat.

Then footsteps ascended the stairs. One set of footsteps, surely a good sign. Would whoever it was be brandishing a torch, a crucifix, or, in Ira's case, a Star of David? If only I had a vampire's fangs. At this point, I'd use them, not to drain vital juices but, like any cornered beast, to rend.

It was Dr. Jones's assistant Chris, who served as the boys' RA. On his shoulders fell this uncomfortable duty. The NSF program and its intense togetherness would be continuing for another three weeks.

He couldn't dismiss me, because I'd done nothing but check out library books, like any good student. Somehow he had to make peace.

He did so by ignoring the truth and encouraging everyone in the program to do the same. Denial. It does save lives. The boys were concerned; they'd come to him, he gently explained. "But I can't believe that you're a homosexual choosing to make your presence known," Chris stated flatly. Perhaps he thought I would have to be effeminate, crinoline-clad, to be truly queer. Perhaps only a rigorous schedule of mincing and tittering would convince him. Or perhaps he realized that I was indeed gay and that the best thing to do under the circumstances was to encourage me to officially renounce an identity that had proven dangerous. I felt like Galileo: Yes, the earth is flat. Chris was asking me to lie to make life easier for all of us.

I wouldn't lie and claim to be straight, but I wouldn't insist on my homosexuality either. He'd given us both an out, an early version of "Don't ask, don't tell." I was sixteen years old; I was frightened; I was not a career activist; I was far away from supportive queer friends. So I said nothing. I gave him the silence he needed to smooth things over.

Chris left briefly, only to herd up my two roommates Jim and Kenny. "Now, shake hands and let's forget this misunderstanding," Chris insisted. As Jim stepped forward and gingerly gripped my hand, our eyes met. His face was flushed, his stare was full of fear. I couldn't believe it. He was terrified of me. I, who was not yet bitter, angry, and irritable, as I am at forty. Still the sixteen-year-old Jeff, I was a nonviolent idealist, a shy intellectual, a Southern boy who tried to be polite and kind in every situation. It would take me many years to realize that such fear, in different degrees and different circumstances, is the sort that sometimes kills.

Everyone seemed grateful to escape this unpleasantness, and, in the remaining weeks of the program, the topic surfaced only rarely. Tonia, the Gossip Queen, whose loose tongue had started the semi-scandal, attempted suicide for no reason the rest of us were ever to learn, and within days she was sent home.

We remaining students spent a week at a biology field station near Lake Norris, Tennessee, studying limnology with a local expert who discoursed on lake microorganisms and aquatic plants. One day, to my amazement, I discovered a dead scorpion on the floor of the lab. Recalling my father's stories of his World War II days in the Sahara and such creatures' penchant for dark sleeping places, I idly wondered if I could coax one into Ira's shoe the next time he took a nap. Then, as now, I have a crippling inability to forgive.

One morning, Sally, a quiet classmate, did a sudden cartwheel as she, Sue, and I strolled through a clearing toward the classroom. Her shirt briefly slipped up, exposing bare breasts. How much simpler life must be, I mused, for those boys who would find that sight arousing. That afternoon, as we all floated about the lake in a pontoon boat, a sudden thunderstorm broke loose. I sat on the deck in my swimsuit, cross-legged, head thrown back, welcoming the passionate violence of the sky, surges of rain crashing over me like the foamy cascades of Abram's Falls. Laughing and shivering, I knew what I felt was ecstasy, a taste of things to come.

On the drive back to the field station, a crescent moon rose with silver certainty over a tobacco barn's silhouette and into lavender sky. One more night there, time to enjoy a bonfire, songs, marshmallows, to listen to crickets and watch fireflies flicker. Then back to the campus of Emory and Henry for a few more days of class. Our time together was almost up.

The afternoon we returned from Lake Norris, I sat on the porch swing reading Hermann Hesse's novel *Damien*. Kenny joined me on the swing with a book of his own. A few minutes passed in scholarly silence. Then, stretching, I rested my arm across the back of the swing. Kenny looked around nervously. Did he think that, blind with desire, I was trying surreptitiously to work my arm around him in order to slip my hand down his shirt? "Oh, for God's sake!" I snarled. "Sorry," he blushed, moving to the opposite end of the swing, and then, by slow degrees, with studied casualness, onto the porch steps and so out into the shade of the nearest tree. No use taking a chance when the possibility of infection might be present.

The last evening of the NSF program, in an old cabin on the campus, we shared a farewell dinner, during which tongue-in-cheek awards were given out. I received "The Gayest," which Ira announced before passing over the mock certificate. Everyone laughed nervously. I smiled good-naturedly, thinking of Luther the Truly Vicious Killer Swan, the churning pond waters, the shrieks subsiding to silence. I would never have to see these kids again.

But a few I would heartily miss, after six intense weeks together. At the dinner's end, Knoxville Katie hugged me hard and whispered, "You're cool; don't you forget it," before heading off to pack. The next morning Sue and Lisa left early, and I saw them off. As she stepped into her mother's car, Sue took off her chi necklace and put it around my neck. I watched the cars disappear, then sat alone on the steps of the biology building in the thick fog of a summer dawn and cried.

For several years I corresponded with my Emory and Henry favorites before our lives sped up in college and we eventually lost touch. In one letter Katie confessed to me that she had recently realized that she was bisexual and thanked me for enduring what I had that summer, for it had helped her come to terms with her own sexuality. Sue told me of a mini-reunion in New York in 1978, a car ride during which Ira had discussed me contemptuously and a drunken Lauren, from the backseat, had growled, "So what's so wrong with homosexuality?!" thus effectively shutting him up. I like to think that flaxen-haired amazon has delighted many a lesbian since I last saw her, and that Ira, though lucky enough to have escaped Luther's voracity, has long ago fallen prey to a snapping piranha swarm of predatory drag queens.

March 1999 I attended the Appalachian Studies Association Conference in Abingdon, Virginia, the first time I'd been back to that part of the state since 1976. When I presented my paper on gay life in Appalachia, I was applauded strenuously by an audience composed of many gays and lesbians. Their enthusiasm was, I suspect, less a comment on the paper's quality than it was evidence that many mountain queers are desperately eager to read material on a topic so little acknowledged or discussed.

Afterward, my lover John and I spent the night at the luxurious Martha Washington Inn, which I hadn't visited since I was sixteen. That evening we attended a performance at the Barter Theater and I thought of that teenager hearing for the first time the work of Anne Sexton, a writer who would teach him how effectively a poet can use pain.

On the way home, John and I drove through the campus of Emory and Henry. The layout of the buildings came back to me in a rush: the boys' dorm, the biology building, the library abrim with dangerous books, the chapel, cafeteria, and duck pond. No sign of Luther in the gray wintry drizzle, no bare-chested boys lunging about on the tennis courts, no Front Runner lookalike. He's probably plump, balding, and married like myself. Perhaps his son is now as old as he was the day I saw him shirtless, lounging in the hot shade beneath the oak trees.

This November, at a friend's invitation, I will be reading poetry at Emory and Henry, almost twenty-five years after my memorable summer there. I will wear Sue's chi beneath a suitably academic dress shirt and blazer. When I look over the audience, I will remember their faces, the ones who knew me for six weeks in 1976, when I was still a sheltered boy, the ones who treated me with kindness. I will try to imagine, in one empty seat (for there are always those at poetry readings), that boy himself—shaggy, sparsely bearded, frightened into silence. When he looks up at me and smiles, I will begin to speak.

ꑦ 7　　　　　　　　　Small-Town Boy

Greg Herren

Everyone in Corinth knew that Floyd Hackworth was a mean drunk, and everybody knew that sometimes he beat on his wife Billie Jean. Billie Jean usually worked the lunch shift at the diner, and make up never could cover up a black eye or a fat lip. Nobody talked about it much. When they did, they always lowered their voices and shook their heads. Nobody thought much of the Hackworths, anyway. They lived in a trailer on the outskirts of town.

"That's something bound to come to a bad end," my aunt Vee said to my mother one Saturday afternoon when they were shelling peas. "You mark my words, Theresa, it's going come to a bad end." She emptied her beer can and put in the can where they were tossing the hollowed husks.

I heard about what Billie Jean did one morning when I rode my bike down to the A&P to get a gallon of milk. I was spinning the rack with comic books in it, itching to spend the dollar I had in my pocket when I heard Mrs. Lockhart, who taught English at the high school.

"She shot him dead." I turned and looked over at where she was standing by a huge pile of oranges. She was talking to Darlene Moss, who did hair at A Touch of Class. "He hit her one too many times, I reckon, and she went and got her brother's shotgun and shot him. In the head. I hear there was blood and brains all over her living room." She let out a little giggle with just a hint of hysteria in it. "I guess her furniture is all ruined, not that it matters. Billie Jean never had nothing that didn't come from the Goodwill in Tuscaloosa." She saw me and smiled big. Her graying black hair was pulled back in a bun at the top of her head. She was wearing powder and rouge and a yellow dress. She always went about her business dressed like she was going to church. "Bobby Rutledge!"

"Ma'am." I nodded at her.

"You starting high school this fall?"

I nodded.

She wagged her finger at me. "You better not be as much trouble as your brothers!"

I nodded. "No, ma'am." I escaped down the cleaning goods aisle, past the mops and brooms and detergents and bleaches. The cold air of the refrigerated area brought goosebumps up on my bare legs. I grabbed a gallon of milk. As I stood in the 8 Items or Less line, I could see Mrs. Lockhart and Darlene still standing by the oranges, talking. I paid for the milk and walked back into the heat. I put the milk in the basket of my bike and started pedaling.

I pedaled down the main street, past the Woolworth's and the bank and my daddy's hardware store. My older brother Danny was standing out on the sidewalk signing for a delivery. He was home from Auburn for the summer, working for Daddy and saving money so he wouldn't have to work when he went back to school. He was wearing the blue button-down shirt and a pair of bell-bottom jeans. His blonde hair glinted in the hot sun. He had been the quarterback the year we almost won the state championship. He waved at me when I went by. I cut across the street and turned.

Aunt Vee's old beat-up Impala was in the carport next to Mama's green station wagon. The Impala had a big dent in the rear fender that was starting to rust out. I put my bike down in the grass and walked into the cool of the air-conditioned house. I went into the kitchen and put the milk in the refrigerator. Mama and Aunt Vee were sitting at the kitchen table. Mama was drinking a glass of iced tea. An open can of Budweiser was sitting in front of Aunt Vee. I gave Mama her change.

"You didn't buy any comic books?" Mama asked. She looked tired. Mama always looked tired.

"No, ma'am."

"He's the readingest boy." Aunt Vee said. She was wearing a red scarf tied around her head, trying to hide her curlers. She didn't have any makeup on. She had a sharp chin and nose, a face that was all sharp pointed angles. She had a small white scar on the side of her nose where she'd had a wart removed. She was the librarian at the high school. She tapped her Pall Mall into an overflowing ashtray. "What book you reading now?" She smiled. Her face still looked hard.

"The Mystery of the Aztec Warrior." I said. "The Hardy Boys." I turned to Mama. "I'm going to ride over to the library."

She looked at the clock on the wall. "Well, you need to be at baseball practice at four; don't forget."

"I won't."

"I reckon Gary Hackworth won't be there today." Aunt Vee said, blowing out a cloud of smoke.

"Ma'am?" I looked at her.

"Vee!" My mother's voice was sharp.

"He's gonna find out soon enough." Vee tapped an ash into her beer can. "Gary's mama went and shot his daddy. Good enough for him, if you ask me." She peered at me with her small brown eyes. "Friend of yours, ain't he?"

"Yes, ma'am."

"You oughtn't to allow that, Theresa." Aunt Vee turned her little eyes back to Mama. "You know no Hackworth ever amounted to nothing."

Mama sighed. "Go on to the library."

I got on my bike. The sky was blue, cloudless. I started pedaling. The library was downtown, just past the A&P. I sailed down Main Street. Danny wasn't in front of the hardware store anymore. I kept pedaling, through the intersection where the Tuscaloosa road bisected Main Street. That was where Corinth's one traffic light was. The library was there, on the corner, but I kept going past it. After the library was the high school and the football field. The sign on the football field still read Happy Graduation Seniors, even though graduation had been a month earlier. I kept riding, past the houses until I reached the edge of town. I turned up Tarleton's Road. It was only paved for about a block and then turned into gravel and red dirt.

The Hackworth trailer was about three blocks off Main Street, set in a field. There was a rusting old Ford pickup in the yard up on blocks. I stopped at the mailbox and stared at it. There was yellow tape that said CRIME SCENE DO NOT CROSS all over fluttering in the wind across the front porch. I stood there for a few moments, staring.

"You looking for Gary?"

Betty Sue Box lived across the road from the Hackworths. I looked at her. "Yes, ma'am."

She was wearing a shapeless plaid cotton house dress that had been washed about twenty times too many. Her wrinkled face was crowned with black cat-eye glasses with rhinestones in the points. Her gray hair was all done up in pin curlers with bobby pins poking out at various places. Her feet were bare in the red dirt. She put a hand on her hip. Fat hanging from her arm jiggled. "He's up the road at his brother's." She shook her head. "Terrible what happened, ain't it?"

"Yes, ma'am."

"I was always telling Billie Jean she ought to run that jackass off, but she wouldn't listen to me." She grimaced, exposing tobacco yellowed teeth. She waved her hands in the air, her arms jiggling. "But what the hell do I know?"

"Yes, ma'am."

"You starting high school this fall, Bobby?"

"Yes, ma'am."

"You gonna be a ball player like your brothers?"

"Yes, ma'am."

"Good." She nodded. "That'll keep you out of trouble."

"Yes, ma'am." I got back on my bike and started riding up the road. I knew where Trent Hackworth's trailer was. Gary and I used to sneak up there sometimes and go through Trent's nudie magazines. There was always a supply of marijuana in his nightstand table, and he didn't care if Gary and I pinched some from time to time. At least that's what Gary said. I never questioned Gary. Trent Hackworth scared me. He worked days at the rubber glove factory just outside of town. He wore his brown hair shoulder length, had a mustache and goatee and listened to music like Pink Floyd and Led Zeppelin. My dad called him a hippie because of his hair. Trent's midnight blue Trans Am wasn't parked in front of his trailer when I got there, but I could hear music from inside the trailer. Fleetwood Mac. The *Rumours* album.

I put my bike down in the red dirt and knocked on the screen door. The other door was open. I stood there waiting for a moment, then I heard movement in the back of the trailer. Christine McVie was singing "You Make Loving Fun."

"Hey, Bobby."

Gary opened the screen door and came out on the porch. Even though we were the same age, he was at least five inches taller than me. His brown hair hung down past his ears. His blue eyes were reddish. He was only wearing a pair of cut-off jeans that gripped him tightly. His shoulders were broad, and his body was lean and hard muscled. Hairs were sprouting around his nipples and coarse black hair trailed from his navel down into his cut-offs. His legs were also covered with black hair. He'd always been a big boy, even back in kindergarten. Then everyone seemed big to a runt like me.

"You doing OK?"

He shrugged and flicked the butt of his cigarette into the dirt. "If she was gonna shoot him she should've done it a long time ago."

"You going to practice?"

"I don't know."

We stood there, not speaking for a moment. Fleetwood Mac played on. "Aw, hell, you wanna go down to the river and get high?" Gary said.

"What about practice?"

"Not for hours." Gary shrugged. "Maybe being high would make you play better."

I was a lousy baseball player. I was lousy at all sports. My brothers were all natural athletes. Everyone expected me to be the same. Gary was the only person who knew how much I hated sports. Gary also kept the other kids from picking on me. "Maybe."

The album ended while Gary rolled the joint in the kitchen. The still was pervasive. Flies buzzing. Crickets chirping. A car driving by. A dog barking somewhere. He finished rolling and picked up a lighter and we walked out the front door. Behind the trailer the woods started, and we walked through, not talking, side by side, Gary every once in a while picking up a rock and throwing it against a tree. He had a strong arm. He was the best pitcher on our baseball team, the quarterback on our football team. People said that when Gary was a senior the high school might have a shot at winning the state championships in football and baseball, and Gary was sure as shit getting a college scholarship to play ball. Gary never seemed to care much about that. He played because he liked to, was what he said. If he stopped liking it he'd stop playing.

Corinth was nestled in a curve of the Sipsey River. The river wasn't much, and if it didn't rain it got shallow enough in places to walk across. It never seemed to move much when it was low, more like a big patch of soupy orange mud. The banks were about six feet above the river. We sat down on the edge of the bank. All it was good for was catching catfish, but most of the time they weren't fit to eat.

Gary lit the joint and took a deep inhale and passed it to me. I took a hit, holding the smoke in for as long as I could, like Gary had taught me. We sat there in silence, smoking the pot, listening to the birds and the bugs.

"I can't believe she finally did it," he said finally.

"Were you there?"

"I was up at Trent's." He shrugged. "She sent me up there. Mrs. Wires called to tell her he'd been drinking, so she sent me up to Trent's. We heard the shot, though."

"I'm sorry."

"Don't be." He tossed a rock into the river, which swallowed it with a gulp. "She shoulda done it a long time ago, when he broke Trent's arm."

"Will she go to jail?"

"Sheriff Kidwell didn't think so. He took her in though, and she's not back yet, so who knows?"

"If she goes to jail what'll you do?"

"Live with Trent I guess, or my aunt in Fayette."

"Fayette?"

He looked at me and smiled. "Don't cry, sissy boy."

"Don't call me that!" I hated that more than anything. It was what the other kids said when he wasn't around. So what if I wasn't good at sports? So what if I'd rather stay home and read?

"Sorry."

"What?"

"I said I was sorry."

I stared at him. He never said sorry to me before whenever he was mean to me. And he could be really mean sometimes. It was a small price to pay for him protecting me. "Oh."

He gave me a crooked grin. "Sissy boy."

That was my cue to launch myself at him, and we tumbled away backward from the riverbank. He was about forty pounds heavier and a lot stronger. It was futile; it always was. He always wound up overpowering me and holding me down, straddling me, but it was fun. I liked the feeling of struggling with him. I knew he would never hurt me. Sometimes he would let me get an advantage, but only if he felt like it, and could always take it back away from me. This time, though, we rolled over and over in the grass, trying to get ahold of each other, until we ended up with him on his back and me lying on top him.

We lay there, panting. I knew I should probably get off, but I didn't want to.

"I don't know what I'm gonna do," he said quietly. The bluish eyes grew wetter.

I didn't know what to say. Gary never cried, not even the time last summer when a couple of big kids from the black high school jumped him and stole his bike. He'd fought back and they had beaten him up pretty bad.

A tear rolled out of his left eye.

I brought my hand up and wiped it off.

He smiled. "Tough guys don't cry, right?" His voice broke. He put his arms around me and squeezed me.

"It'll be okay." I whispered. "Your mom won't go to jail, you'll see."

"Yeah." He shifted his weight and rolled me over. He was on top of me now, my legs spread.

"Hey, you asshole." I struggled. He'd done it on purpose, to catch me off guard, so he could get the upper hand . . .

He kissed me. On the mouth.

I stared up at him.

He smiled, and brought his mouth back down to mine again.

I opened my mouth, and tasted his. It was cigarette and pot smoke, but it tasted wonderful. Then his tongue was in my mouth and I sucked on it softly. His pelvis was grinding back and forth on mine, and I could feel his hardness through his jeans and mine. Then I brought my legs up and around his waist and we lay there rocking, our mouths together, and I ran my hands up and down his bare back. His skin was smooth and firm but hot to the touch, and it felt so good.

He got off of me and still smiling, undid his cut-offs and slipped them off. I could see his dick sticking up, long and hard, and he was pulling off my shirt and then undoing my shorts and then my underwear was off and so was his. He sat there, pulling on his dick. I sat there in the sun, watching him for a few minutes, then reached out with my left hand and moved his out of the way. It felt hard but somehow soft, and I started moving my hand up and down. He closed his eyes, moaned, and leaned back. I started pulling on mine too, my eyes never leaving his beautiful, lean, hard body.

The sound of our breathing came faster and faster as my hands moved. Gary's face was expressionless, smooth, eyes closed, mouth slightly open. His chest moved up and down with every breath, every breath that was coming faster now, breaths that were more shallow now rather than deep. He began to moan a little bit, moans that grew slightly louder each time, until his entire body stiffened and his eyes opened wide. I could feel his dick in my hand tensing, then I felt his climax starting, his dick gathering itself, and then it came, bullets of sticky white that shot up onto his chest and stomach, mixing with the sweat and glistening in the sun. He gasped with each launch, breathing very fast and quick. I felt mine start, but kept stroking him as my own started, much more intense and explosive than any time before in the bathroom at home or in my bedroom.

We sat there for a few minutes, the silence surrounding and cloaking us, our eyes locked. Then he looked away.

"Gary—"

"Just don't say anything." He pushed my hand away, and grabbed his underwear and wiped his chest and stomach off. His voice was low, threatening. "Don't you say anything."

I grabbed one of my socks and used it as a towel, being careful not to look at him, not talking.

"I ought to kick your little faggot ass."

I looked up at him. He was standing, fastening his cut-offs. I stood up and started getting dressed again. My eyes were filling with tears, and my lower lip was trembling. I will not cry, I told myself. I will not cry.

"Go on home, faggot."

I looked at him. His face was twisted with contempt and loathing.

I left. I walked back to the trailer, where my bike was lying in the dirt. I told myself not to run, although every instinct told me to run. He might come after me; he might beat me up because of what I had done. What if he told people? People already thought I was a sissy. How could I ever face anyone ever again? How could I . . .

I got on my bike and rode home.

Gary didn't come to practice. Coach McDonald gathered us all around, and told us that Gary had gone to live with his aunt in Fayette until the police knew what to do with Billie Jean. He said that we should all pray for Gary and his mama.

We paired up to play catch and warm up. I usually played catch with Gary, so I just sat there for a minute. "Hey, Wheeler."

I looked up. Jay Whitsitt was standing there. He was missing a front tooth and had a scar on his chin. He was one of our best batters. "Yeah?"

"Wanna play catch?"

I'd known Jay since first grade, and he was one of the kids who hissed "sissy boy" at me when I walked by. "Yeah, sure." I stood up.

"Sorry about Gary," he said, idly tossing a baseball in his hand.

"Yeah. Well, his daddy had it coming, right?"

He grinned. "Yeah. That's what my mama says." He threw the ball to me.

I caught it and lobbed it back. "Yeah."

"Think we can win the league without Gary?"

I shrugged. "He was our best pitcher, but we'll have to make do, I guess." Just like I will, I thought to myself.

Just like I will.

And My Heart Goes On

                                      Jameson Currier

On my twenty-fifth birthday my mother explained to me how I was
born. We were sitting in the kitchen of the house where she had lived
for seventeen years, the house I had grown up in, a two-story suburban ranch with a half acre of land in the back yard and the swing set
still standing, now dented and rusty.

I had come to visit her in Atlanta for the weekend, a stopover on
my way home to New York City from a vacation in Fort Lauderdale.
My mother, once a slender, breezy Southern woman, now reminded
me more of my grandmother: round and pudgy with curly, cottony
white hair and silver wire-rim eyeglasses. She had finished her morning cup of coffee and was now opening cabinets and the refrigerator,
withdrawing flour, eggs, measuring spoons, milk, all the ingredients
she needed to bake a cake from scratch.

"Your favorite," she said in that light drawl of hers which could
stretch the syllables of any word into a sentence. "Pineapple upside-
down," she announced proudly, as though it were a secret. "Because
it's your birthday."

She stopped and retrieved a large mixing bowl from the cabinet beneath the kitchen counter and as she straightened herself up, her face
flushed and she let out a tiny giggle. "I never told you this," she began, "but one weekend when I was about seven, no, I guess seven-
and-a-half months pregnant with you, your father took me along with
his Scout troop to Red Line Mountain. They were all camping out by
the creek, but your dad had made me stay in one of the cabins by the
Information Center. Well, they all got up early to hike to the top of
Red Line and help the forestry service put markers on a new path, and
I was to meet them later that night back at their campsite. I woke up
early and got so bored sitting around and walking back and forth to
the stream that I decided I would walk up the main road and meet

them at the observation point at the top. Red Line really isn't a big mountain, you know.

"Well, it started getting hot. It turned real fast into one of those awful hazy, humid Indian summer days when you just can't breathe, and here I was walking up this winding road that was just all dirt and sand and gravel and you know, it just wasn't fun. I hadn't brought anything along to eat or drink and by the time I got just half way up I was exhausted. So I sat down and right then a pickup truck comes down from the top of the mountain and the driver stopped when he saw me by the side of the road. This old farmer opened the door and asked me if I was okay and I said yeah, but just a little hot, and then he asked me if I wanted a ride back down to the Information Center. I said sure, because I thought at least I was tired enough now to take a nap. Well, down we went on that bumpy road and that truck, which must have been made before they invented shock absorbers, just kept going bump-de-bump-de-bump all the way down. That road seemed endless. By the time we reached the Center I had gone into labor. Thank God that old man had sense enough to stick around and take me to the hospital.

"You were less than five pounds when you were born," she smiled. "Four pounds, eleven and three-quarters ounces to be exact," she said, opening the top of the package of flour and placing the measuring cup on the counter space in front of her. "You were a premie," she added. "We were really worried about you."

As I walked out of the kitchen and up the stairs to my old bedroom, I realized I found my mother's story humorous, part of some gothic Southern charm I had always invented about her and my family. For a while, I retold the story of how I was born to my friends in Manhattan, at a party or at a bar or when I was out on a date. I tried to use it to explain a lot about me; why I never wanted to live in the South, how the mere smell of dirt sent me rushing toward civilization. I used it to rationalize why I always wanted to get out of suburbia, moving away from quirky, middle-class-All-American-too-Christian parents.

I joked that it accounted for my determination to provide myself with a college education, and how I used that education to find employment in New York City. I felt it answered why I sometimes became compulsively neat: cleaning, washing, filing, sorting. And I thought it explained why I preferred to read a book instead of going camping or hiking or anywhere that meant following a dusty, rocky path. My mother had, after all these years, given me the reason for my own quirkiness.

* * *

Not long after I heard my mother's story, I had an operation to repair an inguinal hernia. I'd spent a few years working out, trying to put my body in better shape, only to wake one hot July morning with a swelling in my groin so severe I could not bear to even wear cotton briefs. I'd never been an athletic child; a season on a little league baseball team as an outfielder (where the ball seldom appeared); and an attempt at intramural basketball in high school (where I never saw the ball, either, due to being shorter than the other players); and my attempt to transform my physique into something other than its scrawny frame had clearly backfired in a way I hadn't expected.

My doctor wasn't at all convinced that it was entirely due to straining too hard with heavy weights at the gym, and offered another possibility, that the hernia could have been present since birth. Whatever its cause, I lived through the operation and a painful six-week recuperation period just as I had such childhood illnesses and accidents as tonsillitis, chicken pox, measles, and a broken arm. To assuage my mother's concern over the operation which involved spinal anesthesia and to amend her fear that that my hernia could be hereditary, I flew down South to have the operation, staying a few days at her home before flying back to Manhattan.

It wasn't long after that that I began to feel a change in my vision. I had been working long hours as a theatrical publicist, reading small-print newspapers for tearsheets for clients, and fighting off severe headaches which I had attributed, at first, to on-the-job stress. One evening as I made my way through Times Square to deliver some tickets and press releases, I noticed that my long-range vision was blurring. Through a friend, I found the name of an ophthalmologist in the West Village near my apartment.

I'd worn eyeglasses for reading since a child, having been diagnosed with astigmatism, and had spent a year of adolescence doing a series of exercises of looking through hand-held prisms to strengthen the muscles of my left eye (I had been diagnosed with a "wandering eye" as a boy—something which sounds now as an adult as so unnecessary to want to correct). At the back of my mind was the idea that because of technological advances in the making of contact lenses, I could get soft lenses, which might change my green eyes to blue.

The doctor, a stocky, handsome man in his late thirties with deep brown eyes, gave me a stronger reading prescription and then said it was impossible for me to wear contact lenses because I had unusually large cataracts for my age growing in my eyes. I wasn't alarmed by the news, but found it strange that this had never been detected before, and I agreed to return in six weeks in order for the doctor to measure the growth of the cataracts. In the interim I discussed my diagnosis with friends and co-workers who urged me to seek a second opinion.

Instead, I decided to return to the doctor for a second measurement and decide on a second opinion after that appointment, once I learned exactly how severe these growing cataracts were. When I arrived to see the ophthalmologist for the second appointment, the doorman of the building where his office was located told me that the doctor had moved and had not left a forwarding address.

This news took me by surprise and I walked to the corner and then back to the building again, wondering if I had made a mistake about the location. I asked the doorman again about the doctor. I had only been there a few weeks before, and told him that there had been no contact with me about the office closing. Then came his response, "He wasn't well, you know." As I left, thinking I could locate his office via the phone book, I remembered there had been some fumbling during my first appointment about whether or not I had shown up on the right date.

And then I heard through my friend who had recommended the ophthalmologist that the doctor had died. I went to another ophthalmologist, this one recommended through a co-worker, who said I had not a single cataract and I ordered tinted contacts. But the story doesn't end there. Not long after that first eye doctor died, I also went to visit my general physician to take an HIV test for the first time.

This was a period in the mid-1980s when every little skin blemish and bug bite and unexplained bruise was causing me considerable worry. As my doctor listened to my heightened panic over sexual partners who were ill and the story of a co-worker who had died, before withdrawing my blood, he tested my blood pressure, my reflexes, my breathing, and my heartbeat and determined that I had a heart murmur.

"It's not a cause for alarm at this point," he said. "But I'd like you to go for some tests so that we can measure it against future readings." He explained that a murmur is usually the result of an irregular flow of blood through the heart and it rarely affects the overall health. I answered a few questions about my general health and the health of my family members, and somewhere in the doctor's explanation, there was a hint of a possibility that my heart murmur could have underlying hereditary causes.

A few days later I arrived at a cardiology clinic on Madison Avenue and, at the age of twenty-nine, was subjected to a series of stress tests that were also being administered that day to a seventy-three year-old man, walking on a treadmill strapped with wires and plugs and bands attached to different points of my body. After the exams were over and I was told nothing of their diagnosis; the reports were to be sent to my doctor.

While I was waiting for the elevator to leave the clinic, I had a premonition of my own death, that if I was lucky enough to survive the AIDS epidemic, then I most likely would die of a heart attack. I never went back to that facility for other measurements. Instead, life intruded: My job consumed my energy, and my murmur receded into my subconscious mind, and I began to find myself among a growing number of friends and co-workers who were testing HIV positive and growing ill, while learning that I, myself, had thus far escaped the virus.

Months later, fighting off a bout of stress which landed in a spot beneath my right shoulder blade, I went to a chiropractor who had been recommended by an actor whom I was dating. Like the optometrist, the chiropractor was a darkly attractive fellow. I undressed and went through his inspection of my body, answering questions as he manipulated muscle groups around my back, neck, and legs. At the end of the examination, he told me that my spine was crooked and that I would need several follow-up appointments to begin to correct it. Instead of returning to him, I went back to my general physician and asked for antidepressants.

Over the years as I have moved from apartment to apartment and changed physicians with different jobs and different health insurance plans, I have learned to tell my doctors about my heart murmur. Every single one has become alarmed by it; over the last two decades I have ended up in clinics from Beth Israel Hospital to Cornell Medical Center to be measured and monitored, testing the strength of my heart through noninvasive cardiology exams such as electrocardiograms, MRIs, and ultrasound echocardiographs, only to be thanked for my time and sent on my way.

I sense that some day down the road that I will be presented with bad news: a decision between surgery or death. But as for now, at forty-four, other than recommendations for antibiotics when I had some dental work done, my heart has not interfered with my day-to-day life. I have used it and abused it as well as ringing it emotionally dry, from living in a six-floor walkup that always left me panting for breath to breaking up with a boyfriend and dropping to an alarmingly thin shell of myself after subsiding for weeks on nothing but anti-depressants and booze.

* * *

I was raised as a Southern Methodist and though my parents were not strict, certain things were simply not discussed. Even though it was the era of free love, inside our home sexual matters were hidden, suppressed, or not talked about at all. We were made to go to church every Sunday—Sunday school and worship services following, and brought back again in the evenings for choir practices and youth fellowship groups. My parents set out to raise their children via an accepted standard version of morals, a belief in honesty, freedom, and trust, instilling their offspring with equal portions of politeness and guilt.

But by the age of thirteen I knew I was different from my parents, detached by some other schism than the separation of generations. I became aware that I was attracted to men; I began studying them carefully—the way the sweat formed on my father as he mowed the yard bare-chested, the way dark hair wrapped around my band instructor's wrists, the way the older boys at school touched themselves as they showered in the locker room.

I started locking myself in my bedroom, staring at the pictures of athletes in magazines, memorizing the firmness and energy of their bodies, fantasizing they were next to me, touching me, wanting me, needing me. I read every book I could find on sex, even the ones my parents kept hidden in my father's workroom in the basement, alarmed and even more confused by the descriptions of homosexuality as a deviation and a perversion.

Almost every gay man can list certain pinpoints of recognition on his trajectory toward gay self-identification, even if he hadn't admitted the possibility to himself at that period in his life; in retrospect, it's clear that it was a moment of gay awareness. The signs are obvious to me now that this happened to me long before I left the South for Manhattan. I remember at the age of fourteen comparing definitions of homosexuality in the different dictionaries of my library. Even earlier I recall a boyish fascination for comic book super heroes, morphing into a sweating discomfort while watching Hercules movies.

Growing up in the South I felt only my difference from my family and others. I wanted to change the way I talked, the way I thought, and I wanted to change the people around me into different persons. Yet one thing a gay Southern boy learns early is to keep his difference to himself or face ridicule. I flattened my accent, hid my desire to be campy, and set about constructing my life into two camps: those who might be gay or sympathetic, and those who most definitely were not. Because of their narrow religious view, my parents were part of the latter group in my mind, and I began to withdraw from them in regard to my life.

There were many years as an adult when I disregarded my parents, presuming geographical distance would keep us out of each other's thoughts, believing any discussion of my life would make them embarrassed, ashamed, or unable to accept and understand. Parents, of course, do not want their children to be different from themselves. But the truth is I could not shake the imprints that they had left on me, both mental and physical. Even now, every day in front of the bathroom mirror, I notice my father's face and hairline, and my skin, the translucent color of my mother's, has become a patchwork of blue veins so close to the surface they resemble the tattoo of a roadmap.

Even though she had been there for visits to see her sister, my aunt, my mother hated and feared New York City; she had gathered enough suspicion of the city simply from watching the nightly news. When I settled there the year after I graduated college, she was worried I would starve, that the building where I lived would burn down, or that I would be mugged late at night while waiting for the subway.

Right after I had moved to Manhattan, we spoke every Sunday on the phone and after quizzing me about my job, my furniture, my friends, what I had eaten for dinner the night before, her voice would take on the petite, Southern-belle quality that I knew was the end of our conversation. "Why don't you come home and live?" she would ask.

I would answer with something like "Not yet," or "I can't," or "I'm not ready," never what I was really thinking. What I really felt was the truth but was too impolite for a Southern man to express: that where she was, where she lived, was not my home anymore.

I never told my mother many things about my life in New York; many details I knew would upset her. I told her about the jobs I had, what the city looked like, what the weather was like, and how I wanted to furnish the apartment where I lived. I remember telling her about the apartment I shared on Bleecker Street, a top-story walk-up with a floor so lopsided in the kitchen that we had to wedge a piece of wood underneath the refrigerator to keep it from rolling against the front door. But I never told her that one night, after a heavy rain, as I brushed my teeth before going to sleep, the plaster ceiling collapsed on top of my bed and had I been there, in the bed asleep, I would now be dead.

But I did tell her about the new friends I was making and a few of the things we did together. I told her about going to the movies and plays, and trips to the beach or Atlantic City or Boston or the Hamptons. At first she used to ask me if I had met any nice girls; then one Sunday I noticed the question had stopped, maybe she realized something in the fact that most of my friends were male.

My decision not to tell her I preferred to sleep with men was not because I was ashamed of my life, it was just that stating the fact would serve no purpose to either one of us; it would not change our relationship. She was my mother and I was her son, we loved each other, and she was there and I was here.

I didn't tell her that the true reason why I left home was not so much to pursue a graduate degree at New York University but to openly explore gay life in the West Village without any parental intrusion. Such things were not really necessary for parents to know about their child.

And I never told my mother about the night walking home alone when I decided to take a short cut through Washington Square. When

I reached the park I saw a man beating a woman in the shadows of the fountain. I yelled and as I approached them I was jumped from behind. I managed to stay on my feet but suddenly there was a fist headed toward my eye. I lost my wallet and my keys and my pride that night.

The next time I saw my mother, six months later, she noticed the scar above my left eyebrow. I said I had fallen in my apartment, tripped over the phone cord and hit my head against the side of my bedroom bureau. I told her it was nothing; it looked worse than it really was.

And as the years went by I held more and more things back from my mother. I didn't tell her about the friends who were dying, or the ones I was taking care of, hoping that they would survive. I never told her about the married man I dated who took me on an expensive trip to Palm Springs and Los Angeles, never told her, either, of the time I was threatened with losing a theatrical job when it was discovered I was having an affair with a member of the cast.

I never told my mother about the time I returned to Atlanta on business because I wanted to spend my evenings checking out the gay club scene I had heard about for so many years but had never fully experienced. I never told her about the trip to Chicago I made to see a musical I had written performed because I was sleeping with the composer. Never told her, either, that I, like her father, have, as the years progressed, developed a "tendency to imbibe too much."

Once, when I returned home to attend my niece's wedding, I brought with me my own bottle of wine, hiding it in my suitcase and drinking in my bedroom after the rest of the household was asleep. Another time, during a period when I was a cigarette smoker, I excused myself to do errands in the car in order to smoke and not be seen by my mother. My parents never approved of these habits in my older brother and younger sisters, and even before I had come out as gay to them, I had enough facts on my side to weigh in their disapproval of the way I was living my life.

And I never told her about the cataracts, my back problem, and certainly nothing about my heart murmur. Once, when she visited me in Pennsylvania where I was living at the time, she mentioned that I looked unhappy and distracted. It would be another year before I summoned up the courage to let her know I was gay and what she didn't know then was that I had just ended an unhappy affair with a man.

She twisted her hands together and said, "You know, honey, you can tell me anything you want." And I sensed then that perhaps she understood more about my life than I wished her to know. For in the next breath she asked me about my health; mothers possess instincts their children spend years trying to comprehend.

At the time I was only suffering from depression and trying to stop smoking to give my life some sense of a different direction. But I opted not to discuss this with her. I had learned from my father that there are things a Southern gentleman simply does not talk about with a Southern woman, particularly his mother. (At the time my father was battling prostate cancer and even between father and son, the discussion of its progress was limited to simple phrases, "Doin' fine" and "Doc says there's hope.")

This never prevented my mother from telling me stories about her own illnesses, her arthritis, her hiatal hernia, and her trips to the dermatologist at age seventy-one to remove deposits which had blemished her forehead, or the illnesses my grandmother suffered, my mother's mother, the memory loss of Alzheimer's, the hip replacement while in the nursing home, a second stroke which left her immobile.

My mother felt that by telling her stories, filling up the empty spaces between us with sound, that she was reconnecting us as we had been years before as mother and infant son, and in a way she did.

The last time I saw her; a weekend in the Poconos while my father searched for his genealogical roots in the area; she talked incessantly about the irritation her metal jewelry was causing to her skin. A watch she had worn on the drive north had made the area of her wrist break out into red welts that had crusted over after she had applied a cortisone creme. I had arrived with a cold at the lodge where they were staying. The cold had progressively become worse during my stay with them, so bad in fact, that I worried about it transforming into something more serious.

It was a beautiful fall weekend, sunny and cool, and the maples, oaks, and hickories full of orange, yellow, and red leaves had transformed the mountainside into tufts of color. But this was the second serious cold I had suffered in the space of two months and I had admitted that fact to my mother upon my arrival. All I wanted was to stay inside, lie on the couch, sleep or watch TV, and get better.

My mother twisted her hands nervously and urged me to eat or drink something every few minutes. "I hope none of this is my fault," she said, when I had drained another glass of orange juice.

"What do you mean?" I asked.

"You being so sickly," she said.

"I'm not sickly," I answered defensively. "I'm just sick."

"You were such a sickly baby," she said. "You got all the stuff babies get right on cue."

"So that hardly makes it unusual," I said.

"I never told you this," she added. "But we didn't expect you to live when you were born. You were so tiny; we were all so worried." Her eyes had taken on a wet, ashamed look and she tilted her heavy body forward in the chair as she spoke in a soft tone so that my father, napping in the other room, could not possibly hear.

"You had to stay at the hospital for something like two weeks in an incubator," she said. "Your daddy went to visit you every day, but I had your brother at home to take care of and I couldn't always make it there, and I was so worried about you. I was just so worried about you not making it and my not being there for you. So we convinced the hospital to install an incubator at the house. It was the first time they had ever done it. They set it up in the living room. We had to rearrange everything. A nurse came out and stayed over at the house to make sure it went okay." She leaned back, pleased with herself, and she lifted the corner of her lip into a crooked smile that I clearly recognized as one I also inherited.

"You were so, so tiny," she added. "All I wanted to do was hold you but the doctors wouldn't let me. So when no one was around I would lift you up out of that stupid glass box and hold you in my arms. I think it made you want to live. I didn't care what any of those silly doctors said; it didn't hurt you, did it? I didn't hurt you, did I, honey? You're not damaged goods."

Of course I didn't respond to this. It's impossible to say if my mother did any damage. As far as I am concerned, in comparison with other gay men of my generation, my own health travails, my heart murmur included, play simply like minor skin irritations. And as for affairs of the heart, most have been of my own doing and undoing. But the older I become the clearer it is to me that my parents provided me with a basic education in survival and faith, passing along a few genetic traits in the mix as well.

I now understand how my mother felt standing over that glass incubator looking at her child struggling to live in a small, enclosed glass box. She not only gave me life, but she also passed along a will to help and hold someone in their arms, something I've been searching for since the day I left home.

9   That Dog Won't Hunt

Christopher Wynn

My father took me hunting one time. I had been quietly waiting in dread, knowing the day would come. I prayed for illness, for bad weather, the Second Coming of Christ, anything . . . but none of it was to be. I was going hunting.

This would be no casual outing in the woods either. Father would be decked out in head-to-toe camouflage; there would be a pointing dog or two leading the way; and we'd both be brandishing live firearms. Charlton Heston would probably stop by for dinner the night before.

The only thing more heinous than my father's suburban obsession with the great outdoors was the fact that he wanted to include me in it. This was going to be a time of father and son bonding, a rite of passage. My father surely understood from the beginning that there was something different about me. I had a certain sensibility not usually associated with the sport of hunting; but I suspect he was hoping I was merely artistic, overly imaginative, and sensitive. As it would turn out, I was all of those things, and gay to boot.

I sensed a forced hunting expedition was coming the moment those first copies of *Outdoorsman* magazine arrived at our front door. Soon, I also noticed the small purchases for items like binoculars and water canteens. Finally, before even my mother realized what was happening, an entire arsenal of rifles had been bought and installed in our home. Dad even started making his own bullets at a workstation assembled in a spare bedroom. This had officially become serious.

The point of no return ultimately came with the arrival of the hunting dogs, which consisted of three gently used, slightly unsuspecting pointers. Dad even built an unsightly kennel on our property just to house the smelly new additions to our family. Unfortunately for my father, the dogs would cooperate with his visions of hunting grandeur about as much as I would.

The first dog, Fritz, was picked up from an aged and crusty farmer outside town. Fritz was a German Shorthaired Pointer named after a member of the famous Von Eric wrestling family. This should have been our first red flag because, while he eventually became a great pet, which only further antagonized my father, Fritz was a lousy hunting dog.

I named our second dog Daisy, after the female character from the *Dukes of Hazzard* TV show. Daisy was a great pointer and full of promise (in sharp contrast to the *actress* playing the TV version of Daisy). Right on cue, however, the dark forces of hunting that seemed to plague my father lashed out again. Daisy was struck with a bizarre hip condition that forced us to have her put to sleep.

Finally, all hopes rested on a big, dopey English pointer named John (a name he came with, thank you). My father meticulously trained John for action using a quail decoy tied to a string. He would bob it up and down, driving the dog into a sniffing, pointing frenzy. John was an excellent pointer in the backyard, but things would quickly sour during his first time in the field.

John's first real quail hunt coincided, tragically, with my own. I should have sworn allegiance to an animal rights group and insisted on staying home.

The infamous outing happened on an overcast Texas day. Father drove us all in the pickup. I sat silently in the cab beside him; John stood wobbling in the truck bed, digging his paws in to remain standing upright. I watched behind me as the dog insisted on leaning over the side of the vehicle, causing his lips to flap and billow in the wind, and one of his ears to fold backward in an unnatural and slightly unholy-looking position.

We arrived at our wooded destination. A shotgun was quickly slapped into my hands. I had only fired my shotgun a few times at the shooting range, so I felt a bit unsteady. My arm still felt sore even from that earlier effort. Hastily, I was drug into the brush along with our confused but eager English pointer. Dad was, of course, wearing so much camouflage that he only needed a few tree branches ducttaped to his head to disappear completely. I had chosen a less survivalist combination of jeans and a tan T-shirt. The three of us traipsed through the woods for over an hour like some sportsman version of *The Blair Witch Project.*

I was beginning to think that hunting really wasn't that bad when we came upon our first group of quail feeding on the ground. Seeing the demure, brown birds for the first time, I felt a sharp stab of guilt cut through my heart. I suddenly had the urge to take one home as a pet.

Before I could make this suggestion, my father froze. He stretched an arm out across my chest, motioning for me to likewise be still. I did and even went so far as to quit breathing altogether. Our prized pointer, John, went utterly silent as he focused his cold, wet nose in the direction of the unsuspecting birds.

With surprisingly good skill, my father aimed his shotgun and cracked off a loud round of gunfire. The quail erupted into the air with a furious flapping of wings and throaty cries of alarm.

Just as quickly, John galloped off back toward the truck, I fled screaming toward some nearby trees, and my father was left to stand there alone in the brush, cursing us both.

Later, upon regrouping, we realized that John, Dad's final hope for a suitable hunting dog, had apparently been emotionally traumatized as a pup and was now gun-shy. And me? Well, the jury was still out.

As quickly as they had come . . . John, the kennel, the guns, were all gone. Dad effectively buried all memories of his Grizzly Adams outdoorsman fantasies.

My reprieve from father/son bonding would not last long, however. Like most men of his generation, my father was searching for a shared activity for us to do together in order to relate. The idea of simply sitting me down with a soda and having a heart to heart would have been far too awkward and simply wasn't done in the South. Instead, he plotted to engage me in a new series of male bonding activities.

Archery equipment began arriving a month after our hunting fiasco. Never one to do things halfway, we soon had several bows, an assortment of arrows, and five bales of hay trucked in for target practice. While I found tormenting neighborhood children with my bow and arrow mildly amusing, I couldn't seem to take archery seriously as a sport. My father was not amused.

After piling the archery equipment into the storage shed, we made room for the fishing boat, with underwater sonar, and then the jet-ski boat, with five sets of water skis. After that came the snorkeling equipment and the diving gear, then the Harley-Davidson motorcycles. My father was having fun, and probably a midlife crisis; but I remained largely unimpressed. None of these activities became that magical shared interest that my father was searching for with me.

I simply preferred spending my time writing poetry, playing music, and otherwise remaining holed up in my bedroom. This drove my father nuts and he became even more determined to get me outside and involved in some sort of father and son activity.

Since I was "too snotty" to participate in any of the supposedly fun outings my father tried to instigate, he decided it was time to get practical and teach me the things that every man should know. This would not include sex of course, since every young man is expected to figure that out from magazines and the current media like his father did. Also, this might have opened the door to a discussion of my confused sexual feelings, and that was territory nobody was interested in shedding light on at that time. No, father was going to teach me about something far more useful—the art of suburban maintenance.

First up was maintaining the cars. I was led out on a Saturday morning to watch and learn as father poked under the hood of our Cadillac DeVille. "Now, first you want to check your dipstick to see where the engine oil level is," he said, just before looking over to find me engrossed in a doodlebug crossing the driveway. I saw an expression of disgust on his face that I had not seen since I was age five. That was the time he was letting the car warm up on a cold morning and came outside to find me pretending to be a rock star. I was playing a fake guitar and gyrating amidst the white smoke pouring out of the exhaust pipe.

After giving up on car maintenance, we moved on to the most sacred suburban tradition handed down from father to son . . . the mowing of the lawn.

Growing up, my family lived in a substantial house with an even more substantial lawn. My father proudly purchased a genuine John Deere riding mower to maintain our grounds to baseball field standards. He then decided to turn me loose on just the backyard portion to cut my teeth on lawn care.

Carefully, father coached and trained me, monitoring my passes to ensure exacting standards of crisscrossing lines in the grass. While Dad was busy practically inspecting my mowing passes with a measuring tape, I would be sweating and feeling nauseous in the Texas summer heat.

Father eventually decided that I was ready to cut the grass on my own. He sent me off on the riding mower and went inside the house to enjoy a glass of iced tea. Unfortunately, his satisfaction did not last long. He soon looked out the window to discover that I had run up onto a rocky slope and knocked myself off the mower. The hungry, grass-eating machine was now barreling across our backyard, unattended and completely out of control. The engine was spouting black smoke as it greedily took out whole chunks of lawn and monkey grass landscaping in its path.

While I remained sprawled out on the ground, struggling to maintain consciousness and get up before the John Deere came back my way, father sprang into action. Within minutes, he had jumped up and mounted the runaway mower and brought it to a standstill by killing the engine. The sudden silence was deafening. All I could hear was my father's heavy, angry breathing as he sat atop our now impotent mower and surveyed the sporadic lines cut into his lawn.

My father continued to try to impart the importance of domestic maintenance to me, even after I was forbidden from ever touching our grass again.

"You'll need to know how to do these things some day," he told me one blustery winter morning. He had drug me underneath our house to patch a burst water pipe.

"Dad," I responded, straining to hold the flashlight steady while scanning for large spiders, "That's why I'm going to have to either make a lot of money or live in an apartment the rest of my life."

My father eventually resigned to allow me to sit in my room and do "whatever it was I did in there." Having given up on trying to connect with me through the traditional methods, he would sit down on occasion and read some of my poetry or listen to a song I had written on my keyboard. He would usually end his visit by looking over at me and asking if I was capable of writing something other than a funeral dirge.

My father just didn't get it. How could he? I was going through the coming-out process before the days of *Ellen* and *Will & Grace,* when conservative straight parents across America would laugh at the antics of "Just Jack." These were the days before a time when being gay would be rendered almost chic compared to previous cultural standards.

I can't be too harsh, however. My father did not have much of a reference for relating to a son in general, much less a gay son. He was five years old when a train struck down and killed his own father in a freak accident. His dad had been working as a brakeman on a California railroad at the time. My father and his older brother were then abruptly relocated across the country to a relative's house in Pittsburgh. His mother went to work in a dress shop to support the family. Later, when my dad's mother remarried, he and his brother would be told to keep quiet and not make any waves about their new stepfather. It was understood that, if a choice needed to be made between them or the new man in the house, they would be the ones to go.

When I get frustrated with trying to communicate and be understood by my father, I try to remember his perspective and where he's coming from. It makes it easier to see why he keeps his feelings and emotions bottled up inside. It helps me understand why being an artist who thrives on intense emotion is such a potentially unsettling reality for my dad. Being gay just adds another dimension to that. He had never known anyone who was gay prior to his own son coming out.

When I was in junior high school, the girl who lived next door to us bleached my hair ultra-blond. My father took one look at my head and said; "I guess it's fine if you want to look gay."

This was the first time I ever even heard him say the word. I think his reference at that point was little more than photos of a pride parade on the ten o'clock news. His words stuck with me though. Not only because they smacked of a truth that was buried deep inside my emerging identity, but also because I could feel so clearly his disapproval.

By the time I understood and admitted that I was a gay man, I was almost twenty and living on my own while going to college. My mother simply asked me the question one day. I told her the truth. She took it relatively well, as well as could be expected. I asked her to tell Father for me. Somehow, I just couldn't bear to do that part myself. She did.

The next time I went over to my parent's house, my father pulled me aside in the kitchen. "Come here," he said. He was starting to cry, so I knew what this was about. My father wrapped his arms tightly around me and then broke down into heavy sobs. He cried so hard that his back was shaking and his hands were trembling. This was one of the few times I've ever seen him cry. He finally said to me in a broken voice, "I want you to know that you're my son, and no matter what happens . . . I love you."

I quickly broke down myself. It remains the most honest moment I've ever experienced with my dad.

Since that moment, my father and I have been on a journey to reconnect. It is as if somehow just giving "it" a name—gay—removed some of the mystery; and we both feel somehow freer and better able to communicate. There is no longer a big secret standing between us.

Gradually, my father began asking more questions about my experience. When did I first suspect? How did I know for sure? He seemed to eventually make peace with the idea that this was who I was and that it was not a phase or a form of experimentation. He eventually began asking about my new social life; he urged me to be safe when it came to sex; and he told a few friends and family members about his gay son.

My father has come a long way. He still can't bear to see two men kiss, but he is now the first one to offer my boyfriend and me help with a car-buying decision or assistance in reclaiming some neglected landscaping. He now even takes pleasure in having us over to cook up steaks, red and juicy, on his patio grill.

It is now, during these wonderful times of reconnection, that I look back and begin to look differently at my childhood with my father. I begin to feel guilty. I wish I had been the kind of son who wanted to share great adventures with him. I wish I had been the kind of young man who would have been there to help duct-tape those branches to his head for a hunting trip or share in his enthusiasm for the sweet purr of a Harley-Davidson engine. He would have liked that.

Instead, I was happier growing up to stay inside, writing my stories and scribbling my poetry. This was a trait my father did not anticipate in me, but has come to love and respect. Likewise, being gay was a trait he did not expect in me, and while he may not understand it, he respects the man that I am and the man that I now share my life with.

My dad remains a restless spirit who refuses to go quietly into middle-aged, white-collared stagnation. He still craves adventure and experience and has a thirst for the outdoors. (Unfortunately for him, he also has my mother, a woman who is terrified of water, hates to sweat, and considers adventure to be braving Saturday afternoon traffic to go to the shopping mall. You can't blame the man for trying, however.)

My dad is a man of such few words that it is ironic that I would grow up to become a man who earns a living off his words. If I had a better use of language right now, I'd tell him thank you, because the best parts of him rubbed off on me anyway.

Just like him, when I feel a passion for something, I dive right in . . . pushing fears, popular opinions, and even rational thinking aside. Sure, the details are different. I'm experimenting with a new form of poetry, perhaps, instead of hiking a mountain trail; but just the same, I learn everything I can about my new interest, experience it from every angle and, of course, buy every possible accessory related to it that's known to man.

Also, like my father, the accessories may all wind up in the back of a storage shed when it's over, and my prized hunting dog becomes a really expensive pet; but at least I gave it a shot. At least I tried. And when the day is done, I can say proudly, like him . . . that somehow I chose life, for better or for worse; and this is something I know he would be proud of.

〜 10   Unfinished Business

Durrell Mackey

After parking his car in the airport parking lot, Ralph got out of the car, walked a short distance to the United Airlines terminal, and took the escalator to Gate 24. Zora sat in a black leather chair at Gate 24 at Oakland International Airport. She was tense. Her hair was pulled back in a bun and she was wearing baggy blue jeans, gold earrings, and a red tank top. Her shoes were flat and black. She looked at her watch; it was 8:30 p.m. She was reading the *Oakland Tribune,* smoking Salems. He stared at Zora and thought, "I've got unfinished business with her and I'm sure she's thinking the same thing about me."

"Zora!"

"Ralph, baby, how are you doing?" she said. She stood upon her tiptoes, kissed him on the cheek, and hugged him close.

"I'm doing good. How about you Zora?" he asked.

"Fine now, but that layover in Kansas City was frightful. I thought Memphis was a hick town, but I've never seen so many hostile white folks in such cramped quarters as I did at that airport. They were sitting in bars like rattlesnakes watching O.J. lead a caravan of LA cops in the slowest car chase in history. I swear to God and another illegal alien, I was worried about being sent to you in a body bag," she said.

"Zora, you're a mess. Come on. Let's get your luggage and head on out," he said.

"What I really need is a wicked shot of Hennessey," Zora said, and laughed. They walked briskly toward the baggage claims area.

"I could use a strong dose of it myself," he said smiling and beginning to relax. "Jesus. It feels awkward as hell seeing her again after two years. I've got to find some way to right the wrongs I perpetrated on Zora. This visit could be the beginning of a new relationship with her, not based on romance but a coming of terms, with each other on our own terms," he thought.

Zora had two tiny suitcases and a crinkled Saks Fifth Avenue shopping bag full of lingerie. Once they made it to the car, Ralph opened the trunk of his car and tossed the luggage in.

As they drove away from the airport, Zora lit a cigarette, took a drag, and exhaled. Ralph rolled down his window and activated the sunroof. They were silent for a few moments.

"Damn. Zora, you still smoke like a train," he said.

"I know, Ralph. I'm still trying to quit, but it's easier said than done. Would you like for me to put it out?"

"For your own sake, I would. It's entirely up to you, though. They're your lungs, not mine. Zora, I wish you could stay for more than two days," he lied. Then he said, "So that we can catch up on some juicy gossip."

"Gossip. Child, I've never known you to like gossip. You've been watching way too much *Oprah* for me," she laughed, stubbed out her cigarette in the ashtray, and quickly lit up another one.

Zora watched the sailboats that drifted on San Francisco Bay. Ralph looked at the oval face of a little black boy riding in a blue station wagon. The child's face mashed up against the window of the car reminded him of his own face when he was a little boy. At six years old he'd learned he was not like other little boys. He had a way about him. He enjoyed putting together Lionel trains and building skateboards, reading his mother's soap opera magazines. Sports didn't interest him; climbing trees always put holes in his jeans.

Little Ralph had been in love with his best friend Herbert after they'd only spent one night together. That night, he got so tangled up into a knot with Herbert until he didn't know where he began and Herbert ended. They'd dissolved into a human pretzel. Before the night was able to move out of the way and make room for daylight, Ralph's virginity was lost to Herbert, a twelve-year-old little boy with the heart of a man.

The traffic on Interstate 8 stalled.

Zora was about to bring Ralph's memories further back to a dark night where he had found himself after his first love Herbert moved with his family to Mobile.

"I never stopped loving you, little Ralph," Zora said.

The words "little Ralph" jolted him like a cattle prod.

It was the end of Indian summer in the small shipyard town of Mosswood, Georgia. Ralph's mother, Ludie, was going out on a date.

"Bye, Sam. Don't let little Ralph stay up too late. I'll be back before midnight," Ludie said.

"I won't, Sis. Go on out and have yourself some fun. I'll see you later," Sam said, closing the door. Sam took off his dirty overalls, sat in a chair in the living room, spread his legs apart, and turned off the lights. Sam's penis became erect.

"Little Ralph, a bogeyman's in your room, but don't be afraid to come over here and sit on my lap," he said.

"Uncle Sam, it's dark in here and I'm scared," Ralph said.

"If you be a good boy and do what I ask you to do, I'm going to buy you a big birthday cake with six pretty little candles on it. I love you, little Ralph," he said.

"I don't want to, Uncle Sam! I want my mama!" Ralph said, exiting his bedroom and running toward the front door.

Ralph made it as far as the porch before Sam cornered and grabbed him by the collar. He stripped off Ralph's trousers, undies, and threw him face down on the warm carpet. He violently penetrated Ralph's ass. Sharp, swift, electric, and splinterlike sensations shot throughout his body. Ralph bled. He could hear Mahalia Jackson's song, "What a Friend We Have in Jesus," in the background playing on the radio.

"Awwwwww! Stop! No! No! Mammmmma! You're hurting me, Uncle Sam!" Ralph said.

"Shut up, or I'll make it hurt even more!" Sam said. Ralph grew numb from his waist down. Sam came and quickly withdrew his huge penis out of Little Ralph's rectum. Ralph raised up on his hands and knees and slowly crawled to his room, lay down on his bed and cried. Sam followed Ralph into his bedroom.

"Nigga, if you ever tell anybody what I did, I'll break your motherfucking neck! Do you hear me?" he said.

"I hear you, Uncle Sam," he said sobbing.

As the traffic on the freeway slowed, Ralph's daydream came to a halt. Zora turned to look at his face. Sweat was falling from his temples.

"Ralph, baby, you look like you've just seen a ghost," she said and took a napkin out of her tiny purse and dabbed at his face.

"I did Zora. I did."

"Make him get the fuck out of your car because I don't get along very well with ghosts. Ralph, I said I'm still in love with you."

"I'm sorry. My mind was somewhere else. Somewhere I never want to go back to. But yeah, I didn't stop caring about you either, Zora."

"But you never really loved me, Ralph. Did you?"

"I loved you, Zora, but I was in love with Bobby."

"Bobby! That lowdown punk ass faggot. He stole you from me."

Ralph wondered if it would all come down to this but he didn't expect it so soon and of all places inside of his car on the way home from the airport. He couldn't ignore Zora, any more than he could close his eyes and drive. He responded out of obligation rather than feeling insulted.

"For heaven's sake, Zora, why are you doing this to yourself and to me? You quit me before I met Bobby."

Zora's eyes were wet with tears. Ralph handed her his handkerchief and she dried her eyes, blew her nose, and looked at herself in a small compact mirror. After a few minutes, she regained her composure and became cheerful again.

A nervous tic kept Ralph's right eye twitching uncontrollably. By 9:30 p.m. they arrived at Ralph's house. He helped her out of the car, retrieved her luggage, placed it in the guest bedroom, and fixed them both a cocktail. Ralph sat in a black leather loveseat in the middle of the living room. Zora sat in a chair in the room, facing Ralph. She took a sip of Hennessey, lit a cigarette, took a drag, and exhaled.

The urge to hold Zora in his arms was overwhelming. He didn't expect this. Regardless of how many nights he'd rocked and cradled Bobby in his arms, Zora was equivalent to the last hurrah. Not just a female, but the last chance to connect with the straight part of his life that he'd put away over the last two years.

Now, he knew that there would be no other woman in his life like Zora. She drew to a close his era of ambivalence. Something had changed, though, in two years: he was no longer ashamed of his urges to be with another man. He didn't feel as though he was being unfaithful when he'd take that second look at an attractive man. Or afraid of what a slight touch or deep conversation with a man might lead to.

Zora's misgivings about coming to visit Ralph were soothed by the burning liquor that trickled down her throat and made her memories of Ralph crystal clear. It wasn't a contest to see if she could win him back. One month after she'd moved back to Memphis she concocted a plot to force Ralph back into her arms. She was going to feign pregnancy and threaten him with a paternity suit. That was an old trick and beneath her as a woman. She couldn't go through that sort of stress any more than she could attempt suicide. So she resigned herself with believing that the good Lord gives and takes away. She blamed God for taking Ralph, not any lack of desirability on her part.

After mulling over her thoughts, Zora asked Ralph if she could take a shower. Ralph nodded and smiled. Moments later, Ralph could hear through the open bathroom door the water rushing up against the walls and shower curtain. As the warm water drenched her body, Zora thought about the way they were the last time she was with him.

They were at a photograph studio at the Fashion Center in San Francisco. They wore Macy's fall fashion collections in a benefit for the San Francisco AIDS Foundation. Zora was snazzy in a strapless peach evening gown that looked as if it had been painted on her. Ralph was decked out in a black tux.

"Damn, Macy's is lucky like a motherfucker to have us don their wardrobe. Look at us. Shit. You can't touch this," Zora said, twirling, twisting, and flaunting her lithe figure in front of a floor-to-ceiling mirror.

"Tell me about it," Ralph said. He strutted like a peacock.

"Let's go out tonight after we're done with the last photo shots and do dinner in Union Square or go out dancing. I want to wax that ass," she said.

"You know me. I'm always RWA. Ready, willing, and able. Let's do Club Universe. Zora, I can't believe we've been together for two years," he said and nibbled her ear.

She giggled.

"Ralph, why are you always staring at the other male models? I watched you looking at Denny at rehearsals last week like you were in a trance," she said.

"I just appreciate a good-looking man, that's all," he lied.

Zora drove her car to Club Universe. Ralph sat in the passenger's seat and took in the sights and sounds of the city. The smoke and dusty haze in Club Universe made Ralph's eyes water and burn. Zora sat at the bar, decked out in basic black, her hair in tiny ringlets. Ralph wore black leather pants. He had checked his jacket and shirt. He was topless.

"I'm tired of dancing. I want to go home. These pumps are kicking my ass!" she said.

"I feel you; let's go," he said.

They walked out of the club hand in hand. When they reached the car, Zora handed him the car keys.

"Do you mind driving?" she asked.

"No problem," he said.

As he drove across the San Francisco Bay Bridge, Zora dozed off to sleep. She woke up when the car rolled over gravel in her unpaved driveway. The blinds at Zora's apartment were shut tight. Her porch light was on. They got out of the car and she followed him up to the front door. Ralph twisted his key into the door and opened it. A lamp in the living room highlighted a sparse but neatly furnished Oakland bungalow in Jack London Square. She sat down on the sofa. Both of her feet were swollen. They disrobed. Ralph went into the bathroom and ran a bubble bath and sat in the tub. Zora tiptoed in and straddled his thighs. The slightest thrust of her pelvic muscles drove him deeper and deeper into chartered territory.

"Oh, Ralph! Deeper! Deeper! That's it! Right there! Ohhhhhhh!" she said.

Ralph was nonorgasmic.

"My hero!" she said, laughing, and pulling Ralph's member out of her. Then she said, "Ralph, I'm concerned about the slips of paper I found in your wallet with the first names of men and their telephone numbers."

"You've been going through my wallet. I'll be goddamn," he said.

"I read your journal, followed you to the sex clubs two weeks ago, and waited up for you all night last week when you didn't come home," she said.

"So now you know. I'm gay, and you've been doing surveillance, stalking and spying on me. Who gave you the right to snoop through my personal belongings anyway? Waiting up for me as if I was a piss ass teenager," he said.

"Well, if you don't think I care enough about you, then get the fuck out of my house! I'm moving back to Memphis tomorrow," she said, before stepping out of the bathtub. She grabbed a towel and hurried to her bedroom.

These memories made her wish she'd never met him at all. She wondered if she'd made a mistake by coming out to California to visit with him. Was she still trapped under his curse?

Ralph sat out in his living room looking over the plans for his fifteen-year high school reunion. Ralph heard Zora yell for some soap, and when Ralph brought the soap into the bathroom, Zora made a pass at him.

"Ohhhhhh! I want some dick so badddddd!"

Ralph felt awkward. He handed the soap to Zora over the top of the shower curtains. He pretended as if he didn't hear her words and left the bathroom as if she wasn't talking to him but to the passions the liquor had stirred up inside her.

Zora finished her shower and came out into the living room wearing a leopard pantsuit, her hair tied up in a white towel. She poured herself a drink and lit a cigarette at Ralph's bar, then walked over to the sofa and sat down. Zora faced Ralph.

"Why did you accept my invitation to see me again, Zora, after three long years? When I invited you to visit, I was only being polite. Couldn't you have just said kiss my ass and let the past rest in peace as the dead do?" he said as he finished a can of beer.

"The dead don't rest in peace, Ralph. I know, because I'm one of the walking dead and I'm not resting in peace. Ralph, real penis envy is when a woman in love with a fag realizes that she can't compete with another man for his love. I don't have a dick dangling between my legs. That is what you prefer, isn't it, Ralph?" she said and blew a gust of smoke toward the ceiling.

"What I prefer is to live my life the way I want to live it. I'm glad as hell to be gay. I'm not a fag, Zora. My grandmother told me a fag is a burnt piece of wood. All I ever wanted from you was to be treated with dignity and respect, and that's something you could never give to me. I'm no longer living a two-faced lie. I'm out and free, Zora. As free as the air in this room," he said.

"You were always free to leave, Ralph. We weren't married," she said as she sipped her drink.

"Not to each other, but you carried on as if you were still married to your dead ex-husband. Carrying his memory around on your little skinny wrists. I never cheated on you, like you thought. I brought it on home to you."

"Ralph, you always were a pathological liar. And you still are. I'm giving you a chance to fess up with the truth for once in your sorry little life. Mama's boy. From the beginning of our relationship, I always suspected you were gay."

Ralph wanted to act surprised at Zora's revelation that his secret life was never really a secret to her but he couldn't. He remembered her complaints about his solemn moods, his interest in male erotica, his need for male approval, and his lack of passionate sexual desire for her. Zora was a front. Someone he could take to class reunions, dinner parties, nightclubs, and even to his mama. He would show the world that since he was born gay in a homophobic world, he'd outdo straight men and become the whoremonger. He'd out-macho his male peers, beat his women, and lust in his heart for every piece of pussy that strolled across God's green earth.

"If you knew I was gay why did you stay with me so long?" he asked.

"I thought you were different and that it was just a phase you were going through. I listened to you talk in your sleep about your encounters and heard your nightmares about Uncle Sam," she said.

"A phase? At twenty-eight? Oh please! All I know is when we split up I finally established my identity as a gay man. I only had half a life with you. Now I've got a full one," he said.

"You can change, Ralph. There are doctors and therapy. What's going to happen to you when you begin to age and that rock-hard body of yours turns soft and starts to sag?"

"I should have a fucking awesome video collection by then. Besides, I'm committed to Bobby. He's not only good to me, but he's good for me. I'm not leaving him," he said.

"Like you did to me motherfucker," she said.

"You cut up my clothes, burned my journal, threatened my life, and kicked me out of your house. It was Bobby who picked me up off of the streets, took me into his home, arms, and heart. I've been there ever since and it is where I'm going to stay until death do us part," he said.

"Where is your boyfriend, anyway? Cheating on you the way you did to me?" she said.

"I trust him. If it was legal, I'd marry him. If I had a uterus, ovaries, and fallopian tubes, I'd have his baby. Do I look worried to you? If he's cheating on me with a woman, then she's giving him something that I can't. I'm man enough to accept that. If it's with another man, then as a man if I really want to keep him, it's my job to compete well enough to bring him back to me. If I lose, then I'll wish him well. I don't have the time for bullshit. That's more than I can say for you. You're not blind. You see that Bobby's not here, but he told me to tell you he'd be home shortly. Here, he gave me these flowers to give to you," he said, handing her a bouquet of long-stemmed red roses.

"Shit. I'm not dead yet. I don't need flowers. He'll see the pit of hell before I do. Black bastard. He probably has AIDS," she said as she took the flowers, walked over to the trashcan, and dumped them.

"Like I said, he'll be home in a few minutes and I want to see you tell him that to his face. Zora, girl, you need help," he said.

"Help, my ass!" she said.

Zora went into the guest room and slammed the door. Ralph massaged the tension that settled in the middle of his eyeballs and temples. He thought about Bobby the way you'd think when there's trouble and you know that help is on the way.

The bartender dimmed the lights, turned the music off and began to close the bar. Bobby's eyes zoomed in on Ralph like a pair of binoculars.

"Hi! I'm Bobby. I've wanted to meet you all night long. I love your slanted dark brown eyes."

"Hey, thanks." Ralph gushed. "I'm Ralph," he said, grinning and shaking Bobby's hand. Then he said, "I was watching you too. I don't deal with rejection too good, though. So I waited for you to make the first move. Sorry, I don't mean to sound like a whiner, but I don't have a crib to sleep in tonight. My girlfriend put me out."

"Check it. I've got plenty of room at my place. Come on. Let's go. I only live two blocks away."

"I'm game."

The house was dark inside. They stumbled through the darkness, found the bedroom, and stripped buck naked. Bobby's dark face, hair, and hands smelled like sweet tobacco. His lips tasted like wet molasses. Bobby looked up under his pillow, found a rubber and put it on. Their nude bodies entwined, rose up and down like high tides.

"Oh, baby. Don't stop. Please don't stop. Yeahhhh. I'm—."

"Me toooooooooo!" Ralph said. They lay quiet, nose to nose.

"There's something I want you to know," Bobby said.

"What?" Ralph asked.

"I'm HIV positive," Bobby said.

Ralph didn't blink. His eyes narrowed. He turned his back to Bobby and looked at a photograph sitting on the nightstand of Bobby with a young black woman and a little girl dressed like a Barbie doll. He turned back around and faced Bobby.

"I'm not," Ralph said.

"I assume everybody I come into contact with is HIV positive. Ralph, I'm scared, but I can't keep hiding for the rest of my life. None of us really knows what we are anymore."

"I know, baby. I'm gonna make sure that you'll never be lonely again, if you only let me," Ralph said, and shuddered.

"I'd turn down a billion dollars if it meant I could trade it in on a cure. Wash my blood clean of the scourge," Bobby said, his eyes watering.

Under the low shadows of a dim light above their heads, Ralph spotted the tracks of a tear that froze halfway between Bobby's eye and the corner of his mouth. Ralph kissed the tear and licked it from Bobby's face.

"See, I'm not afraid," Ralph said.

"But Ralph, if I die, then you will be alone. Isn't that just as risky as getting sick or falling in love?" Bobby asked.

"Living is risky. If you fall in love with me, it'll be the greatest and most glorious risk of them all," Ralph said.

"All I know Ralph, is that on this night, lying here in your arms, I'm falling in love with you. For better or worse," he said.

"In sickness and health," Ralph said.

"Till death do us part," Bobby vowed.

Bobby was cursed with the gift of smelling trouble miles away. When he pulled into his driveway, the porch light was off and the blinds in the living room were open. He could see Ralph's back slumped in a chair. He looked for Zora and she was nowhere in sight.

Bobby got out of the car and went into the house. Before he set the Styrofoam tray full of leftover soul food on the coffee table, Bobby could see by the expression on Ralph's face that trouble had found a beachhead between Zora and Ralph. He hung up his jacket and pulled Ralph close. He didn't ask questions, but instead coaxed Ralph into sitting down and began to massage his shoulders and the nape of his neck.

"Baby, I'm so sorry about dinner, but Zora and I got carried away," Ralph said as he turned around and looked into Bobby's chestnut eyes.

"Sweetheart, don't stress out about it. It's all right. I stopped by Lois The Pie Queen Café over in Oakland and he hooked me up with some black-eyed peas and stuffed bell peppers. Man, I'm good to go!" he said trying to cheer Ralph up.

"I didn't even prepare dinner for Zora," he confessed.

"Wow. That bad, huh?"

"Well, we had to rehash a lot of old stuff. Man, demons can be a motherfucker!" he said.

"You telling me? I know the deal. Look, let me make you some coffee. I think you can use it real bad," Bobby said as he winked and playfully nudged Ralph's chin.

"I'll go and fetch, Zora," he said.

"Cool."

Zora was standing in the hallway listening and watching Ralph and Bobby. Ralph brought her into the kitchen to meet Bobby. Instead of shaking her hand, Bobby reached out and hugged Zora. He held her for a few moments. He could feel her body shake as she began to cry.

"I'm so sorry. I didn't mean to interfere with anybody. I just couldn't pass up Ralph's invitation," she moaned.

"Interfering? Zora, you're not interfering with us. We're all family now. Don't you see? Ralph still loves you, and whatever he loves I'm crazy about," Bobby consoled.

"You really mean that?"

"Is O.J. Simpson guilty?"

"As sin," she said, laughing and regaining her composure. She gave Bobby a small kiss on the cheek before she gently pulled away from him.

Bobby went into the kitchen, poured three cups of coffee, and brought them back out on a small tray. He set the tray on the coffee table and handed a cup of coffee to Zora and Ralph. He picked up a cup and took a sip.

"Have some coffee. We're all gonna be up for a long time," Bobby said. He looked at Ralph and then said, "Right, Boo?"

"Yeah, baby, a long, long time," he said.

"Excuse me guys, but I've got a telephone call to make." Zora took a sip of coffee and lit a cigarette, then walked into the hallway, picked up the telephone, and dialed.

"Hello."

"Hi, Ludie. This is Zora. Girl, how you been doing?"

"Zora? I'm doing fine, but Lord have mercy, child, I haven't heard from you since you moved back to Memphis. I thought Ralph and Bobby told me you were coming to visit the Bay Area for a spell."

"I'm already out here. I got in this evening. I'm staying with Ralph and Bobby."

"Ralph and Bobby? Child, are you out of your mind?"

"Honey, relax. We're not exactly having an orgy," she chuckled.

"I was thinking more like a war!"

"Ralph don't know it yet, but I'm leaving to go back to Memphis tomorrow morning."

"So soon? Honey, you just got out here. Mercy! You young folks sure waste a lot of time and good money. Flying from one part of the world to the next as if you've got wings."

"I still thought I could change him, Ludie, but now I realize that you can't make someone love you if they don't. I'm giving up. Ralph's hopelessly in love with Bobby and he's happy. I've never seen him like this before. I'm letting the past go."

"You are a smart girl, Zora."

"I'm only calling because I'd planned to come over to see you and have dinner, just me, you, and Ralph. See if you could put a bug in Ralph's ear. Tell him he's got a lot of nerve passing me up. A sure thing."

"You can still come over for dinner. Tell me about all those fine men in Memphis, breaking down your door to get at you," Ludie chuckled.

"Ludie, since moving back home. I've placed my love so high upon a shelf no one can get to it. Not even me," she said.

"Well, baby, when you get back home you go climb right on back up there on that shelf and you make your love come down. Use a footstool, if you have to. Love should never be so far away from a woman that she can't even touch it."

"You've always been a practical woman. Good-bye, Ludie."

"Bye, baby, and keep in touch. You hear?"

"I will."

Zora hung up the telephone and walked back into the living room, where Ralph was softly stroking Bobby's brow. Zora sat down next to Ralph and gazed into his eyes. He turned away from Bobby, smiled at her, and hugged her tight.

"I heard what you said to Mama on the telephone. I was listening on the other line. A girl named Zora taught me how to eavesdrop."

"Always be my friend, Ralph," she said.

"I will, Zora. I will."

The next day, Ralph drove Zora back to the airport. She caught an afternoon flight back to Memphis and promised to invite Ralph and Bobby for a visit.

On his way home from the airport, he sped along the I-80 freeway, passed through Emeryville, Berkeley, and Albany. He looked out on the San Francisco Bay, and watched its teal green waters roar up against the shore. He felt a sense of continuity. A seagull flew above the sea and it made him think how he would feel if he had wings and could fly. Ralph had come to terms with a very special part of his life and it would take more than the wings of a bird to make him soar as high as he was feeling right now.

༼ 11   A Southern Reflection

P. J. Gray

I looked into the bathroom mirror and I saw age. I examined the noticeable lines of my face with careful consideration. As I poked and tugged at my skin's remaining elasticity, my concentration slowly melted.

An image immediately flashed before me, then became focused. I could see my small, childlike hand reaching down and touching a block of freshly cut live oak. My fingers drew along the circular rings of the fleshy exposed trunk—touching nature's own timeline. I recalled the smell of the wood so clearly and could picture my father's stately pose with his ax in hand. A grove of moss-covered oaks and sand pines surrounded him. I vaguely remembered his explanation of the rings—a simple and intelligent prose incorporating the concepts of age and wisdom. My father was as eloquent as Billy Graham behind a podium and as handsome as Rhett Butler ever was. He always had a way with words, even during the most laborious takes. His words were as lyrical and refined as his Southern accent. I would later realize that my attraction to certain Southern men was in direct relation to my perception of him.

I was suddenly propelled back to the bathroom mirror and regained consciousness. Somehow, I had miraculously shaved my face without a scratch. The hot water from the sink faucet clouded the mirror and bathroom like an August afternoon over a Florida bayou. As I breathed the warm, humid air, I wiped the mirror clean and began to stare into the aperture of my memories.

The recollections of my Southern upbringing consumed me. I could almost feel the blinding sun as it baked the manicured lawns and homes of my neighborhood along the white, sandy beaches of the Florida panhandle. I could feel the stifling heat from the black asphalt tempting to burn my feet through my favorite pair of blue and white flip-flops—the pair my mama bought me from TG&Y. And, I began to see all of the shirtless, barefooted teenage boys of my youth. Their skin was tanned, freckled, and smooth like polished leather. Their summer attire consisted only of a pair of faded, frayed Sears Wrangler cut-offs, the occasional Band-Aid, and a healthy dose of testosterone. I could almost smell the saltwater in the air pouring from the Gulf of Mexico—an aroma made even more distinct when combined with the odor of Ucatan sun-tanning oil. That scent reminded me of Toby. Funny, I had not thought of Toby for years.

Toby became my next-door neighbor in the summer of 1977, the day after my twelfth birthday. After his father's death, his mother sold their farm and moved from the northern part of the county near the Alabama state line in order to open a tourist gift shop near the beach. I fondly recall the day they moved into their house and the first time I saw him through my bedroom window. It was a warm, breezy July afternoon—the kind that Floridians without air-conditioning prefer. His open bedroom window faced mine from only fifty or sixty feet away which made spying that much easier. I secretly watched him unpack his belongings for several hours, oblivious of time. He completely fascinated me.

Eventually, he noticed my stare and cautiously approached his window ledge. At first, I tried to move from his line of sight, but I was too late. As we studied each other, I knew that I was looking at someone differently and in a way that I did not fully understand. We slowly gestured to each other and exchanged an awkward "hey." His wavy red hair was as thick and his Southern drawl. His teeth were straight and as white as beach sand. His lips were full and a bit pouty. His body was lean and sportsmanlike and his naturally pale skin was freckled and sunburned. This was an attraction that would soon change my life forever.

It was not long before we became inseparable classmates and friends. Our adolescence was spent fishing, hunting, and camping together. We ran, swam, and surfed together. We shared a love for softball tournaments, weight lifting, fried chicken dinners, country music, and family secrets. We spent hours listening to groups like Alabama and the Oak Ridge Boys. Although we socialized with other kids from school, our friendship grew stronger as did my feelings for him, both emotionally and physically. I became increasingly confused by these feelings and somehow found a way to successfully suppress them. Fortunately, I found solace in the privacy of my bedroom, spending what seemed like hours consumed with carnal thoughts.

Before we knew it, we were attending high school and struggling through the rituals of early adulthood. During the summer prior to our senior year, we were hired as lifeguards by a local hotel. Toby persuaded me to accept the job in order to prevent him from working at his mother's gift shop. By now, he had become very athletic and was an exceptional swimmer with exceptional features. These, of course, did not go unnoticed by the local sorority set. Toby was aware of his good looks but never seemed too egotistical. He dated girls from our school occasionally but never seemed committed.

The days of lifeguarding on the beach were sunny, hot, and mostly uneventful. Our time was filled with annoying tourists, lost children, jellyfish stings, and hours of self-reflection. Fortunately, I could always rely on Toby to make the time more enjoyable. In fact, I took every possible opportunity to admire his body when he wasn't looking. I would sit on the guard tower for hours pretending to comb the shoreline for helpless swimmers while I watched him distribute beach chairs and umbrellas or converse with other guys on the beach.

By the summer's end, I had convinced myself that the infatuation was futile. I could not run the risk of losing our friendship in order to confess my true feelings for him. It just wasn't worth it. At that age, I knew that I wasn't completely prepared to come out despite the realization or acceptance of my homosexuality.

A feeling of dread passed through me as I shook myself out of the past. I found myself still standing in front of the bathroom sink. My morning routine was unforgiving. I continued to concentrate on the present but to no avail. My thoughts of Toby and the beach haunted me. They were too vivid—too powerful. I entered the shower blindly and allowed the warm water to pour over me. In an instant, I was back on the beach.

On the last day of the season, we decided to take our time closing up the beach. We laughed and reminisced about the summer as we gathered the rental chairs, flags, and equipment. The large sun fell on the horizon as the sky turned the most beautiful shades of orange and violet. By the time we finished our work, the beach was deserted and peaceful. The Gulf water retreated with a surprising calm.

Toby was first to climb the lifeguard tower and sat on its edge. From the sand, I watched him absorb the sunset with a certain sense of longing. And just when I thought he had forgotten where he was, Toby glanced down at me. As dusk continued to envelop the sky around us, we stared at each other for what seemed like an eternity. He smiled an unusual smile at me and gestured to join him atop the tower. Although I was a bit confused by his signals, I still couldn't help myself. Whether I knew his intentions or not, I couldn't afford to miss the chance to be alone with him, even if I had to pretend the moment was nothing but a fantasy. He grabbed my hand as I reached the top of the ladder and began the chuckle under his breath as I sat beside him.

"What's up?" I said cautiously. "What's so funny?"

"I'm sorry. I guess it's nervous energy or something," he replied, wearing a coy grin.

"Nervous? About what?"

"I've been thinking about it for a while—I'm not sure how long— but it's been a while," he answered vaguely.

"What is it? C'mon, you can tell me. We're friends, right?" I asked as I carefully put my arm around the back of his neck.

"Yeah, that's just it." His look turned serious as he studied my face. "You're one of my best friends and I feel that I can trust you. So, I've got to tell you this. Uh . . ."

"Tell me. Just say it."

Suddenly, he turned his head and forced his lips to mine. I was so startled that I quickly pulled away and for a moment. We looked at each other as if it were the first day we met through the bedroom windows.

"God, I'm sorry," he said under his breath as he turned away. "I'm sorry."

Before I could think anything to say, I put my hand on his to get his attention; and as he turned to me, I quickly leaned over and kissed him again. This time neither of us pulled away. The kiss was comfortable and awkward, familiar and new all at the same time. As we slowly separated, the reality of broken boundaries immerged and we suddenly broke into a brief bout of nervous laughter trying to study our emotions.

In an instant, the memory was shattered by my clock radio alarm blaring from the bedroom nightstand. I looked into the bathroom mirror only to see a faint outline of my reflection buried beneath the thick layer of condensation. The hot water had turned cool. As I turned the faucet handle, I stared at my hand—the hand that once touched Toby's young, sun-kissed face. Then, I wiped the moisture from the mirror and faced the reality of time and distance. I also caught a reflection of a smile.

⤳ 12   Breath

Kelly McQuain

SUMMER 1982

Lungs ache white hot as you hide beneath the water, a stream of bubbles rising slowly to the surface. You won't let Ricky pin you down again, no siree—jealous of your earlier dive, how you mastered something he can't do.

Relive the moment: arcing from the springing board, body pitching into the air, arms and legs narrowing, needle-thin. Spiked hands parted water in a clean rush, liquid blue surrounding you, a chlorine tingle sweet on your skin. Surfacing to the sight of Artie leaving his lifeguard chair and walking to the deep end of the Y's pool to compliment you—a snap of his fingers, a thumbs up. His off-center smile flashed, *Real potential, buddy.* Artie's shoulders are wide and his arms are firm—his jaw square as a coal shovel blade. His broad chest tapers to his waist in a streamlined V, a superhero from one of your comic books. Your eyes glaze at the sight of him. Has Ricky Pierce noticed those stolen glances, how they last too long? Is that why he tortures you?

Beneath the water, your lungs burn, cells turning to cinders, but still you ignore the urge to surface for air. You practice leg kicks and punches, fight the pressure, trying to force each blow as fast as in air. Water dulls momentum but hones muscle. You want to be, need to be, as powerful as Artie—blond hair and blue eyes, the build beneath his tight orange T-shirt as strong as Aquaman's.

Finally you surface. Chlorine-fogged eyes peer past splashing kids to spy Ricky on the bench next to Artie's chair. His eyes flare wide when he notices your head pop up. He shoots you the bird. Artie glances down, but Ricky turns the gesture into a quick scratch of his nose, a cowboy-casual brush of middle finger against skin.

Artie sighs, leans toward Ricky, his words getting swallowed by the din of the pool—splashing boys and laughing girls, the jabber of little kids hugging Styrofoam floaters. The noise swirls into the moss green arches of the Y's vaulted ceiling, then swoops down again, its echo ringing in your ears as your arms and legs scissor back and forth. You lip read Artie's words to Ricky, who can get back in the pool now if he promises to behave. Treading water, you feel betrayed.

Ricky stands, offers a salute to lifeguard Artie, then marches toward the deep end where the diving board is. As he nears a group of girls gathered at the six-foot marker, he snags a thumb in his shorts, hoists his cut-offs over bony hips, swaggers like a rogue. The girls splash water at his wiry legs, and he leans over their heads, pretends to spit, causing the girls to shriek and dive beneath the pool's foamy surface. Ricky glances over his shoulder, knowing he shouldn't be fooling around, but Artie is off breaking up a skirmish among the little kids. Only your eyes are upon him, taking him in, watching Ricky's lip curl at the sight of you before turning away—back to his graceless canonballing off the dive.

You kick forward, sharking beneath the surface, eyes stinging as you navigate the wavy limbs of goofing children. Streamlined, slippery as an eel, you won't let Ricky Pierce hold you under again, won't let his fingers squeeze your throat tight as you watch the breath bubble from your lungs. Damn Ricky to hell. You will be quick and powerful next time, you will stretch your lungs till they balloon inside you—twin oxygen tanks lasting minutes, hours, days, forever. This is your world now. Underwater is a dream you can swim inside, live inside. Almost.

Even time turns fluid as you float to the surface then dolphin down again—endless mammal repetition. Each submersion lasts a little longer than the one before. Thoughts fracture. You want to stack them neat inside you—*Everything in its place,* Momma says, her new baby on its way and all your old toys and clothes packed in boxes stacked inside your sister's room. *Can't Ally keep the baby?* you asked just last night, *Can't you put the crib in her room?*—let you keep your own. *No,* Momma said, *I'll need the baby's room next to mine, close in case it cries at night, gets the croup, forgets how to breathe as babies sometimes do.* And so you're pushed around, shoved aside, put wherever a boy can fit. In a girl's room with posters of TV hunks on the walls, *Starsky and Hutch, Dukes of Hazzard,*

Fonzie from *Happy Days*—Hollywood eyes staring down at you in the dark, twinkling, winking, *We know what you're thinking.*

At five till four, Ricky foregoes cannonballing and slinks toward the boy's locker room, beating the end-of-swim rush. Maybe he'll be gone by the time you go change. Swimming past stragglers, you head toward the deep end, trying to wring Open Swim of a few last minutes of pleasure before heading to the showers. In the deep end, the diving board stands free. Climbing out of the pool, you know what to do. Head to the board, grab the cold metal poles, hoist yourself up the tall ladder. Time for one last dive, and your heart leaps with anticipation of that moment when gravity shifts and flight turns to falling. Excitement jolts through you, a flash of lightning down your spine. Maybe if this dive outshines your last, Artie will ask you to stay after the other kids have gone. He'll be waiting there as you surface, offering a hand up as you climb out of the pool. He will rub your wet hair and compliment your form, share secret tips for making your next plunge even better. Maybe he'll strip off his shirt, legs and arms flexing as he climbs the high board to show you how its done. You can see him, launching forward with a bounce, body rising, snapping over, arms arrowing toward the water. In your mind's eye, his golden skin flashes as he slashes the water, his dreamy dissolve fading into rings of foam.

You stand atop the board now, pool gleaming before you, snakes of light writhing beneath its surface, You breathe deep the chemical air of the county Y. One good dive, and Artie's friendship is yours.

Thought whirls, dizzy in your brain as your feet bounce against the board. You launch yourself a little too soon, twisting your body wrong as the blue pool rushes forward too fast for your limbs to angle out. Your arms cut awkwardly through the surface, your stomach wallops against the water, air bubbling from your lungs as you sink beneath the spume, water surrounding you like birth in reverse.

You surface, gasping for air, feeling as panicked as when Ricky Pierce attacked you. You swim toward the shallows, trying to calm the tremors from your body, your limbs hacking ungraceful swaths. Before you're even halfway there, Artie walks to the poolside and blows his whistle. "Everybody out!"

Four o'clock. You take your time, slowly gliding to the edge of the pool, not wanting to leave the water, its comforting coolness, the way it moves over your skin like someone's hands. But Artie impatiently twirls his silver whistle. He points at you and says, "Out, buddy." He has the only dry hair in the place—long on top, slightly curly, falling in his eyes. You'd like to grow your hair like that but Momma would complain. Swimming to the ladder, you find yourself once more wishing that Artie had given Ricky Pierce more than a measly ten-minute time-out, that he truly was your buddy. No surprise then that when you climb from the water, Artie's eyes have resettled on some other kid—your heart again cheated.

As you head into the changing wing, the hoots and jeers of boys ricochet off the tiled walls. From the shower room to your left, a curtain of steam billows. You hide your Batman beach towel behind a radiator and walk in to rinse the chlorine from your skin. A warm cloud envelops you. Arms folded against your chest, you rotate slowly in the center of the room, searching for a free space beneath the showerheads lining the walls. The steam parts, revealing Ricky Pierce standing in a corner, his hands busy working a bar of soap in foamy streaks up and down his arms. His cut-offs lay at his feet. As he turns to you he reaches back to glide the soap along his buttocks. A first whisper of hair sluices down his chest to the top of his belly, its thin dark line an exclamation mark dotted by his navel. Sneering at you, Ricky runs the bar of soap down his grown-up cock, daring you to strip down, too.

You want to run from the room, but it's too late. As you step beneath an empty showerhead, Ricky slurs your name. "Andy-pansy," he calls, and a chuckle ripples through room, all the guys watching you. "Stupid cocksucker. You shouldn't of got me in trouble with your pal, Artie."

Head under the hot shower, you glare at Ricky through a wavering veil. "He's not my pal."

Ricky's eyes redden, something feral. "Andy-pansy, you think you're hot shit. But I know someone whose shit is hotter. Maybe someday you can kiss my ass and find out."

"You're just mad 'cause I dive better than you."

"Oh, right." Ricky winks at the other boys. "Real Olympic material here. Special Olympics, that is."

Though Ricky's buddies snicker at the joke, a few of the youngest boys scurry from the room; others pull back, hugging tiled walls, waiting to see what happens next. Ricky doesn't let them down. He bunches up his wet shorts in a tight ball and hurls them at you, laughs when you duck and they spatter the wall. "Toss 'em back," Ricky orders.

"You're crazy."

Ricky snaps back his head then thrusts forward, spitting out a gooey hocker that flies across the room to smack against your chest. Water won't wash the slug shape off; you have to flick it, watch the slick wad curl white and sticky on the concrete floor, a tiny apostrophe heading down the drain.

"Toss 'em back!" Ricky yells. "Or I launch another throat oyster."

Hating yourself, you kick his shorts back to him.

"Stupid," Ricky says as he catches his cut-offs. You brace yourself should he throw them again. But Ricky surprises you, merely slinging the wet shorts over his shoulder. Gears grind inside his brain as he searches for the most hurtful words to say to you. "Know what I ought to do?" he finally says. "I ought to go upstairs and hide behind the snack machine. Lay in wait in the lobby till your sweet old mommy comes to walk you home. Then I'll leap out and punch her in her big fat stomach."

"No you won't, Ricky."

"I'll knock her down and jump on her belly and smash it open like a jack-o'-lantern."

"Stop it, Ricky."

"Then I'll stamp my flip-flops on her big bouncy milk udders. *Yeeha!*" Water flies as Ricky dances, smacking the soles of his feet hard against the floor. "Hog blubber mommy, hog blubber mommy—"

"You can't hurt her—she's *pregnant.*" You say it like a magic word, an incantation to keep Ricky at bay.

All it does is make him cease his little jig. "I know that, you dumb retard." Ricky moves in close. "I just don't want any more Andy-Pansies popping out of her." His hand on your throat, pushing you back against the wall. Hot spray enveloping both of you, water running down Ricky's nose, spilling over his blood red lips as he tells the other boys to clear out—something they do without protest.

When they are gone, Ricky smacks his hand hard against your cheek. "You know how your mommy got that way? Someone's prick juiced her snatch, that's how." He takes your hand inside his own, forcing your fingers apart and down, tight in the space between both your bodies. As he closes your hand around his cock, his eyes tighten their lock on you, daring you to look down. You can feel him hardening in your grip. Don't you dare look down.

"Bet it wasn't even your drunken daddy who done it. Bet it was that retard with the paper route. Bet it was some nigger hobo who spiked her pussy good. Maybe the two of them together, retard and nigger, gang-banging your old lady like the sloppy cunt she is. Better prepare yourself, Andy-Pansy. Nine months' incubation and out pops a jigaboo retard, black as burnt toast!"

He punches you hard in the stomach then pulls away laughing, penis bobbing with each chortle, mocking you. *Take it back,* you want to yell, but all breath has left you; you slide down the cold tile wall, the words left to curdle inside your gut.

And then Ricky lurches close again. "Poor Andy-pansy. Did I hurt your feelings? Maybe you need a pacifier. Take my prick up your little cocksucker lips, why don't you? I'll juice your throat, you fucking queer." He tries to pin you against the wall.

But somehow you gather enough strength to push back, even though Ricky is stronger and your limbs still feel underwater. You push hard. Ricky jerks to the side, a bullfighter's deft pivot that causes your momentum to send you crashing to the floor. "Give this to Mommy," Ricky says, kicking your stomach. He turns to leave, his still-hard prick jutting slightly ahead of him like a pink-tipped divining rod.

You crawl into a corner, curl up—crumble inside. Slowly breath returns to your body. The pain in your belly subsides to a dull ache, loose and liquid, moving through you like slow poison. Why does Ricky Pierce hate you? Why does this telltale difference circulate beneath your skin like blood? For a long time you sit there huddled tight, hoping the steam will sweat out the answer, hoping the water will wash it away.

* * *

Later, alone in the changing room, you find your locker door ajar, your shoes and shirt missing. At least your shorts and underpants are there, so you slip them on then wring the water from your wet trunks and wrap them in your beach towel. Searching, you discover one flip-flop in the wastebasket, the other in a puddle of water surrounding a clogged floor drain. You put them on, then hunt the room for the

T-shirt Daddy bought for you as a back-to-school gift last year—an old favorite now. Where is it? Everyone has cleared out, and there is no one to ask for help. Only after opening and closing all the locker doors do you give up hope. Ricky must have taken it, coveting the Wonder Woman decal on the front, the way Lynda Carter glistened in her star-spangled suit. You never should have worn it here. Momma will yell at your carelessness, but she should have bought you a lock like you asked. Your feet squish against the wet floor as you head for the bathroom to make a pit stop.

And there you find your Wonder Woman shirt, sopping in the urinal. You tell yourself maybe you didn't like it so much after all. It wasn't your favorite. It wasn't. The smell of human waste is heavy in the room, enough to make you gag. You glance back to the locker room, afraid Ricky Pierce might be lurking behind you, ready with his hyena laugh. But the room is empty. You step to the other urinal and take aim at a small gray toilet freshener, dwindled to the size of a cough drop. It's Ricky Pierce's eye and you're pissing on it like he pissed on your shirt. The smell of urine is thick, and you hold your breath as you go. When you leave the bathroom, Wonder Woman stays behind.

Upstairs, Momma still hasn't arrived, though you're the last kid left. You check behind the snack machines to make sure Ricky isn't hiding out. But only Artie remains in the deserted foyer, and he's behind the paneled partition of the check-in booth, filling out paperwork. Used to be Daddy picked you up, but no longer. You miss your time with him, alone in the truck. Daddy barely says anything, but you like that. If he noticed at all that your shirt was gone, he'd simply say time to get a new one. He'd rev the motor and you'd feel the thrum of the engine as the truck pulled into traffic. You could close your eyes, rest your head on the window, feel the air rush through your hair. You could be going anywhere with Daddy, him so quiet you could get a word in edgewise, not like chatterbox Momma. Maybe you'd tell him how Ricky Pierce looks ugly behind his big buckteeth, Daddy knowing it's not true but there's a need to make something up, some imperfection Ricky has beyond hating you. Maybe the two of you wouldn't say anything at all, you'd just sink back into the seat and let the hum of the engine soak into your body, eyes closed as you wait for Daddy to reach over and muss your hair in a way you'll never grow tired of.

But after fifteen more minutes, Momma finally walks into the Y, wrapped in her orange maternity muumuu, red strands coming loose from her swept-back hair, and suddenly you're embarrassed by Momma's prize-pumpkin stomach, like you're the one who did this to her. It doesn't matter that you have felt the baby kick inside her when she's let her guard down, stretched out snoring on the sofa in the living room, your hand gliding soft over her belly. *A bun in the oven,* you've heard Daddy joke, and it makes you picture illustrations from old Golden Books, a witch baking Hansel. Seeing Momma waddle in now, belly as round as a potbelly stove, your thoughts shame you. You worry that what Ricky Pierce said might come true. The doctor has told Momma not to smoke, but still she sneaks Lucky Strikes or Salems when Daddy's not around. You wish you had a pair of X-ray glasses, the kind advertised in comic books. You want to know if Momma's baby's brain has been burned to ash and cinder, if its lungs have been charred even before it's drawn breath. Ricky's shrill voice haunts you. *Nine months' incubation and out pops . . .*

"Ready?" Momma asks, impatience in her voice. You pull your eyes from her stomach to her face, flushed from climbing the stairs outside. With the back of her meaty hand, Momma wipes oily sweat from her brow. "Then gather your crap up," Momma says, "'cause I got errands to run. Your sister's at Grandma's. You can stay there." You figure you're almost off the hook—then Momma's forehead wrinkles. "Where's your shirt?"

"Lost." The small sound an air bubble.

"What do you mean, lost?" Momma's voice loud, rising so high Artie looks up from the window of the check-in office.

In your heart, *Please, Momma, just let this be.* "Someone stole it."

"You probably forgot where you put it, the way you are." Momma sighs like she's sucking in all the air in the room. "You'd lose your balls if you didn't have a sack to carry 'em in. I better go look myself."

Momma crosses to the office and raps her knuckles on the window. Someone's lit a match beneath your heart. Fire burns. Blood boils. You hope your face doesn't give you away as you watch Artie put down his clipboard, then listen patiently to Momma, who explains why it's time for a scavenger hunt. Next to her, Artie looks younger— the college student he is. Not quite his own man. He glances over to you with a look of pity that cuts you to the bone. Forcing a smile, he opens the door and leads Momma downstairs. In silence, you follow.

Back in the changing room, while Momma searches, you sit on a bench and wring tight the toweled swim trunks in your hands. The smell of chlorine lingers in the air. Momma flips open locker doors, glancing inside them one by one. Artie leans against the tiled wall, swinging his whistle in the air and looking bored. Suddenly Momma turns to you and swats your arm. "Help me," she says. You stand up and start opening doors, surprised to see even Artie joining in.

The three of you search row after row of lockers, all empty. Momma's lips pinch tight as she closes the last door. You're about to breathe a sigh of relief, but then her eyes light on the bathroom alcove. She starts to head in.

Your lungs tighten inside your chest. More than anything, you don't want Momma and Artie to see your shame, how much Ricky Pierce hates you. You pray a kindhearted janitor already fished out your shirt and threw it away, but you know you're not that lucky. Momma steps through the archway.

The pressure in the room coils around you like a snake, squeezing the air from your lungs. Momma's sharp *a-ha!* rises from the bathroom, and the hold on you tightens, so sharp you think you could black out at any second. You want Artie to throw his superhero arms around your body and rescue you. But you're too weak to move, too weak to ask for help. You watch in silence as Momma reaches back into the locker room and grabs from a bench a plastic bag some kid forgot to carry his swimsuit home in. She disappears back into the alcove only to walk out seconds later, her hand protected inside the bag as she waves the sopping T-shirt high in the air.

"What's this?" she asks, a schoolteacher tone in her voice.

You look at Artie, who stares at the shirt, trying hard not to laugh.

"Who did this?" Momma wants to know.

There is not enough air in your lungs to answer.

She steps forward till her big stomach nearly knocks you over. Artie is laughing for real now and you hate him. He knows who did this, he has to. Why won't he stick up for you?

"You better tell me," Momma says.

Artie's stare burns into your body; his laughter singes your ears.

Momma shoots him a dirty look before turning back to you. "Okay, mister, if that's the way you want it." She reverses the plastic bag over her hand so that the urine-soaked shirt is tucked neatly inside. She chucks the bag hard into your gut like a football. "You can wash it yourself."

Artie flattens himself against the wall as Momma marches past him and heads upstairs. You turn to follow her. Artie touches your shoulder as you pass and says, "Stay cool, buddy." But his words carry no comfort; hurt burns like a forest fire inside you, blazing a steady path. With great effort you force in a lungful of air and tear past Artie, up the steps till Momma's lumbering form blocks your way.

* * *

Momma smokes a Salem on the drive to Grandma Rose's house, even though her doctor has strictly forbidden it. You worry the smoke will scorch her baby's lungs, turn it into a monstrous mutation. But you are also strangely grateful for the silence Momma's bad habit brings. The bag with the Wonder Woman shirt rests in your lap, a smelly lump. You imagine Ricky's germs leaking through, tainting you forever.

Momma turns onto Kerens Avenue, pulls to the curb in front of Grandma's gray house, her Dodge Rambler jerking to a halt. You don't move; you're numb inside, a missing body hidden underwater. Momma grumbles as she reaches over you to unlatch your door, her swollen stomach pressing against your side as she tells you to scoot. You squeeze out the half-open door and stand dumbly on the grassy bank of the sidewalk, swim trunks in hand, staring at Momma through the passenger window. She places another cigarette between her lips, eyes scrunching up as she raises a lit match and cups her palm around the flame. Two drags before her new Salem catches. She breathes in deep, tosses the match away. Catching you staring, Momma gives you a hard look. "I've only had two today," she tells you, but her eyes shrink and you know it's a lie. Still Momma won't give up. "And I've only smoked those because you frustrate me so much." She reaches for the bag you left lying in the front seat. You hurry to go.

"Hold on there, Superman," Momma calls. You turn to see her lifting the plastic bag, leaning toward you. "You forgot Wonder Woman here." She lobs the bag at you. It smacks you hard off guard in the chest, and your arms fumble to catch it. A few drops of urine spatter your skin, the toxic liquid burning you like acid. "See if your grandma will let you wash your shirt here," Momma calls, and without a second look she is speeding off to the store.

You wipe your wet chest with your rolled-up beach towel, but the beads of urine only seem to swirl into a larger area of contamination. Your whole chest burns with humiliation. You're a little boy Cain, marked and cursed to walk the earth.

You don't feel like going in and telling Grandma you're here, being forced to explain to her what's in the bag. So you head around back to where you can hear your sister Allison playing. Alongside the house bloom tiger lilies, yellow and orange, the kind that grow around backwoods outhouses—shithouse flowers, your Daddy calls them. A light mist blurs the brightness of their colors, the water spraying from a garden hose that hasn't been tightened right to the spigot at the side of the house. You follow the green hose around the house as it coils through flowers and grass like a garden snake.

In the backyard, Allison and her friend Janet Lambetti leap a whirling sprinkler. Allison can't swim yet but still she likes to get wet. Long red hair plasters her skull; her thick hips gleam pale beneath the late afternoon sun, and her flowery green one-piece bathing suit clings to her like a second skin. A hazy rainbow glows inside the spray of water, and the girls dance wildly around the shimmering colors, their shouts and screams ringing in your ears. You pass close by them, the sprinkler scattering diamonds of water over your chest and shoulders. You rub the water into your skin, trying to wash off the burn of contamination.

Allison cups her hands to splash you. You back out of firing range, leaning against Grandma Rose's chestnut tree. Sitting in the shade, you breathe deep the smell of grass and clover, your lungs feeling full at last. Fuzzy dandelions parachute across the chain link fence from a neighbor's overgrown yard, bits of white fluff landing on the pile of towels and dolls and candy that the girls have assembled beneath the tree. You steal one of their candy cigarettes and stick it in your mouth, trying to look tough. Maybe it will soothe you the way it soothes Momma; maybe it will blacken and burn the feelings growing inside you. Overhead, the chestnut tree's arching branches form a canopy that blocks out the sun, the sky, everyone else—almost as good as being underwater or walking alone in the woods near Cheat River. You suck thoughtfully on the sweet cigarette, shaping the hard sugar into a point. You realize you are hungry. You reach for another candy cigarette. If one feels this good, why not try two?

"Hey!" cries Allison. "Them's mine. Why don't you come and play?"

You throw down her cigarette pack and tell her not to let Grandma know she saw you. Allison wants to know why. "Just because," you tell her. She sighs and crosses her heart—nine years old and still such a kid. She can throw you that wounded look all she wants, but you won't let it get to you today.

You leave Grandma's street, following the tracks on which old coal trains used to run, stepping on weeds that now grow between the ties. Past the edge of town, you climb the hill that shortcuts to home. Soon the noisy rush of Seneca falls away completely, replaced by the cicada call of the woods. You take deep breaths as you trudge uphill, letting the mountain air fill your body until you almost forget about the bag still clutched in your left hand, the souvenir it contains. In the distance, you hear the rush of Cheat River winding through a valley in the woods, and you wish had the energy to walk the extra distance to it. But you're tired and hungry from swimming all day. This trail is shortest, dropping down half a mile before your house, on the far edge of old Mr. Beaman's property, across from the dirt road leading to home.

Walking there, you think of Ricky Pierce again. In a million different ways he dies inside your mind: Acid, piranha tank, black widow in his shoe. Gunshot, pipe bomb, machete in his skull. Kryptonite, holy water, a stake through his heart. And once you're sure he's dead completely, your mind's eye can't help but reassemble him again—changing the wiring of his heart until he is not a threat but a friend, a goofball buddy you can slurp a Mountain Dew with, read comics together, let sleep over in your room. But then you remember you don't have your own room anymore. A new baby is coming. All you have is the shrinking space inside of you. More and more, the world tears away what comforts you can muster.

Scrambling down the mountain, you edge out of the woods, then study the ramshackle row of pens that shelter Mr. Beaman's hunting dogs. They're sure to kick up a ruckus as you pass through his yard, sending old man Beaman flying from his house, shotgun raised in the air. You make a run for it anyway, leaping from the brushy hillside and tearing through Beaman's tomato patch, his dogs going wild, howling and tearing at their cages. Halfway across, you notice Beaman's truck gone. You slow down, catch your breath. The yowling of the dogs is a barb in your ears, hot and hurtful as Ricky's taunts, as shrill and splitting as Momma when she bosses you around. You push their images from your head as you breathe in slow and purposeful. Casually you select a couple of plump tomatoes from Beaman's tethered vines, biting into one, letting its summer-sweet tang wet your tongue, its juices spill down your chin. The other tomato you hurl through the air, its soft red sphere exploding against the chicken-wire mesh of the dog pens. You watch the rich juice spray like blood, feeling good inside, knowing old man Beaman will shit his pants when he sees what you've done.

⚘ 13   All About Trent

Thomas L. Long

The bookstore going out of business isn't about me, but I still feel really ashamed and I'm really in touch with some very old grief issues. I'm not going out in public to bars or anything because I'm too devastated to talk about it. I just want to wear black crepe and put a black wreath on my door for a year. I know I'm only twenty-four, but this was going to be my first step in building a queer business empire, and now it has to go out of business, just before I was getting ready to leave and move to Chicago to sort out my next move. Jonathan feels pretty bad about having to close the business, but anyway he wasn't that involved in the day-to-day operation lately. He started it in October 1969 after he moved away from New York and back to the South; he was *over* New York. Ahead of his time. *Over* New York in 1969; what a pioneer! This store was the first queer bookstore in the South. In the beginning Jonathan called it an "alternative bookstore"—doesn't that sound so retro? Love it. Back in those days, it was against the law for perverts to run a business or gather in public. I really admire him.

We had sex the first time we met; he wanted to get into a relationship right away. Too heavy for me; so he settled on making me assistant manager of this store. Business was already declining so it wasn't really more than a part-time job, but just enough to teach me the nuts and bolts of business. I have this really chichi MBA from Duke's Fuqua School of Business—the Fuck You School of Business—but I didn't want to go the New York–Wall Street–Richmond–Atlanta– Charlotte route that my classmates were hungry for. Jonathan really taught me a lot about business and about networking. From one store in 1969 he branched out almost every five years all over the South. He knows everybody, so I've hooked up with some very successful queer men. And they've been so sweet to me during

the store's long parade to the grave. I was just devastated when Jonathan told me he would file for bankruptcy: How can you do this to
me? I told him. It's just like my father's death all over again. I get connected and established and start to feel secure about myself and then
this important male figure in my life just abandons me. You bet I've
got a lot of grief work to go through. What has really hurt me, though,
is that Jonathan made his decision without consulting me and in a
week locked the doors and went to bankruptcy court. What about a
liquidation sale? I asked him. It would give me a chance to bring
some closure to all the business relationships I'd made in the year and
a half that I'd worked for him. We could go out in style, process our
sadness. He just told me, Trent, apply for unemployment and talk to
my lawyer about filing a claim for back pay.

What a rejection; it's a good thing I'd been telling everybody that I
was going to move to Chicago in September. Buddy Lothar, though,
has been very sweet. He's the Virginia's Hams heir and a big-time
presidential campaign contributor. He called me from Ruritania—
he's the U.S. ambassador there—and said, Trent, sugah, I heard about
the bidness going south; get yo'self to the airport today; there's a
ticket there in your name, fly over here, and let Buddy take care a you
for a while. We'll get you set up in something else real quick. You interested in a gay rental car bidness?—I tell you, isn't Buddy just
sweet?

I'm going to take a long time to sort all this out. What a bummer—
just when I'm starting my career, my first professional position ends
with the store going out of business. How's that going to look on my
resume? Thank God for Lars Hendrikson out in Minneapolis; he's the
big medical information technologies guru and entrepreneur. He told
me I had a place to stay with him and Carlos as long as I wanted or
needed one. I think it might be interesting to work for him, but I'd
need to be really clear about boundaries with him and Carlos. We've
sometimes gotten into these weird "scenes"; I'd sort of like to be
Lars's lover or maybe just a fuck buddy, but if I went to work with
him—maybe something like vice president for concept development
which is something that I'd be really good at since I'm a very high
"N" on the Myers-Briggs Type Inventory—I couldn't still do those
scenes, especially if I was living with them. Boundaries; boundaries
are everything. I didn't always have them, so here I am always trying
to be some older man's butt-whore-little-boy-protégé-apprentice-

neophyte-personal-assistant and getting fucked every which way because I don't maintain boundaries. Father issues. Just when I came to acknowledge that I wanted my father to fuck me, he goes and dies. Talk about guilt and disappointment! Men are always doing that to me. And I'm always worried that my love is going to kill some man or he's going to leave me. Can you blame me for always having my resignation letter in my pocket?

That's why I'm so hurt by Jonathan's not letting me run a going-out-of-business sale. I'm not some disposable twinkette; I have feelings; I have needs. But I've discovered all sorts of new strength and endurance. It's like my therapist says—and he always whispers this while twisting his nipple piercing—"Sweetheart, if you can't stand the pain, get out of the dungeon." Ludovic Rothkind—*the* Rothkinds, *ancienne* European banking, money so old it's before there was money—has really helped me put it in perspective: *Ma petite coquine, ce n'est pas de toi.* So French; so fatalist; so true. I can let it go; it's not about me.

ᒪC 14   The Yard Sale

George Singer

Jeff and Victor had caught many yard sales in their ten years together as a couple. In fact, when Victor was offered a teaching position at the Georgia State University School of Law and they decided to leave their beloved LA, their house in the canyon, and all their West Hollywood A-list friends, Jeff and Victor consoled themselves that at least the yard sales might be better in Atlanta.

And so on this, their first free Saturday since arriving in Georgia, Jeff drove the Land Rover while Victor rode shotgun in the passenger seat. Victor had recently dyed his chestnut-brown hair a shocking yellow that he told Jeff would make him seem cooler to his students. Today, Victor was unshaven and the brown stubble against the yellow was a bit unsettling to Jeff, but when Victor smiled at him sweetly, Jeff just smiled back.

It didn't matter if the boys were cruising LA or hightailing it through the backwoods of Georgia, Jeff and Victor went in search only of the things they collected—toys. Early, early GI Joes or Barbie's boyfriend, Ken. Stangl dishes, but only the Windfall pattern. Ouija boards, pre-1960 and made out of real wood. Old Macintosh computers. Sony flip clocks from the 1970s. And almost all literary first editions.

Jeff's famous blue eyes peered out warily from inside the Land Rover. He hadn't known what to expect of Atlanta. At first, before he'd left the well-heeled Buckhead, Jeff had thought Atlanta wasn't really all that different from LA. The same suburban sprawl. The same displaced small-towners looking for a great big urban experience, that made Atlanta, like LA, filled with out-of-towners.

But then Victor had found this yard sale in the classifieds of *The Atlanta Journal-Constitution* and they left the homogeny of Buckhead and drove into a world of small, boxy, 1960s-built suburbs, which Victor referred to, somewhat ominously, as *Dukes of Hazzard*-Land. The vegetation got thick and so did the air. It was here, for the first time since leaving California, that Jeff saw, tucked away here and there on the bumper of a Dodge Ram, dangling provocatively from the occasional porch, the unmistakable bloody red and black of the Confederate flag. "Not quite like LA anymore," Jeff thought, his hands sweaty on the leather steering wheel of the Land Rover, which suddenly felt to Jeff *too conspicuous* as they pulled up in front of a heavily shaded, small, gray ranch where a magic-markered sign said simply, "Yard Sale."

The lawn was patchy brown and dry, strewn with cardboard boxes that could be filled with great *finds,* but were, most likely, just junk.

The Yard Sale Lady was a redhead in her late forties, wearing a pink sundress. She squinted out from under her enormous straw sun hat while she took in Jeff and Victor. In spite of her enormous straw hat, her exposed freckled skin still looked dusted by blush where the sun had reddened it.

"This was my father's place," the Yard Sale Lady told Jeff and Victor. "He just passed. He was one of those fathers whose kids just hated him. *Hated him.* Neither me or my five sisters had talked to him for at least the past ten years." The Yard Sale Lady squinted and turned ugly before she said, "He was one mean son of a bitch.

"I was the last one to get here this week. After my five sisters picked over the place and took everything that was worth anything— this is all that's left for me." She gestured to her father's things, the ones no one had wanted, that were now spread out all over the lawn. "Barely good enough for an old-fashioned yard sale."

Victor looked discreetly at Jeff and Jeff understood that behind his sunglasses, Victor was crossing his eyes in a gesture that said, "The Yard Sale Lady is *insane.*"

She went on. "I'm just trying to get enough out of all this not to have to put my plane ticket back to Virginia on my Visa." Then she smiled eagerly, not at all self-conscious of her badly neglected teeth.

Victor smiled back at her politely, as if she had said nothing at all, then walked off to begin his examination of the boxes.

Jeff lingered and listened to her thoughtfully. It had crossed his mind to be very polite. Across the street, in the window of the neighbor's tiny ranch, a Confederate flag hung in the window instead of a curtain. Jeff didn't want to piss off the Yard Sale Lady; he was afraid she might start screaming, "Faggots!"

Instead, Jeff put on his concerned look, so well practiced on his patients back in LA. It worked on the Yard Sale Lady. She liked Dr. Jeff's blue eyes and she *loved* having someone listen to her lay out the whole bitter tragedy between her and the five sisters. Jeff told her he had worked at Cedars-Sinai and the Yard Sale Lady knew all about the hospital. Cedars-Sinai was where the stars went in and out of through the pages of *The National Enquirer, The Star,* and *The Globe.* She was very impressed with Dr. Jeff.

Victor had poked into a moldy cardboard box and recognized an important book to any collector of American literature. It was missing its book jacket and the green binding was too faded to read, but Victor knew immediately it was an early edition of *The Great Gatsby.*

Victor flipped it open to the copyright page for the famous Scribner's A that would have marked it a true coveted first. There was no A.

He closed the book and almost put it back, before Victor remembered Scribner's didn't start using their famous A until 1927! *The Great Gatsby* came out before 1927, didn't it? Victor opened the book again. He saw 1925 on the copyright page and in roman numerals on the title page. It was an authentic first edition of *The Great Gatsby.* Inside, Victor swooned.

"All the books are just two dollars," the Yard Sale Lady called. Victor barely heard her. His head went off like a clanging, bell-ringing, slot machine jackpot. "FIND! FIND! FIND!"

Victor paid the Yard Sale Lady. Worried that his excitement might make her suspicious, Victor chatted inanely by way of distraction.

"I grew up outside Atlanta," Victor told her, sounding just a little more Southern, "but I never lived here in Atlanta proper. I moved away to LA. We just moved back. Well, I just moved back and dragged Jeff with me. I got a job teaching at the Georgia State University College of Law. I'm a law professor there."

Victor smiled at the Yard Sale Lady. He noticed she didn't seem at all impressed. Perhaps it was his too-yellow hair.

She just smiled and said, "I just knew you two guys would buy something." She took the book from Victor and started to wrap it in a week-old piece of *The Atlanta Journal-Constitution.*

"Oh, that's OK," Victor said, grabbing the book back and pressing it under his arm to protect it from her.

Jeff was examining a Bakelite-handled eggbeater when Victor asked him coyly, "Find anything?"

Jeff smiled and held up a brown plastic mug with a tiny version of that great Farrah Fawcett erect-nippled 1970s poster laminated onto it. Farrah smiled BIG at Victor.

"Nice. But it's not this, child," Victor said, smug and Southern as he held out the book for Jeff to examine.

Jeff's blue eyes widened as he took the book from Victor for a closer inspection. He flipped to the copyright page just as Victor had done. "Sorry, Victor," Jeff said with his own Boston smirk back at Victor.

But Victor's eyes gleamed at Jeff, fresh with excitement, so ready to pounce and prove Jeff wrong. *Victor seems very sure of himself,* Jeff thought, and then he remembered.

"Oh right. Nineteen twenty-seven," he said, a smile creeping across his face as he nodded in approval at Victor. "Very nice. Very nice."

Victor remembered how much he loved Jeff. Not just because he gave up his job at Cedars-Sinai to follow Victor to Atlanta, but because he also knew that Scribner's didn't start using their famous As until 1927.

"And does she know?" asked Jeff, looking over at the Yard Sale Lady for a second.

Victor winced slightly.

"Victor. Didn't you hear what she said about her five sisters?" Jeff asked.

Victor didn't say anything.

"And the ticket to Virginia? Come on now, Victor. We can't do that to her." Jeff was using his *patient* voice. He asked Victor, "How much did you pay for it?"

"Two dollars," Victor told him.

"What's it worth?" Jeff asked.

"With no dust jacket? Four hundred," Victor answered, unable to resist showing off to Jeff that he knew exactly how much it was worth.

"Give her three hundred," Jeff commanded.

Victor's whole face scrunched up with the absurdity of it. "Are you crazy? No." The discussion, as far as Victor was concerned, was over.

But then Jeff said evenly, "I left Cedars-Sinai for you."

Victor's left eyebrow arched. He knew it would eventually come to this. He just didn't think it would happen so soon. Over something so small.

Jeff waited, but Victor said nothing. Jeff walked off toward the Yard Sale Lady, waving the book above his head and calling, "We were just looking at this book. You can't sell this book for two dollars. This book is valuable."

"What? Really?" asked the Yard Sale Lady. "Like how much?"

Jeff looked back toward Victor for help. Victor noticed how much older Jeff looked with all the gray that had recently appeared in his goatee.

Victor looked at the grass. "I could give you two hundred for it," he whispered.

The Yard Sale Lady said, "Shit! I could take it!" Then she beamed. "I'm just glad you didn't get in your car and drive off a hundred miles and then find out it was worth two *hundred* dollars." She laughed, and it became a hacking, phlegm-filled cough.

"And I want to get this Farrah mug," Jeff said, holding up the mug.

"Oh, you can have the Farrah mug. Shit! Take the Farrah mug." The Yard Sale Lady laughed again and this time it didn't turn into a cough.

Victor took out his wallet and the Yard Sale Lady thrust out her open palm. Victor cursed that he had only twenties as he piled the crisp bills, fresh from the ATM machine, twenty by twenty, into her waiting palm. Toward the end, the Yard Sale Lady, overcome with excitement, began counting out loud. "One hundred sixty! One hundred eighty!!!! TWO hundred!!!! Shit! Is this my day or what?" Victor put his wallet into his pants. He was sad. This transaction had robbed him of the delicious pleasure he would have received in recounting the tale of his *Great Gatsby* find at the all-boy cocktail parties back in Buckhead.

The Yard Sale Lady reached out and put her hand on Victor's arm. She said to him, deeply moved, "Thank you so much for being good people, Mister. God bless you."

Victor was astonished to find utter and complete sincerity in her face. He quickly looked away and walked to the car. He had done more than enough to appease Jeff already today. Thanking her would have simply been taking things too far.

Jeff wasn't bothered. Victor's cynicism was part of his charm. From the passenger side of the Land Rover, Victor could see Jeff thanking the Yard Sale Lady, even shaking her hand.

She waved heartily as they pulled away, as if they were friends.

Victor examined the book in silence.

"You always wanted a copy of *The Great Gatsby*," Jeff said, finally.

Victor nodded, still holding the book.

Jeff persisted, "Two hundred dollars was still a good deal."

Victor, whose years as a lawyer had taught him how to take any thought to virtually any conclusion, decided that he was, after all, a Good Samaritan. Hadn't the Yard Sale Lady said he was *good people?*

"We don't belong in LA anyway," Victor blurted out. Jeff's eyes twinkled with the hint of a smile. The yards of Atlanta certainly had yielded greater finds than the manicured lawns of LA.

I left Cedars-Sinai for you.

Jeff replayed the moment over and over in his mind with relish. It was the first time in their ten years together that the doctor had rendered the lawyer utterly speechless.

I left Cedars-Sinai for you.

Jeff wondered if it would have as potent an effect on Victor the next time. He smiled and looked forward to finding out.

ᔕℂ 15　　　　　　　　　　Escape Artist

John Michael Trumbo

Straw. Hay.

Fresh cut, crisp hay.

Or, hay that has lain there for decades, refusing to rot. There on the barn floor.

Chewed, worm-holed planks.

Flakes of decades-old red paint peeling off the wood. I pick at it, up close. Run my boot across the surface, stripping it nearly clean.

I like to hide here—in the barn. Up the wooden ladder, in the loft.

Or, in the grain cellar.

There are plenty of places to hide in here. Not from anything—or anyone—in particular; just to hide—inside my own world—safe.

I'm Ford. My dad named me after his pickup, which he loves. Only I don't like it that much, riding in it. It's all rusted and stuff. I can even see the ground under my feet from the hole in the passenger side's floor.

Like I said, it's all beat-up and I hate riding in it. I'm afraid my friends will see me in it and laugh 'cause it's not very cool. "Farm boy," they'll say. But I'm not. Dad may have been born on a farm but not me.

Once, he had to take me to school in it 'cause I missed my bus, and I guess the hood wasn't latched in front all the way or something 'cause when we got out onto Route 7 the thing flew up in our faces! At first, I was scared—we couldn't see anything. Then I realized we were all right and got embarrassed when Dad pulled over to fix it. I didn't want anyone to see me in it, or climbing out of it at school, especially with the hood all messed up. I just hung my head and slumped down real low. I guess that's kind of dumb, but I did.

Anyway, I'm not a farm boy, but most of my relatives are, like my cousin Carl. My parents built our house in the woods which is almost bad enough. We live on a dirt road that never gets plowed during the winter, so if it snows a lot you're stuck. And in the summer you have to keep the windows in the car rolled up 'cause the dust is so thick. That also means I have to wash the car a lot.

We're a lot closer to big cities than my relatives. I think my mom and dad didn't want their kids—me and my brother—to grow up on a farm like they did. I think they wanted better than that.

I have one friend on my road, Dale, who I hang out with. Otherwise, I usually just hang out by myself, playing or makin' up stuff. My mom told me I should make more friends but I told her that Dale is my friend. "I know," she said, "but wouldn't you like to have more friends other than Dale?"

"No. Why?" I asked.

"Well, because the more friends you have the more fun you can have. Don't you know some other boys at school who you like?"

"Sure. But I see them at school all day long. I'd rather just hang out with Dale, or watch TV or something."

"I just think you'd enjoy yourself more having other little friends around."

"But I do enjoy myself already." I had no idea what she was getting at. She finally gave up and returned to her work. She was ironing and getting ready for dinner.

My mom's pretty. She has wavy, brown hair and brown eyes like mine. All my relatives—especially the ones on my dad's side of the family—constantly remind me that I look more like her than my dad. My Uncle John makes fun of me and says: "You look like a *Miller*," like that's bad. But he's big and fat anyway, so who cares?

I usually watch cartoons with Dale. My brother doesn't like cartoons. He's four years older than me and he likes to act like he's a lot older. Dale and I lay on the floor in the den to watch TV and sometimes my brother comes in to bug us. "What's on?" he asks.

"Shhh. *Batman*," I answer as the Riddler is about to drop Batman and Robin into a vat of acid, as always.

"That's so juvenile. Don't you have anything better to do?"

"No, except get away from your fat face. Now move so I can see!"

"Just as I thought. Well, I have better things to do with *my* time. 'Bye, loser."

"'Bye, fathead."

I like Dale because he's quiet and he likes the same things that I do. He knows not to talk during *Batman*. I also like spending the night at Dale's house. His mom and dad aren't as strict as mine. They let us stay up late, sleep outside in a tent, and eat dinner in front of the TV. Plus, Dale doesn't have any stupid brothers or sisters to bother us.

Dale has a really short buzz cut like his dad. I think he was in the Army or something (Dale's dad). What's kind of cool is that he walks around their house in his boxer shorts all the time. I wish I could just hang out in boxers like Dale and his dad but my mom buys stupid old Sears briefs. And she'd freak if any of us walked around the house in them.

I also wish I had a buzz cut like them. It looks more comfortable, but Mom says I'm just trying to look like Dale and she won't allow it, which is dumb because lots of guys have buzz cuts and I'm not trying to be like them. Carl, my cousin, has one which I like, but he's a real jerk.

Carl usually never gives me the time of day. He's three years older than me and a freshman in high school. We see each other a few times a year, usually at family reunions or holidays. Last summer, he and I were behind our granddaddy's barn and he asked me if I wanted to smoke a cigarette with him. "You don't have to inhale if you don't think you can handle it," he said when he handed me the lit cigarette.

"It's OK," I said back.

"I just don't want you gettin' sick and pukin' everywhere before we go back to the house."

"Don't worry about it; I've done this before."

Then he goes, "Yeah, right, asshole. You have not."

"Have too," I said. "A couple a times at camp last summer. This kid had some."

"Right! I'm sure you smoked cigs at freakin' church camp! When? Between crafts and 'Kumbaya'? No way; you lie."

"Look, I don't care if you believe me or not, man. I did and that's all that matters. I'm just glad we got out of that family picnic shit." I wanted to change the subject and quick; you never won an argument with Carl. "Man, if Aunt Gladys tries to wrap those big, fat arms around me one more time, I'm really gonna puke."

"Just give me my smoke," he said, sticking his fingers out for it. "If my dad found out I lifted it, he'd kick my ass."

Then, nobody said anything for awhile. The silence kind of floated around us like the cigarette smoke in the air, and it got awkward. It always got weird around Carl. I figured that being related ought to have counted for something—you know, to have stuff in common—but it didn't.

Anyway, we were sitting with our backs up against the barn and I could smell fresh-cut grass from my granddaddy's yard. It smelled dry and kind of musty, like it had been shut up somewhere all summer. You could also smell the chickens, the fresh manure on the garden . . . a bunch of farm smells.

"Race you through the corn," he said all of the sudden.

I thought for a moment. Although I liked just being quiet out here behind the barn, I knew Carl would give me shit if I didn't take him up on his dare. "OK, asshole," I said, trying to sound tough. "You're on. Go!"

We both scrambled to our feet and took off toward the cornfield. The rows began just north of the barn. I took one and Carl took the next. Dry, sharp corn leaves slapped and scratched my arms as I started off, but I didn't let it bother me. I knew it would itch like crap later, though.

"Don't get lost. I'm not comin' to look for ya," Carl shouted.

"Screw you. Don't *you* get lost, wimp," I yelled back.

Sometimes I wondered what would happen if I did get lost in the corn. My brother and I played in the corn a lot when we visited granddaddy's. I loved to get lost in the stalks, then have to find my way out.

I could hear Carl close by but I couldn't see him. Granddaddy's corn was pretty thick and way too tall to see over. In a minute, though, we both reached a clearing in the field where no corn grew; in the middle was a large rock.

"Beat ya," Carl said, almost out of breath.

"Did not," I said.

"Bullshit. Did too."

Carl and I both collapsed on the rock. Nothing but small patches of grass grew in the clearing.

"We could hide out here and not go back to the picnic," Carl said.

"I know; that would be cool. We could go get stuff from the barn and build a little fort here, you know? And not tell anyone?"

Carl was silent.

"It could be just for us, no girls."

"Ever seen a girl?" Carl asked all of the sudden.

"What do you mean, 'have I ever seen a girl?' Of course I have."

"No, stupid. I mean, have you ever seen a girl? Like, with her clothes off?"

I had to think for a minute. "Well, I guess. I walked in on my mom once when she was putting her dress on."

"That doesn't count, stupid. I said a girl!"

"Well then, I guess, no."

"That's what I thought."

"Well, Mr. Smarty-Pants, have you ever seen a girl?" I asked. I wanted to turn his attention away from me. This was uncomfortable again.

"Sure, all the time."

"Where?"

"Places. At school. Sneakin' in the girls' locker room and stuff."

"Sure, I bet."

"Hey, man, it's true. I've seen the stuff all right."

"What stuff?"

"Don't you know anything? Girl stuff."

"Oh, yeah." I wasn't sure what he meant by "girl stuff" and I don't think I really wanted to know, but still, I was curious. "So, like, what stuff?" I finally asked.

"Man, I knew it! You're such a pansy-ass. I knew you didn't know anything."

"Do so."

"Do not! Or you'd know what 'girl stuff' is."

Man, I felt stupid around Carl. I hated when he made fun of me, but he was right. I had no idea what he meant or even what the big deal was. It felt like he was part of some club of guys who all knew stuff about the world but I didn't. I also thought that by hanging out with Carl some of what he knew might rub off on me, but right now I felt like a jerk and just wanted to be away from him.

"You'd probably like some of this, then," Carl said suddenly, grabbing his crotch.

"What?" Now what was he up to?

"You know what I mean." Carl kept grabbing his pants.

"What?" I had to ask again.

"Come on, man. If you don't even know what 'girl stuff' is, then you must want some dick."

"I don't know. I don't think so."

"Yeah, I bet you do. That's why you don't know shit about girls, or care! Even when I was your age I was goin' after chicks. You just want what's in my pants." I just stared at him as he groped himself through his jeans. "I gotta nice one . . . you can make it feel real good for me."

I couldn't respond.

"Come 'ere," he said. "It's OK."

Still nothing.

"Come 'ere, I said!" He reached out for me.

I backed away, slipping off the rock. "No, man, I don't want to. Lay off me."

"Come on, man. You know you want to deep inside. I won't tell anyone."

I wasn't sure what was happening. It kind of felt like when you get in trouble with your dad and you just freeze, waiting for the punishment. You know it's coming; you just don't know exactly when and how much. I had that same funny feeling in my stomach except that I hadn't done anything to Carl.

He moved toward me again. What did he want me to do to him anyway? When I looked up at Carl's face again, he was kind of smiling, like out of half of his mouth. "Come on, man." I still felt like I was doing something wrong, like I was getting into trouble though I wasn't sure why, and I didn't want any part of this.

"I said no. I'm gettin' out of here."

"You are a pansy-ass, you know," Carl yelled as I left our clearing. "You better not even think of telling anyone about this or I'll smash your head in so fast!"

I didn't intend to tell anyone what had happened. I took off into the cornfield, deeper into it instead of going back toward granddaddy's house. The sun was already starting to set and the shadows inside the stalks grew darker but I didn't care. I kept running until I came to another clearing and I dropped onto the hard dirt.

I couldn't hear or see Carl. He was probably headed back toward the house and would tell everyone that I had gotten lost in the corn. I knew my dad would probably start yelling for me, but I wasn't lost, not yet. I laid on the ground and watched a bird sail overhead. I wondered what the bird saw when it looked down; did it even see me? I was probably just a little black dot; a little black dot trying to find its way out of the big puzzle-maze of corn.

But now I felt safer, hiding in the corn. I liked listening to the leaves rustle when the wind blew. It looked like the stalks had their arms crossed, protecting me.

I wasn't angry about what Carl had done—not really—although I probably should have been. If someone had tried to do that to Carl, he probably would have beat the shit out of the guy. But I didn't feel like beating the shit out of Carl; I just felt . . . empty about the whole thing. Maybe Carl was right. Maybe I did want what was in his pants.

At school, I would just kind of listen in the background when other guys started talking about sex stuff. I didn't know what the big deal was. Who would want to put their dick inside another person? I was more interested in watching *Batman, Superman,* and *Speed Racer* cartoons with Dale.

No, I wasn't going to say anything to Carl or anyone else about what he had done. I just tried to forget about it. It was no big deal anyway.

Eventually, I got up and started walking back through the rows of corn the way I had come. It would have been cool if I could have flown up and out of the cornfield like that bird flying around above me. I could have flown over granddaddy's house and seen my family below, and Carl just standing there all stupid, then just kept on flying.

Ephebus

Gerard Wozek

*A form of Sufism involves prolonged contemplation of a beauti-
ful young man—an ephebus—in order to ascend to mystical
states.*

Ferris seems to be on an Ecstasy crash. His head is splayed over the
steering wheel of his 1981 Mercury as a plastic effigy of Shiva dan-
gles from the rearview mirror. He holds up a silver Buddha on a chain
in the light of the open glove compartment and places it on his breastbone. His car engine is still rumbling and the hum seems to move into
mine as he fumbles over outdated highway maps and sweat-damp tis-
sues for a box of gold-wrapped condoms. His emerald nose stud re-
flects a flinty moon.

Ferris leaves his clothes in a heap on the floor of his car. His oak-
brown skin seems glazed with flecks of ice as he steps onto the gravelly parking lot. "I'll meet you at my teepee." He looks at me, grinning, with a cottonwood twig falling between the gap in his teeth.

From the front seat of my station wagon, I watch his lithe naked
body become a hazy streak as he merges with the dew-laced evergreen trees and bushes. As he edges his way into the thicket, I imagine Ferris grazing the tips of blackberry bushes, their purple crowns
breaking onto his smooth shoulder blades. I think of his cloudy breath
in the damp night air mingling with the sound of crickets and owl
screeches. I see him wiping the gritty sweat from his forehead, his
cock jostling to the rhythms of his half-trot through the woods, his
nipples erect in the Southern twilight air.

I shift backward in the front seat of my car and listen to the sound
of men drumming in the field that lies just beyond the wooded camp-
ground. I hear their banshee wailing and sudden dog yelps. I count
their gravelly shouts. I detect their rattles and tom-toms from across
the Radical Faerie sanctuary, a place where men come to gather,

camp on the land, and celebrate the turning seasons. There is merry-making in the bowl of this Tennessee valley and *soul churning,* as the faeries like to call it, going on everywhere in this secluded park. Even from this distant vantage point, I can smell their musky sweat, feel their pulses jangle, and merge with their crooked yodels and rising heat.

I move my hand across my crotch and feel a tingle that moves up into my belly. I glance across my dashboard, at crushed Styrofoam cups, a used-up evergreen air freshener and assorted chewing gum wrappers. On the seat next to me is an old *Gay Times* with a muscle-bound stud in a leather harness on the cover and I look right through his stare. I'm almost indifferent to this squat pose, the model's oiled biceps, his overtly masculine jut. For a moment I think back to my porno collection at home, my ten thousand downloads of uncut cocks from off the Internet, my towering stacks of *Torsos* and *Manhunters* that are meaningless for me now. I hold my breath for one instant on the edge of the woods, then decide to make my way toward the teepee.

Bonfires are burning all around the camp area tonight. I inhale a sooty fog as I open my car door and follow the circuitous footpath into the brush. The ringed moon sifts through branches of trees, illuminating cigarette butts and used condoms left on the muddy trail. I step over prints left by animals and I try to forget the city where I live, the concrete and Plexiglas, the rush of the subway, the stifling pace. I want to forget my job as an insurance broker. I want to forget the incessant ring of my cell phone. I want to lose my paranoia of looking over my shoulder when it is dark on my street. I want to fall into a natural state of being. I want to wake up to feel my own heart racing with anticipation for the day. I want to slip into a state of tranquil grace.

I glance at the map handed to me at the sign-up post and note the references to unmarked graves of Civil War soldiers buried under my feet. I become more conscious of my own pulse thinking of handsome young Southern boys, barely men, who have turned into mulch and gravel underneath these woods.

I approach a clearing and notice a shudder behind a thin cluster of pine limbs where Ferris fumbles with a wool army blanket spread out at the entrance of his roomy tent. He is prone on his hands and knees, tucking the edge of this dark cloth into a rock cluster. The slick sweat on his freckled back throws back a soft glow. I rub my palms over the rough folds of birchbark and wait for my breathing to calm.

He is wearing a long skirt constructed from willows and supple grapevines and a mishmash tiara fashioned from scrap tin and painted acorns. He prances about the open bluff that overlooks the Tennessee pasture. He sings a few lines of "Don't Cry for Me, Argentina" in a deliberately exaggerated Southern drawl, while throwing crumpled daisy petals into the nocturnal spring air.

"You can call me Ferris or you can call me Dewballs," his voice seems to shudder then bounce off of the gutted rock formations of the nearby caverns. "I'm bursting with juice for you."

His mottled hair seems to be animated all on its own, like Medusa's serpents writhing and hissing into the airless pitch. The last flecks of twilight linger inside the recesses of his deep-set eyes. Something about his smile suggests genuine warmth, something that I could never find in the urban rancor of Chicago. He slowly lifts the beaded flap of a stand-alone teepee made from animal skins and old Confederate flags and with a gentle turn of his head he motions me inside.

"Genuflect at the altar first." There is a hint of whimsy in his voice, as though one could almost believe in the fey kind of world he is attempting to bring into being. He lights a kerosene lamp and my head scrapes the needle edges of an inverted antler mobile. On top of a shaved tree stump he has placed several polished river stones, an effigy of a goddess with a lion's head, assorted bronze deities, a feathered kachina doll, a cracked Mexican Mother Mary nightlight, and a tall white taper melting over an empty beer bottle.

We both kneel at the makeshift altar and Ferris lifts a string of amber beads from around his neck and places it next to the smooth, dark rocks. He gently touches my thigh with the furry end of a wheat stalk that sends goosebumps up my spine. "I knew when I saw you at the welcome post, we'd become fast friends," he says rubbing rose oil on his wrists. The tent air is damp and the thick deerskin walls hold in the heady essence of incense and musk.

"I'm still covered with city dust, so you'll have to forgive me but I'm not used to such sincere openness. Do you camp out here often?" My hand grazes over the fur tarp on the floor of the lean-to and I accidentally knock over a tall stack of magazines that have been set next to the fat log.

"I am the essence of camp, my dear," he laughs as he opens a locket swinging from around his neck with a picture of Bette Davis in it. "I never did get over that dress she wore in *Jezebel!*"

As I attempt to straighten the pile of *Gentleman's Quarterlys* and *Fashion Mode* magazines, I notice that the issues are dated from several years back. "Why are you saving these old style magazines?"

Ferris searches out a fading picture from *Uomo, the Italian Male Fashion Magazine.* "Don'tcha recognize the stud on this cover?" The boy in the photograph is handsome, dressed in a tailored blue Armani suit with eyes that hold in sophisticated aloofness. He seems to radiate a glow as though he were a hallowed apostle.

"Debonair." My response seems to float awkwardly in the pagan atmosphere.

"Are you ready for your mystery date?" He hands me an advertisement for a designer's cologne featuring the same striking lad, now standing knee-deep in a swirling body of water. The model's taupe linen pants are soaked, revealing the seductive outline of his crotch.

"It's you." My words almost form a question. I closely scrutinize his unshaven face in the dim lantern light. His blue eyes are unmistakable. The same sexy teenager that had posed in these foreign glamour magazines is dressed in semidrag in this cockeyed tent tonight.

"There was this guy I met in Belgium once," he begins to speak very deliberately, keeping a lit match hovering over the wicks of several small candles. "He'd collect all of my fashion spreads, then cover his bedroom walls with them. He even sent me a picture of his shrine. The guy claimed he would just float through those images, as though he were levitating or something. He said it made jerking off kind of spiritual."

"What was it like to be someone's fantasy?" I touch the full lips on one of his photographs.

"It did nothing for me." His voice seems to suddenly halt the persistent drumming that pervades the air. "I mean the Navajos have this belief that if you take a picture of someone, you are stealing their spirit. I became this pornographic dream for a herd of strangers I never even knew and I'm telling you, lovey, it never brought anything truly fulfilling back to me."

"And so you've come here."

"I came out here to whirl with the dervishes I s'pose." Ferris closes his eyes and starts to drift into reverie. "There is a circle of men, very

Southern, mostly from the recesses of Georgia and Tennessee, who really make an attempt at cherishing one another's erotic energy. They bond in an attempt to heal what has been damaged or to rekindle natural loving instincts that have been submerged. That's what is meant by men coming together in a faerie circle."

"But what do you mean by *very* Southern?"

"Oh, you probably have this image of icy mint juleps and Paul Newman playing the role of Brick in *Cat on a Hot Tin Roof* or something." Ferris throws his head back and his eyes appear larger.

"Well, I remember the characters in that Tennessee Williams' play had this image of Brick as someone he really wasn't."

"You've got it, love," Ferris looks down at an image of himself hawking designer cologne. "I suppose you could say that I was Brick; well, at least I was when I was younger. My family had these expectations for me. And I played along, always very gracious, always well-mannered with my obligatory 'yes sir' at the end of each sentence. But there was a wilder spirit growing in me. I suppose I took the very best of my *Southerness* and tempered it—well—came to terms with it anyway."

"You mean you fix a mean fried catfish and cornbread, line your black-eyed peas up perfectly on a fork, and wipe your lips with a napkin after every bite."

"Stereotypes aside, my sweet Yankee," Ferris begins to mimic a tipsy Vivian Leigh, "I bake a fierce pecan pie, I always hold open a door for a lady, and, yes, I do wipe up after my voracious bites."

"I have this idea of chivalry being linked to what is uniquely Southern."

"Chivalrous in the sense that I believe in nobility and courage. Southern men have always felt the need to light passionate fires for whatever cause they were obliged to." Ferris points outside past the half-open flap of his teepee. Colonel Braxton Bragg led his brigade over Lookout Mountain in the 'Battle Above the Clouds'."

"Sounds romantic."

"Yes, Southerners have a peculiar way of romanticizing the past, but you know that hundreds of zealous boys were killed during the Civil War. If you meditate on the land here for a period of time you can almost hear the gunshots. I often listen for the ghost stories of young soldiers buried out in those fields, those adolescent desires that were never quite consummated."

"So you believe in ghosts as well?" I inquire with a half-smile.

"How can you not?" There is seriousness in his eyes that I haven't yet seen. "All around us you can feel the spirit of the land. The heroes went to their graves too soon. You ask me what it means to be Southern and I say that it is having a sense of loyalty or faithfulness. The word of a Southern gentleman is linked to a time when all agreements, even implied ones, were binding. This is what our ancestry is made up of and this is what defines the authentic Southern character."

Eight candles blaze and Ferris seems more handsome in this light than even in his expensive soft focus photographs. He carefully lifts a delicate piece of yellowed paper from his altar and begins to read. "Not even losing this battle, not even death will keep us separate."

"What is this?"

"Part of a letter written by the son of my great-great grandmother. He died while fighting in the war between the North and South."

"It's so tragic; so many died." I glance at the intricate, almost calligraphic, handwriting on the paper. "He was writing to his mother?"

"He was writing to another soldier, another young man serving in the war. My family kept this locked away until my sister came across it in an old trunk. She gave it to me." He places the note back and puts a river stone over it. "I know this young soldier kept his word. I know that not even death separates him from his true heart."

Ferris locks his thumbs together and his hands form the image of wings. He listens for something I'm not quite sure of, maybe it is the wind or the sound of singing in the basin, but the stillness is almost unsettling.

"I know that especially in the South it is difficult to be a softer man, but you've somehow managed to dismantle the revered macho image."

"Dismantle is a good word, brick by brick if you will!" Ferris curtsies with his willow skirt.

"Quite a feat considering that everything in our culture calls for us to conform to some image of the masculine male. But somehow you've reclaimed yourself as a being who is more androgynous and . . . " I pause for a moment.

"Humane?"

"Yes, with a gentle, unassuming disposition."

"Why thank you for the compliment, sir." Ferris reaches over and pats my hand. "I guess that's in the demeanor of a Southern gentleman too. Vacation Bible school taught me to never be too proud to know that we're all linked to one another. We're all part of the same fabric, honey lamb, though I'll never get used to that hideous Yankee flag."

Ferris giggles delightfully then places four lit votive candles in a semicircle around the teepee. He tosses dried foxglove and eucalyptus petals around the circumference of the tent and sets several burning incense sticks of jasmine and sandalwood around an outstretched blanket in front of the teepee. The soppy night air seems to carry an electric charge and the resumed drumming outside lends a hypnotic edge to the collage. Ferris, motionless and poised in the axis of the blanket, seems to have momentarily suspended his breathing. He hands me a small bottle of oil and lies down on his stomach. "How about a rub, sexy?"

Kneeling above his sweaty back, I massage clover oil warmed from the heat of my palms over his skin. The heady aroma coils up through my nostrils and I can hear Ferris begin to moan as he falls into the motion of my hands grazing his body. The sinewy ligaments and muscles along his spine and vertebrae begin to ease. I pour out the syrupy unguent over his thighs and legs and work the pungent salve into his buttocks. He lets me undo the supple willow laces that are strewn around his torso and I fall into an almost hypnotic rhythmic motion.

"Let's watch the moon," I whisper. Clasping the furry blanket, he moves toward a clearing near the back of the tent where a fire pit is still aglow with afternoon embers. Ferris lies down on his back and for a long time there is silence. He keeps his hands open and extended then slowly begins to speak.

"And what did you come here for? Are you in conflict with something?"

The words give me an opening. "I feel stifled by the urban rush and the pretense I feel in Chicago. I want to slow down. I want to feel like myself again, connected to whoever that is now."

"Look at me." Ferris speaks in a hush. "I mean, really look at me, and enjoy what you see. When I was younger I was punished for staring at people. It was considered impolite. But I want you to look deeply and don't be ashamed of whatever you're feeling. Let it be a kind of devotion."

I stare lovingly at my newfound friend and feel my body begin to spiral and ascend. My pulse becomes rapid. I don't take his engorged cock into my mouth, but I can taste its oozing crown. I don't encircle his nipples with my tongue, but they rise and become pinpoints for my desire. I don't wedge my hand at his scrotum, but staring down at it, I can sense the sap churning and rising, the tiny muscles clenching. I don't smell the heavy musk scent of his crotch, or lick the beads of perspiration at his underarms and belly. I don't stroke his face, bite his earlobes, kiss his full mouth, or wedge his thick, dark-tipped penis inside of me. But I can taste him, sense his rabid desire, and in this moment, I absorb the pure pulse of his wanting.

Outside, a rowdy group of men passes by with a soundblaster turned up on the Smashing Pumpkins singing "Landslide." The half-drunken imps are singing along with the tune and seem oblivious to our erotic bonding. The drums they are carrying aren't tympani from the Civil War and the long wooden sticks slung over their shoulders aren't Confederate rifles but fishing poles. I touch my lips to my companion's shoulder and I can feel all of the unrequited longing of forgotten young soldiers surging beneath us. It is as though I can feel their pulses laced into the land and they urge me on.

A thousand voices seem to be singing around me, resonating through me as I move my hand over my raised organ as it shoots a hot stream of white balm over Ferris's chest. He rubs the warm, wet, pearls over his own hand then down to his foreskin and he comes instantly. Watching this, the ground underneath my feet appears to tilt.

Ferris opens his eyes and kisses the spunk. "Love medicine." His voice is steady and assured. "So good for us."

I reach down and offer my hands to help him stand up. We embrace, and his slow even breath fills the concave of my ear. My skin prickles and the thin hairs on the back of my neck stand erect. The heat of his body is absorbed into my own as we mesh into one pure throb of light.

"Y'all should spend the night, you know," he half-whispers in his overly dramatic, breathless fashion. "I mean, it would simply be un-Southern to leave now."

"Will you make me grits and coffee in the morning, sir?" I tug at the blanket he holds around himself.

"You have my word."

Ferris moves away from the teepee and into the stirred-up night air, into the black holes that are forest shadows. I follow him, tripping over fallen oak branches. He holds in a deep breath then turns to look back at me, a compass of honey shimmer on his face. The faerie revelers have all gone to bed and the crickets have quieted.

"Feel the heat here?" Ferris holds his hands over a raised mound of earth as though he were warming himself over a bonfire. "All the young soldiers go on dreaming of a peaceful world." He pauses for a moment and looks through the tangle of trees overhead.

He lets the blanket robing his skin drop and I take a snapshot in my mind, then let it go, allowing all of his curvy, boundless, pixie energy to return to him. I look at Ferris and for a moment I flash on the young face he had as a boy model, almost a dead ringer then to Paul Newman. I think of all the images cast over him, the fantasy made up for him by parents who hoped he would be someone different, by strangers who only desired his beautiful skin. It would seem that getting older has helped him to divine what was underneath that glossy image. Something radiant and authentic was always within him and as Ferris would have to agree, "something very Southern."

Tonight a lilac bush rests as a diadem in his auburn hair and flecks of lighting bugs orbit in a golden nimbus around his frame. For a moment, it appears as though he is dancing inside of a wheel with tiny tongues of flame flickering in a hoop around him. I follow him over spindly fir needles and whispering graves back to his teepee. He holds the flap open for me and waits as I enter the place where we can sleep skin to skin, man to man. In dreams I locate that brave, untrammeled spirit that still breathes fire inside of me. Then Ferris and I wake up to feel our pulses pounding in unison, a kind of electric humming that goes on and on.

17   The Kitchen Table

Jay Quinn

Phil touched the table under the lip of its edge, checking for dryness. It was dry to the light impress of his fingertips. The top looked wet, still, though it had been a day and a half since he'd put on the last coat of varnish over the deep cherry stain. Phil saw his reflection on the glossy surface. The afternoon light from the March sun spilled in from the open garage door. He imagined he could see himself from above and below, simultaneously. Deciding it wasn't unpleasant, he produced a smile and squared his shoulders as two sets of himself reared away from each other. Just as suddenly, he bent from the waist and watched as he met himself in the tabletop's gleaming surface.

Phil decided then, at just that moment, that there was nothing wrong with him. The notion that there were many ways to see oneself at once delighted him. He laughed without realizing that he had never been a man given to laughter, or much deep thought. As simply as catching his reflection, he knew many things that had seemed so strange and troubling weren't strange at all. Somehow, reflections don't lie; they just reveal.

Outside and upstairs, Phil heard the screen door to Trace's place slam shut. The bang was followed shortly by the sound of Trace's footsteps, slow and sure, descending the stairs that ran down the side of his place, just outside his kitchen window. Phil moved from the garage out into the drive as Trace hit the bottom step. Seeing Phil there, Trace hesitated and then moved calmly toward his old Jeep Wagoneer. He held two small brass boxes awkwardly in his hands, both wrapped individually in fishing line, the smaller one stacked on the other.

Anticipating his next need, Phil walked to the Wagoneer and opened the door for him. Trace shyly mumbled, "Thanks," and leaned into the car to place the boxes gently on the front seat. Phil hung onto the top of the open door. Their eyes met briefly as Trace straightened to get into the car himself.

"Where are you off to?" Phil asked. Trace reached for the armrest of the door and for a second, Phil thought he would jerk the door from his hands to slam it shut without answering. The second passed. Trace looked up at him reassuringly. "I'm going to take care of something I've been putting off."

Phil nodded and let go of the door. Trace looked away and started the car saying, "I got some supper going. You want to come up and have some spaghetti later on?"

"Sure. I'd like that," Phil replied. Trace gave him a curt nod, but offered a small turning up of his lips in an attempt at a smile to let Phil know he was pleased as he closed the car door.

"I have a surprise for you when you get back," Phil said over the engine noise. Trace looked at him and smiled larger. He shifted the Wagoneer into reverse and Phil stepped away from the car. Once in the street, Trace offered a nod of his head before driving away. Phil resisted the urge to wave, but he did walk down the length of the drive to watch as Trace stopped at the stop sign before turning left past the cottage at the corner and disappeared from sight.

Phil looked the other way down the street toward the beach. The wind off the blue gulf waters was warmer than the chill air just inland. He felt himself reaching toward that warm southern wind. Back home, on Long Island, the wind off the water wouldn't be this warm for weeks. He felt lucky this afternoon. What was it he'd heard Trace say? "It's an ill wind that doesn't blow somebody some good."

Phil looked back in the direction Trace had gone. Trace had been in that ill wind, just like he had. From the street he turned and looked at the house. It was the house the ill wind had blown some good. After six months of work, it looked pretty damn impressive. Coated clean and bright in fresh white paint, its rotten shutters replaced with new ones painted something Trace called "haint blue," the old place looked like a palace compared to what it had when Trace had asked him to look at it.

That was back at the beginning of October. Phil had been living with his son Mikey and his new daughter-in-law, Pauline, since he'd moved down from New York. Mikey was generous to let his old man stay while he was looking for work, but the place was getting crowded. Mikey had just gotten a job, straight out of the Navy, with an air-conditioning company that had a maintenance contract with the base in Pensacola. It was through his job that Mikey had gotten word that there was a guy looking for somebody to fix up an old beach house.

Phil wasn't really sure it was the best way to start out, working on his own, but Mikey made it clear that it was time for Phil to find something that would enable him to move out. Phil understood. He had been twenty-two, the same age as Mikey, when he found himself with a new wife and a baby on the way. The way he looked at it, it was tough enough to start out without having to support your old man. Phil called the number Mikey extended on the back of a light bill envelope.

The next morning, he waited in front of the house not knowing who to expect. The accent of the man who answered the phone was strange. Phil couldn't decide if the man was a redneck, a moulie, or somebody from Maine. The inflections were all mixed up. He was surprised when a slender, blond guy, about his age, showed up in a nice-looking car and introduced himself as Trace Bonnett. The accent was the same, undistorted by the phone lines. Phil listened, trying to place it as he followed Trace around the outside of the house as he pointed out rotten soffit, peeling paint, and detached gutters.

While Trace was searching through a set of keys for the one that would open the front door to the first floor, Phil said, "If you don't mind me asking, where are you from?" The man had looked at him with a hint of a smile and unlocked the door. Stepping into the chaos of discarded furniture and peeling wallpaper, Trace told him he was originally from the Carolina low country, but that he had lived for many years in Boston. "And you've got to be from Lawn Guyland," Trace said with the native inflection. Phil let himself smile in return.

That settled, Trace walked him through both floors of the house explaining that he wanted to make the lower floor a rental and live on the second floor himself. He went on to explain that he would be moving down permanently the first of January, and planned to do all the finish work on the second floor himself. What he needed done immediately, besides the exterior repairs and painting, was the upstairs bathroom and kitchen ripped out completely and then remodeled.

In the upstairs kitchen, Trace leaned against a wall that was to be relocated, looked Phil in the eye and said, "So, what do you think?" Phil turned and walked into the living room without answering. From the side windows and porch, he could see the Gulf. Quickly, he calculated and thought through the job. It was a lot of work to be done by the first of the year. He knew the Florida Panhandle wouldn't be any different than Massapequa, New York: No one would do jack shit for half of December. He hated painting, but he could do it, and the rest, even the electrical. It was a sweet little job.

He heard Trace come into the living room and stand behind him. There was something about the guy that made the hair on the back of his neck stand up, but he couldn't quite put a finger on it. Then, he thought of the first floor.

"You say you want to rent out downstairs," he said and turned to look at Trace who was standing in the light from an east window, the brightness picking out threads of silver in his longish hair. The light also picked out the lines and weathering of the man's face, while making his wary eyes almost gold in the light. Phil dismissed his uneasiness and stumbled ahead, "I'm looking for a place to live. If you'd consider renting to me, I think I could give you a good price and guarantee the work would get done by January."

Trace had looked at him and then turned toward the window. He peered out briefly and then looked back. Phil felt himself examined. He defiantly turned into the gaze and lifted his chin to meet Trace's assessment eye to eye. Trace looked away abruptly and said, "We could give it a shot. If you'll agree to stay until the renovation is complete, we'll talk about a lease then."

Trace's long, slow assessment was discomfiting. It bordered on the personal side of a line that separated casual from intimate. It dawned on Phil then what had been bothering him about his employer to be. He was a fag. The realization didn't bother him. In fact, it made him feel better. He'd been dealing with fags since he turned fifteen years old. He knew from old and recent experience, fags could be useful. All you had to do was treat them nice and as long as they didn't take it the wrong way, they could make life sweet. They were always tipping you good or hooking you up with deals, hoping they'd get a taste of your dick. It was no big deal.

Trace turned away from the window and Phil was pleased to see he had colored slightly. He wasn't bad-looking, for a guy. Phil didn't think it would take too much effort to play up to him. "Tell you what, Mr. Passariello, take tonight and figure up a price. I'll figure out what I need in terms of rent and utilities and we'll get back together tomorrow morning and work it out over coffee." Phil forced all of his charm into a grin and stuck out his hand, taking two steps toward Trace. "It's Phil, and I think you got a deal." Trace took his hand in a dry, surprisingly strong grip, and shook on it. Phil shook his hand until he smiled back.

They spoke of sets of renovation plans and minor details as Trace locked up and they returned downstairs. Phil leaned on the front of his truck, folded his arms across his chest and hooked the heel of his boot on the bumper. Peering back at the front of the house he said, "I think this old place could be a beauty. All she needs is a second chance."

Trace stopped and turned to look at the house. After a moment, he turned to Phil and said, "I think that's what we all need." Phil grunted his agreement and turned to look at Trace. The man caught his look and held it. Phil smiled and Trace said, "I don't see you as a wiseguy. What did you do to earn a nickel upstate?"

Phil looked at Trace in disbelief. Trace's face betrayed no judgment or subterfuge. He simply waited for a response. Phil could feel all of his sudden excitement at the prospect of a place to live and work snatched suddenly away from his grasp. He felt foolish in his arrogant assessment of this guy as another lightweight fag. He snorted and looked away from Trace as he brought his booted foot down from the bumper to rest solidly on the ground next to its mate. "It's a small town, Phil. We both may be outsiders, but I speak the language," Trace said.

Phil shrugged. He wasn't a wiseguy, but he used to work for one. He didn't know how to make the ways of the old neighborhood clear to this odd redneck-Boston hybrid. How could he explain that sometimes you took heat because you knew you'd be taken care of if you did and if you didn't. He'd traded five years in prison for his wife, his kid. Coming out, he'd lost both. Mikey was grown and gone. Gina divorced him for somebody else. For that five years of his life, he'd been rewarded with enough money for a secondhand truck, a few tools, and an invitation to find a new place to live.

He looked back into Trace's patient gaze. "Fuck it," he sighed. Trace lowered his eyes and turned to walk away. Phil panicked slightly; there was too much at stake here to let it end like this. He knew, sooner or later, the question of prison would come up. He had to deal with it now or his reputation in this hick town would be for shit.

"Hey. Wait up a minute, man," Phil said taking a step after him. Trace stopped and turned back. "I took a fall for grand theft. It would have gone a lot harder for me if I hadn't. You know what I'm saying here?" Phil implored. He dropped his arms and opened his hands, palms out. "I did what I hadda do, understand?"

Trace looked him in the eye and said, "I needed to be back in Boston two days ago. I need my house fixed up. I need somebody I can trust to do it and not fuck with me." Phil shoved his hands in the pockets of his jeans and lifted his chin to stare back. He said, "I'm clean. That's all I can tell you."

Trace broke his stare and looked off down the street toward the water. He murmured something Phil didn't catch, then turned back to face him. "Sharpen up your pencil. I ain't got all the fucking money in the world to get this done," Trace said, gesturing at the house behind them. "I'll meet you for coffee at the pier at seven-thirty tomorrow morning," he said, and got into his car without another word.

Now, six months down the road, Phil looked at the house with affection. In many ways, he felt the house was his own. It reflected his pride in himself and in his craftsmanship. He owed Trace for that and he knew it. More than that, he owed him for teaching him how to fit in with and appreciate all the strange people he had arrogantly dismissed as a bunch of ignorant hicks when he first moved down. Phil walked back toward his downstairs porch, remembering the run-in he'd had with the electrical inspector.

The guy looked like freakin' Forrest Gump and acted like an asshole when he came to sign off on the rewiring Phil had done in the new kitchen upstairs. Phil had lost his temper and threatened the guy. As a result, the inspector shut him down. Phil called Trace at his office in Boston to complain. He was greeted with a reception less hospitable and sympathetic then he'd expected.

"You told the electrical inspector *what?*" Trace had demanded. Phil recounted the conversation verbatim. "Phil, these ol' boys don't give a fuck how you did it in New York. Then you had to go and get all Guido on him. What a fucking idiot." Trace paused for a full minute and then said, "Don't do or say a goddamn thing. I'll handle this." He hung up.

In response, Phil had slammed down the phone then went out and got drunk. Late the next afternoon, Trace had pulled up in front of the house with the electrical inspector right behind him. Ignoring Phil, the two men had gone upstairs. Defiant, Phil had followed them up to the second-floor kitchen and listened silently as Trace asked the inspector to explain the problem to him. With a mixture of "aw-shucks" feigned ignorance and genuine respect, he'd listened to the inspector recite the relatively simple problems with the wiring.

"Damn, is that all?" Trace had said. "You mean to tell me I had to get up at three o'clock this morning to fly down here to straighten this out? Shit." He looked at Phil and said coldly, "What made you think you could get in a pissing match with the man who can shut us down?" When Phil didn't answer, Trace pushed a little harder. "Do you think you're capable of getting this done the way he wants it?"

Phil glowered at Trace, but gritted his teeth and nodded. The inspector looked from Trace in his three-piece suit to Phil in his work clothes and made a decision. He said, "No harm done. This man knows what he's doing. He's just not familiar with per-zactly how we do it down here." Trace looked at Phil, expectantly. Taken aback at the inspector's swift change of sides, Phil looked at the inspector and said, "I have a big mouth on top of being stupid. I owe you an apology." The inspector looked at him and smiled. "Ain't nothing but a thang. I can get right hot-headed my own self. Take a look here; I'll show you what you need to do."

After the inspector left with a great deal of goodwill and backslapping, Trace looked at Phil and asked if he had any beer. Phil retrieved a couple from his refrigerator and carried them out to his porch. Trace took a long pull off the bottle and said, "I'm about to give you one more lesson on getting along and fitting in down here. You can take it or leave it, but I expect my house to be ready on the first of January. Understood?"

Phil nodded and took a hit of his own beer. Trace looked him in the eye and said, "You can catch a lot more flies with honey than you can with vinegar. Down here, you're the ignorant asshole, not the other way around. These people don't owe you nothing. Yankee trash looking for a way to get over is a dime a dozen coming in and out of here. You figure out how to say 'yes sir' and 'no sir' and not feel like you're kissing ass and you'll be just fine. If you can't, you let me know now and I'll get somebody who can." Phil had only nodded in reply, stung by the reference to Yankee trash.

Trace drained his beer. "One more thing," he said. Phil looked at him resentfully. "Did you notice how quick our friend the electrical inspector was to take your side, even after you had threatened to kick his ass?" Phil looked away and said, "Yeah? So what?" Trace chuckled, then said, "A working man'll side with one of his own kind over somebody in a three-piece suit every time. You think about how much you have in common with these people and I'm pretty sure you'll figure it all out." Phil didn't know what to say. Trace set his empty beer bottle on the porch rail, stood, and said he had a plane to catch. With that, he was gone.

Remembering that now, Phil realized that incident not only gave him a lesson that worked in the coming weeks, it was exactly the moment he'd begun to grow a grudging respect for Trace. He looked at his watch. Though it was still awhile before he expected him back from his mysterious errand, Phil wanted to have the kitchen table in place when he got back. He wanted everything to be just right.

Phil went into his bathroom and stripped. He shaved carefully, then stepped into the shower. He let the hot water run over him for a long time before he began to lather up. He thought about Trace saying it was easier to catch flies with honey than with vinegar. Remembering that, he played his memories of the weeks since Trace had moved down.

Trace appeared on January second with only a couple of suitcases. True to his word, he planned to work. Right away, he set about painting all the interior rooms upstairs and down, then building kitchen cabinets. He worked longer than he seemed to expect Phil to, only to collapse on an air mattress in his bedroom at the end of the day.

Curious as to his lack of belongings, or a need for the comforts of so much as a radio, Phil asked him when he was expecting the rest of his things. Trace had answered obliquely, saying only that there was no need for things when the box to put them in wasn't finished. Phil had no answer to that, only more questions he felt wouldn't be welcomed.

Phil was not a garrulous man, but he was used to living with people who talked. He liked the company of conversation, even if it was bullshit. Trace seldom spoke except to direct him in his projects or ask him for a hand as he cut wood, assembled it, and mounted the simple, but elegant new kitchen cabinets he was building for the kitchen.

Trace never told a joke. He never offered observations on the town or the weather or the news. After a month of working side by side, Phil knew no more about him than he had when they first met. It both fascinated and rankled Phil. Any attempts on his part to draw the man out of his solitude were met with either a kind of distracted silence or a swift change of conversation back to the work at hand.

Trace maintained a respectful, polite distance between them. He never treated Phil as a hireling, but he never asked him to share so much as a noontime sandwich or a beer at the end of the day. A newcomer, alien and outside, Phil hadn't made any friends in the few months he'd been south. He met Mikey occasionally for a beer, or a Sunday meal, but Mikey and Eileen were so preoccupied with the beginnings of their marriage and Eileen's pregnancy, they made for dull company. His ego still bruised from Gina's abandonment, he found his casual attempts at dating women he met in bars to be thwarted by his lingering resentments from the start.

Phil was lonely. Stuck in such close and constant company with his enigmatic employer, he had nowhere else to focus his attention. As a result, Phil began to watch Trace. He became hyperaware of his routines of rising, of eating, of going for a cold swim or walk on the beach after work. He became fascinated with Trace.

Working side by side, in the house, in the impromptu cabinet shop in the garage, outside, everywhere, Phil began to notice small things about Trace. He noted the angle of his jaw where it cut up sharply to meet below his ear. He watched old freckles scattered across Trace's shoulders deepen to bronze as the skin around them turned gold. He noted the progress of the lightening of the sparse hair on Trace's upper chest from dull gold to platinum. He noticed how his upper arms and thighs hardened from an office worker's slack fullness to the firmness suited to their new function.

When he found himself hidden in the garage to watch as Trace mowed the sparse grass around the house, he became angry with himself. Waking that night from a dream of that scene to find his dick in his hand, hard and demanding, he felt disgusted and desperate. Pleading some made-up visit from relatives, he took off for a few days. He drove east along the rim of the panhandle, stopping at night

to drink and find sullen women enlivened by his novelty and enam-
ored of his dark good looks.

The day before he was due back, Phil woke up to one such
woman's slightly soiled expectations in a trailer park outside Cedar
Key. He pushed the rough urgency of her lipstick-stained lips and
teeth away from his mouth and down to his unresponsive dick.
Closing his eyes as he held her bleached head in his hands, he found
the desired response picturing the backyard of the house.

Phil could see Trace's golden shoulders taper sharply to his small
waist and narrow hips. He saw himself step from the shadows of the
garage and motion Trace inside. In the hot, dusty shadows, he'd force
Trace to his knees, and then push his proud head to his aching crotch.
Trace would unsnap his jeans and pull them down as far as they
would go between his widespread legs. He could feel his hot balls
freed to swing in the cooler air of the shadowy garage. Trace would
open his mouth to take the broad dark head of his dick into the hot,
moist, smallness of his mouth. He would bend over him, forcing the
long length of his dick down his throat. Reaching behind Trace's
kneeling form, he'd slip his large hand down the back of his pants.
Phil could see the waistband rip and give way as his thick, hairy wrist
disappeared down the back of Trace's pants. He felt his fingers part
Trace's confined cheeks as he sought the tight lower entrance to
Trace's body. He'd tease it. Make it ready for him to plow.

Out of his mind and in the close, hot trailer's bedroom, Phil rose to
his knees and rode the woman's mouth to gagging. He only was
aware of Trace's imagined moans as he bucked into him relentlessly.
He felt his dick arch, choking with his cum. Phil spent himself in her
mouth, to her struggling, scratching alarm.

"You son of a bitch," she screamed after he let her go. She spat furiously onto the floor next to the bed and then slapped him. "Get the
fuck out of my house, you fucking pervert." Phil dressed quickly and
moved past her heated, steady stream of curses to the cool, waiting
morning outside. Disgusted with himself and miserable, he drove
four hours straight back to the house.

Driving through the bright tackiness of the innumerable beach
towns along the way, he carefully considered all of the attentions he'd
received from the men who'd wanted him over the years. In high
school, it was skinny, redheaded Shaun MacDonagh. His puppylike
adoration was as plain as the freckles on his face. Stumbling and

blushing, he'd courted Phil with a persistence that was embarrassing. Phil had casually abused him in defense against the taunts of his friends. Finally, he very publicly humiliated the boy to save himself from further embarrassment.

After he married Gina, there was Marty Genovese, who did plumbing work for the company Phil worked for. Sporting a mustache like the biker from the Village People and constantly plaguing Phil with insinuations and unsubtle gropes, Marty had made him so uncomfortable he'd quit and gone to work for another company.

In prison, there was Al Silverman, a former addict dentist, busted repeatedly for selling bogus Percodan and codeine scripts. His shower stares lead to cryptic notes and then outright propositions. Phil tried to be polite, taking his offerings of cigarettes and the occasional joint, but it finally came down to busting him in the mouth to get him to lay off.

The miles ground under the rough tread of truck tires. Unwanted and unbidden, Trace answered each memory. Phil pounded his palms on the steering wheel in frustration. He rammed up the radio's volume and twisted the dial endlessly in an effort to distract himself from the questions that plagued him. From his mental picture slamming his dick into the black-rooted, bleached head of the woman he'd just left, he could almost feel Trace's brighter, shorter hair twisted between his fingers, his mouth wet around his now sore, hard dick. He fought against the image of pinning Trace on the floor, ruthlessly fucking him like he would a woman, watching his face, until the silent, distant man gave in and begged him for it like all the others had before.

Exhausted and defeated, he pulled up at last in the drive behind the beat-up Wagoneer Trace had bought soon after he moved down to stay. Stumbling tired and disoriented by the hours of ceaseless motion and his own dirty dreams, he grabbed the paper bag holding his things and headed straight for his place on the first floor. He didn't want to deal with the living, breathing presence of Trace. He just wanted a shower and some sleep.

Halfway to his door, he heard Trace's screen door slam and looked up to see his unknowing tormentor standing on the porch above him. "Hey," Trace said. Phil stopped and returned the greeting grudgingly. "Come up here a minute. There's something I want you to take a look 'at," Trace said. Phil was about to beg off when he recognized something he'd never heard in Trace's voice before. He sounded happy. He sounded anxious for Phil to respond.

Phil tossed his paper bag luggage onto his porch and turned to go up the stairs. Trace was waiting on the porch. With a smile, he opened the screen door and motioned Phil in ahead of him. Phil entered the empty living room and stopped. Trace stepped around him and walked toward the opening in the back wall which gave into what had been a tiny dining room before Phil had ripped it out to join that space to the kitchen's. Trace turned to Phil with what had become an honest grin.

Phil took the few steps to stand beside him. The kitchen was finished. Since he'd been gone, Trace had lacquered the cabinets white and trimmed them in wood trim resembling rope, painted a glossy deep blue. In what had only been gaping holes in the cabinets, now stood gleaming white appliances. The cabinet tops were covered with shining white tiles for a countertop that continued generously as a backsplash that went up the walls to meet the bottom of the cabinets.

Phil whistled and moved to stand in the middle of the room under the lazily turning ceiling fan. "It's fucking beautiful," he said admiringly. "Who'd you get to do the tile?" Trace followed him into the room and ran his hand lovingly over the countertop. "What you mean, who? I did it. Finished up about three a.m. last night. You missed helping hump up the range and stuff by about thirty minutes," Trace said triumphantly.

Phil shook his head and looked up at the recessed lights whose places had to be cut so tediously out of the beadboard on the ceiling. Trace had painted it the same shade of blue as the rope trim on the cabinets. Phil had wondered at all the extra effort at the time, but now he understood. The effect was cool and clean. It was a room that demanded to be sat in, lived in, eating, laughing, drinking coffee. "Now all we need is a kitchen table," he said without thinking.

When he realized what he said, he felt himself flush deeply. He looked around nervously and stepped quickly back into the living room. Trace followed him with a sudden rushing description of things he wanted to do in the living room. Embarrassed, Phil barely listened as Trace excitedly described the bookcases he wanted to build in. He moved back deeper into the house's bedrooms, describing the closet built-ins he planned for those rooms as well.

Phil hung back and murmured appropriately as he followed Trace from room to room. He no longer trusted his own words. ". . . so we have to get busy. It's no big deal. I've got all the drawings done. If you'll cut, I'll install. I thought we'd bring the table saw and the compound miter saw up to the front porch." Trace paused in his excitement and looked back to find Phil's response.

Phil had been staring at his back, a riot of hatred and growing love battling across his features. He had no idea what showed on his face when Trace turned to look at him. "I'm sorry," Trace said and looked away. "I just went off not even thinking. I'll let you get settled in before I put you back to work." His coolness had returned.

Phil was unexpectedly crushed by the return of polite distance in Trace's tone. He quickly responded, "No, I'm sorry. It sounds great. I'm just sorta wiped out from the trip."

Trace nodded as he walked past him and back out into the hall. He stood, waiting for Phil to leave the room he'd been using as his own. Phil glanced down at the air mattress covered with a twisted set of sheets and two abandoned pillows. He swallowed hard as he moved out the door and down the hall to the living room. By the front door, he paused and looked back at Trace. He said, "I'm anxious to get started. Let me catch a quick shower and I'll be ready to rock and roll."

Trace offered back a tight smile. "No. There's no need for that today. I was up late myself. We'll start in the morning." Phil was miserable at the dismissal. "Are you sure? I can—" Trace interrupted him saying, "No. No problem. I'll see you in the morning." Taking a step back toward Trace, Phil said, "The kitchen, it's fucking incredible." Trace took a step away from him and said, "Thanks." Phil nodded and went downstairs feeling more alone than he had in a long time.

The rush of hot water down the long length of his body felt good. Phil watched it collect the soap's lather and push it downward to puddle like sea froth on the floor of the shower stall. He imagined it carrying away all of the last reservations he had. Not wanting to be lulled into the comfort of any last-minute misgivings, he turned and shut off the hot water tap.

He welcomed the cold shock of the water. He tilted his head back to catch the brunt of it on his face. He turned slowly, lifting one arm, then the other to let it race down his sides. He parted his buttocks to accept the cold rinse and thrust his hips forward to allow the stream to part his pubic hair and circle his dick and balls in a chilling, cleansing circle before shutting the water off completely.

Phil stood still, listening and watching as the water slowed from clear running rivulets off his fingertips, scrotum, and bent face to drips, to drops. He shook his head to clear his ears and hair of water before pulling back the shower curtain and stepping from the shower. He looked for his reflection in the full-length mirror mounted on the back of the bedroom door.

Unfogged, his image repeated itself much clearer here than it had in the surface of the kitchen table. The image betrayed the pride he'd always had in his looks. He'd passed tedious hours working out while in prison. His constant activity and the sunshine on the outside had only improved and toned the color and mass of his chest, ropy muscled arms, and long waist. At forty-four, he was simply more of what he'd been at twenty-two. His hairline, even cruelly exposed by the wet weight of his hair flung back from the forehead, had only retreated a bit on either side of a strong widow's peak. His leonine head was mounted on a thick neck that found its base on broad shoulders. Centered just below the slight swell of his hips was the origin of a thin dark trail of hair that crawled up over his belly and scattered across his upper chest, making his nipples look as thickly lashed as a young girl's eyes.

He cupped and squeezed his cold, shrunken scrotum in one hand and lifted and stroked his dick with the other. He felt both respond with a blooming fullness back to their familiar heft and solid weight at the joining of his legs. He spread his feet shoulder width apart and allowed his genitals their freedom. He traced the edges of his strong thighs with the palms of his hands and looked down past his knees to the lightly furred tops of his feet and long slender toes.

It was a body he appreciated and knew well. It served him, mostly without fail. Convinced of its reliability to perform, he dried himself briskly, recalling the proof of its ability to attract.

* * *

The morning following his return from the desperate trip across the coast, Phil woke early with a sense of unexamined resolve. He dressed quickly, then drove to a nearby fast-food joint. Back at the house before seven, grasping a paper bag containing breakfast in one hand and coffee in the other, he'd kicked at Trace's front door and called him until he appeared, sleepy-eyed and surprised at Phil's offering of breakfast and his understated eagerness to begin work.

For the next two weeks, Phil repeated that process each morning as work on the complicated built-ins progressed throughout the second floor. He concentrated on working as a team with his distant employer. He asked him questions about the details of the cabinetwork and as a result, he came to know more about the man.

"You said you wanted the inside of this place as well thought out as the inside of a ship," he said to Trace as they fitted new drawers into a chest of drawers built into the master bedroom's closet. "What gave you the idea?" he prompted.

"I'm sick of having stuff slung up everywhere," Trace said. "For seventeen years, I lived with shirts draped over chairs, clean towels folded and not put away. I swore, one day when he . . . " He caught himself and stopped. He glanced at Phil, kneeling next to him on the floor. Phil looked back, waiting for him to continue. Trace stood and looked around the room. "I need a plane. This drawer's still sticking toward the back." With that, he left the room.

Phil persisted without pressing him to finish his self-censored revelations. His efforts earned him knowledge of many disjointed facts of Trace's life before he showed up on the Redneck Riviera. Phil was able to piece much together from the puzzle of Trace's disjointed and accidental revelations. He learned Trace had been partners in a successful business that had something to do with high tech R&D. From a few other unguarded comments, Phil put together the facts that Trace's partner in business was his partner in life, or was, until he died.

Though the unguarded asides and fractured bits of narrative came over weeks, Phil was able to ascertain Trace's partner had died in an automobile accident, followed shortly by the death of their dog. Trace sold their business for a sum of money he never disclosed, but Phil knew how much the renovation was costing. He also knew Trace paid him on time, every week as agreed, and the checks were always good.

Phil also persisted with his physical presence. Working on fitting the support rails that ran behind and under the shelves, or reaching to steady and hold a piece of cap trim, Phil would reach behind Trace, encircling him with his arms, lightly touching his chest to his back.

Working above him on a ladder, Phil would pivot on one foot to bring his crotch to Trace's eye-level, inches from his eyes.

This sly, steady physical proximity also confirmed Trace's unspoken attraction to Phil's mere presence. As for Trace's reaction to the intimacy of Phil's increasing physicality, it was never refused, but never reacted to in words. Phil was amused at his own enjoyment of being such a tease. He would strip off his shirt in the heat of midday with all of the torque and hip shifting of a man he'd watched in a detergent commercial on TV. He found himself opening doors for Trace, or volunteering to hump sheets of plywood up the stairs to be cut on the table saw. He handed Trace tools without being asked. He summoned sandwiches out of thin air at lunch and lit Trace's infrequent cigarettes with a lighter he picked up at the gas station for just that purpose.

Trace seemed to respond to all of this growing attention as a flower follows the sun. Phil could feel him gravitate toward him. He would turn suddenly or glance up to find Trace looking at him. Trace never said a word. He would only look away with renewed determination on his face.

Finally, the cabinetwork was done. The shelves and built-ins were sanded and stained or painted. With a happy smile, Trace had turned to Phil as he dropped a paintbrush into an emptied paint can and said, "How about a beer?"

Phil returned his smile with a grin. At Trace's suggestion, they dragged two old porch rockers from the garage and set them side by side, with a cooler between them, to watch the sunset over the water. Phil retrieved his new boom box from his place and tuned into a local station that featured oldies. One beer turned to several as the sun fell spectacularly and night slipped over the gulf waters. They shared both memories the songs evoked and an entire twelve-pack.

Reaching for the last beer simultaneously, their fingers interlocked. Trace jumped and made a move to draw away, but Phil tightened his own around them. He looked at Trace searchingly. Trace sighed and looked away. Phil released his grip on his fingers as Trace stood unsteadily. "I think it's time for me to call it a night," he said. Without looking at Phil, he steadied himself and continued, "You can have the last beer. I'll see you in the morning."

As Trace took a step to move past him, Phil stretched his leg out to rest his foot on the railing, blocking his exit. Trace froze. Phil leaned forward and grabbing his wrist, pulled Trace roughly into his lap. Briefly, Trace allowed himself to flow with the momentum. He rested his face at the muscled joinery of Phil's neck and shoulder. Reaching up, he slid the palm of his hand into the opened panels of Phil's shirt and stroked the hard plane of his chest. Then, abruptly, he pushed away and stood up.

Still firmly holding his wrist, Phil found his face in the darkness. "Do you know the difference between a straight guy and a gay guy?" Trace said quietly. "No, what?" Phil said as he tugged at Trace's arm. Trace jerked his arm free and said, "A six-pack." He stepped over Phil's outstretched leg easily and walked to the screen door. Opening it, he looked back at Phil and said, "If you ever decide you want to try again when you ain't drunk, let me know." Then he went inside, pointedly locking the door behind him.

* * *

Phil rested each foot in turn on the commode and dried his thighs and feet, then neatly folded his towel in thirds and hung it over the bar in the shower. Turning toward the mirror once again, he watched himself as he reached to stroke his chest as Trace had done that night. He rolled his head searching for the memory of Trace's head, snuggled into his neck. In the mirror, his eyes found his dick, lengthening and thickening, untouched, at only the memory. Grasping it, he stroked it to full attention. He let it go and turned to admire and measure its high arching echo to the slight curve of his belly. He wasn't drunk, nor did he plan to be that night.

Phil combed his freshly cut hair with his fingers before striding purposefully to his room. He found fresh boxer shorts, socks, and clean jeans. He dressed rapidly, coaxing his dick down his left thigh before zippering and buttoning his jeans and pulling on the new polo shirt and sneakers he'd bought with a sizeable chunk of his last week's pay. There was nothing left to do now but put the kitchen table in place upstairs and wait for Trace to come home.

It was short work to retrieve the table from the garage and hump it upstairs to Trace's kitchen. Phil placed it carefully in the space between the two windows looking over the street toward the gulf beyond. With equal care, he placed the four antique thumb-back chairs Trace had lined against the opposite wall to wait for a table like this.

Phil stepped back to admire his handiwork and the completed picture Trace must have seen in his mind from the very beginning. The table and chairs gleamed in the kitchen's late afternoon light. On the stove, a pot of red sauce simmered, filling the air with as many memories of Phil's old home and happiness as the actual scent of tomatoes, garlic, and spices.

Looking at the neat, bright kitchen, Phil found himself longing for a sense of home he hadn't allowed himself since he'd been sent to prison. At first, he'd banished the memories of home and comfort in the face of the gray, harsh environment he found himself in to make that place more bearable. Then, three years in, he'd been served with divorce papers. He allowed bitterness to grow in the place of any sense of comfort and security. He hated the rush of longing that overtook him surveying this kitchen, that table, the simmering pot of sauce so clearly meant to be shared with him and him alone. Just as real, a sense of desperation replaced the sense of longing. He understood how much he didn't want to leave this place.

Phil made himself leave the kitchen to wait outside on the porch. He sat in one of the rockers he and Trace had retrieved from the garage the night he'd made a pass at Trace. They had managed to strip and sand away layers of old paint in the odd moments between work on the shelves and cabinets inside. The old rockers' uncertain creaks and gives were silenced by new screws, glue, and several coats of white oil paint. They sat, side by side, waiting for occupants who laughed and shared dreams and cold drinks.

Phil rested his head on the rocker's back and stared up at the haint-blue beadboard ceiling. Trace had explained that the color was magic. It frightened away bad spirits and protected all the entrances to the house. It was an old practice where Trace came from, part voodoo, part signature of a time and place Trace seemed to want to knit together in this home. Low-country and Boston, then and now, all arriving in packing boxes to fill the box Phil had helped make to keep them in.

Phil had eagerly helped him unpack when the moving van finally arrived. Trace had explained he had given a lot of thought to what he'd kept and given away from the house he'd shared with Kevin. Phil took in this first mention of the man's name without comment. He'd seen the single framed picture Trace had of him while he was helping unpack.

The fairly recent photo was taken on a sailboat. Big-boned and Irish, Kevin held Trace from behind, a large mutt nuzzling his ear. Secure and laughing, Trace was relaxed into the man's broad chest, held lovingly by his large hand on his bare stomach. Even in the black and white of the photo, Phil could fill in the green eyes and crisp auburn hair of the man. He grinned a big sloppy grin from behind Trace's laughter caught in the shot. Phil mentally compared the width of Kevin's bare shoulders and thick wrists to his own. He wondered what made Trace love the big red bastard.

He put the picture aside, unable to look at it. He'd removed some packing material and uncovered two brass boxes. The lids were engraved with names and dates. He'd picked up the one that read Kevin Toibin. The contents shifted like sand inside. The other box only said Mack. It was the big man himself, reduced to ashes. Phil had felt an eerie chill come over him, he felt actually touched by a shadow. He looked up to find Trace watching him.

Without a word, he'd taken the box from Phil's hand, reached to pick up the other from the box and placed them high on a living room shelf. Then, he turned and began to search the area around Phil. Phil knew he was looking for the framed picture. He moved some packing material off of it and handed it to Trace. It followed the boxes to the high shelf. Trace turned and said, "I need your help in the kitchen. The dishes and shit will make it in the cabinets a lot quicker with some help."

The regular pattern of the beadboard in the ceiling ordered and calmed Phil's thoughts. In the repetition of the clean straight lines, he could place and sort what he was feeling. He lined up the ache he felt seeing the dead, cold look in Trace's eyes as they worked to put away glasses, plates, and bowls. He placed his longing for a home, this home, in line next.

In the knot of his thoughts, he grabbed the strand that made him selfishly want to fuck Trace roughly into giving him all of the validation he craved. As he pulled that strand, he found the end of the realization that he would do anything to not be alone and outside anymore. Those strands didn't fit nicely into the linear pattern of the ceiling. He couldn't sort them out. He didn't know where the new stinging realization of his own vulnerability and the intense attraction to the silent, grieving man began or ended.

Phil wanted Trace's back securely lodged against his chest, his hand holding Trace's belly. He wanted his dick buried deep inside Trace, anchoring him to him and this place. He wanted to run as hard as he could, down the stairs and far away from the very thing that meant he had become. And Phil wanted not to move from this seat until it was his turn to become ashes in a box, burned clean of any doubt or regrets.

Phil's preoccupation with knots and long lines disappearing down the length of the porch ceiling was dissolved by the sound of the Wagoneer pulling up the oyster-shell drive. He watched as Trace shut off the engine and slowly got out of the car. He shut the door gently and then just stood there. He looked small, and very lost in his own drive.

"Hey," Phil called softly. Trace looked up at him without seeming to see him. "How'd it go?" Phil said awkwardly. Trace just looked up at him, then struggling to keep his voice deep and controlled, he said, "They wondered what the fishing line was for. I asked them how they planned to get those two small boxes down six feet into that child-sized vault. I had . . ."

Phil began to walk toward him as he faltered. By the time he made it to the steps, Trace continued, "I had to convince the priest to bless the grave, after I put the box with Mack's ashes down with Kevin's. He said it was sacreligious . . ." Phil quickened his pace until he was almost running down the stairs. As he turned at the bottom step, Trace turned away and placed his hands palms down on the hood. "I told him I couldn't leave him there alone." As Phil almost ran toward him, Trace dropped his head and began to shudder at the shoulders.

Phil stopped next to him and put his hand firmly on the back of Trace's neck. There was no sound, no sobbing. He turned Trace gently, but firmly, toward him. Trace jerked from his grasp, but didn't move away. He tucked his head and rubbed his eyes on his shoulders as a little boy would. "I'm okay," Trace said firmly. "It's done." He looked up at Phil gratefully and repeated, "I'm okay."

He squared his shoulders, looked Phil in the eye and asked, "You got anything stronger than beer in your place?" Phil nodded, put his arm over Trace's shoulder and steered him through the gathering dusk toward his door. Trace didn't throw off his arm, or resist when Phil steered him inside to his own kitchen. He sat obediently at the small metal patio table Phil had picked up at Wal-Mart. Phil opened the cabinet under the sink and pulled out a bottle of Jack Daniels. He rinsed out a styrofoam cup from the morning's coffee and quietly asked, "Ice?"

Trace nodded and looked dully around the sparse, but clean kitchen. He accepted the drink and watched as Phil settled into the chair opposite him. "Aren't you having one?" He asked. Phil shook his head. Trace looked away and then took a deep swallow of his drink. "I appreciate this," Trace said after awhile.

Phil ached to reach across the table and touch him. He wanted so much to take him in his arms and stroke him as he had Mikey when he was a little boy. He hurt in sympathy and simultaneously he wanted Trace sexually all the more. "It's okay," he said.

They sat silently as Trace nursed his drink and the kitchen's light deepened to near darkness. Trace tipped the cup back to find it empty, the ice long melted and gone. He set the cup on the table and looked at Trace, searching his face. He looked toward the front door and said, "I don't want to go." Huskily, Phil whispered back, "I don't want you to."

Trace turned to look at him again. "I know. But you have to understand. I ain't a tour guide to queer world." Trace dropped his head and continued, "I can't take but so much right now." Phil stood and slowly took the two steps to stand in front of Trace. He reached down and took his bowed face in his hands. "If you only want to fuck me, that's okay . . . just let me know," Trace said. Phil knelt in front of him and lifted his face to meet his own. "But you can't fuck with me. I won't let you fuck with me," Trace said desperately.

Phil let go of his face, and wrapping his arms around Trace's shoulders, pulled him roughly to his knees and into his chest. Swaying gently, he rocked Trace in his arms. Phil could feel the knotted muscles of Trace's back under his hands. He could smell his hair. He could feel his breath at the hollow of his throat. He could feel his heart's insistent thud against his own. "I built us a kitchen table," Phil said simply.

18   Lost Near Jerusalem

Joe Frank Buckner

The forklift slipped its chain, slamming to the warehouse floor, vibrating through Andrew's bones and waking him. He fell asleep shortly after the truck driver picked him up on I-95, just south of Savannah, and slept for the next two hours, even after the truck stopped to be unloaded.

The truck lurched away from the warehouse and Andrew was seething, shooting silent eye darts at the driver for having taken him so many miles off I-95 without waking him. He was annoyed with yet another delay in catching up with his buddies in Daytona before they left for Fort Lauderdale.

His anger grew each time the driver turned the radio volume up while screaming into the citizen's band microphone. The blaring country music would be squelched when the driver talked, providing Andrew the only relief from the music he hated.

"Hey, Bub, would you mind turning Rita McTiresome down a few decibels?"

"That's Reba McEntire," he said, turning to Andrew. "Miss Reba McEntire." As with most of his frequent incendiary arguments, Andrew wouldn't remember much of the one that followed, except for his own last words. "What kind of fucking truck driver are you, anyway?"

"I'm the kind," he said, braking fast, "that leaves smart-assed punk hitchhikers right . . . here . . ."

The driver reached across Andrew, opened the passenger door, and pushed him out with one shove of his wide-open hand. He threw Andrew's backpack at him with such force that he flew backward into the ditch, his stomach catching it, smacking his tight abdomen as if it were the palm of a baseball glove.

Andrew stood in the middle of the unlined potholed country road. Both straight-shot directions were flat, wooded, uninhabited, and seemingly endless. He had no idea which way would take him back to I-95. But he continued on in the direction the truck had gone, walking in the middle of the road, listening for a vehicle or any sound of humanity.

Rain began to fall through the thick humid air, rising back up to him steamily from the hot pavement. He cursed his father and the truck driver, giving them equal credit for his predicament.

His father had purposely left him in a DUI holding cell until certain the last of Andrew's college friends had left for spring break in Florida. He had politicked Andrew out of the charge, but then took away his car and credit card, punishing him by ruining his spring break, or so he thought.

Andrew stole ninety-three dollars from his mother's purse and walked to the intersection of I-95 and Interstate 1, near Fairfield. Those few miles were the most he would have to walk, successfully hitchhiking from Connecticut to wherever he was in South Georgia.

Andrew was as angry as he was lost. He dropped the backpack in the middle of the road and stripped off his shirt when rainwater and sweat trickled down the small of his spine to his crack, tickling the tiny hairs there.

A bobwhite sang out from a nearby oak thicket as Andrew pulled off his jeans and dug in his backpack for a pair of running shorts. Before pulling them up from his knees, he grabbed his bare crotch and yelled obscenities in the direction of the long-gone truck driver and then directed a few more at the quail that continued to serenade him.

Rain on his bare chest cooled his skin as we walked on, but his anger still burned underneath, stinging like hot needles in the constricted muscles from his neck to his groin. He walked to the edge of the ditch to pee and thought about masturbating, violently, to relieve the tension, as he had after his father brought him home from the police station. But he decided he needed that certain edge, that potent anger, to deal with whatever lay ahead.

Forty-two minutes later he reached a crossroads. He had not passed a house, nor had a vehicle of any kind passed him. He was sick of the swampy woods and the steamy heat, but most of all he was sick of the warm rain falling too lightly, like a constant, uncertain tap on his shoulder.

He looked down both sides of the intersecting road for shelter. He saw the rusty tin roof of a house almost overgrown by bushes, trees, and vines.

He stopped under the canopy of a chinaberry tree, listening, sure he heard singing from the porch of the house. He blinked through the bothersome veil of rain as he walked, seeing a boy's hand waving him on.

It was a clapboard shack, never before painted, leaning oddly, as if windblown, away from its crumbling chimney. Massive azaleas grew up high around the front porch, almost touching the eaves, blocking all view of the front windows and the porch.

Andrew smirked at the old Buick Electra beside the house. It was wrecked, rusted, and partially stripped; perched up high on blocks like some old dinosaur with its bones picked nearly clean.

Another casualty, a vintage Kelvinator refrigerator, lay open on its back near the front steps, petunias growing thickly out of it in a profusion of pale lavender and white.

Andrew rolled his eyes up to the young man on the top step.

"Hi. How you?" the stranger asked.

"How do I look?" Andrew stepped up, slinging water from his shoulder length dark hair. "I'm wet and I'm really pissed off."

"Better than bein' wet and pissed on," he said, laughing too loud.

"Brilliant. Tobacco Road High, right?"

"What?" the boy asked, rubbing one bare foot over the arch of the other.

"Nothing." He stood back, looking at the road he had just left. "Where the hell is . . . *this?*"

"May not be educated," he said, giggling, "but I sure know where I am."

"Cute. Just, where am I?"

"'Bout ten miles north of Jerusalem."

"What?"

". . . and about forty miles from I-95."

"Oh, this is great," Andrew said, spinning around, roughly combing his fingers back through his hair. "I don't believe this shit."

"How in the world did somebody like you get himself way out here?"

"Some goddamned . . . "

"Don't you cuss 'round me," raising his hand to heaven. "I'm a Christian."

"Some fat slob, some asshole of a truck driver dumped me out."

"Why'd he want to do that?"

"I didn't like Reba. . . . Oh, it doesn't matter."

He stepped in front of Andrew, shrugging his shoulders, tilting his head boyishly. "What's your name?"

"Andrew Lorillard."

"Well, Andy . . ."

"Don't call me that. Drew . . . but never Andy."

"Please to meet you, Drew," he said, offering his hand as if Andrew had not yet said a word. "I'm Johnny Ray Lastinger."

"Well of course you are," he laughed, barely brushing his palm against the boy's.

"Won't you sit a while, dry out?" he asked, motioning to the swing before sitting on the broken-down old sofa.

"Drew, where you from and where you heading?"

"Connecticut," he said, flopping back on the swing. "Meeting friends in Daytona and then on to Fort Lauderdale for spring break. I'm close enough now I'll just call the guys to come get me."

"Ain't got no phone."

"Of course you don't," Drew laughed, slapping his palms to his forehead. "Why would there be phones in . . . hell?"

"I'd invite you inside for tea to cool you off, wouldn't be iced though, 'cause we ain't got no 'lectric no more." He looked down, losing his smile for the first time. "I'd invite you in anyway, outa the damp, but my pa, he's lyin in there on the floor . . . passed out drunk."

"Oh, really?" Drew asked. "And how long has 'Pa' been prone?"

"He came in 'bout sunrise, yellin' and chasing me round and round, blaming me for his misries, like always. He took a swing at me and fell flat on the floor. And wherever he falls out, that's where I leave 'em and just stay outa the house. He'll yell out for me late this afternoon to come in and scramble him up some eggs."

Drew looked directly at Johnny Ray for the first time just as the boy bit down on his bottom lip, his eyes shifting to the door. He believed him to be no more than his age of nineteen, but he couldn't be sure, for he had an ethereal, Oliver Twist waif look that, depending on lighting, could put him anywhere between fifteen and twenty something.

Drew stopped swinging the instant he saw the white of Johnny Ray's hairless underthigh not covered by his jeans shorts. He had not noticed how well tanned the boy was until he anchored his foot on the edge of the sofa, exposing the promise of still hidden white flesh.

"Does he ever hit you?" Drew asked, watching the boy's fingers pick at the ragged fringe of his cut offs.

"If he can catch me."

"Why?"

"'Cause he ain't got my mama to beat on no more since she ran off with Remer Boyett."

"I'll bet the Jerusalem Junior League was just scandalized."

"What?" Johnny Ray asked, holding his blond hair off his fore-head, blowing air upward.

"Nothing." Drew watched the boy rub his initials engraved on the backpack at his feet.

"You're rich, ain't you, Drew?"

"No, but my son-of-a-bitch father is."

"We're poor as Job's turkey."

"No shit," he laughed, sitting up, resting his elbows on his knees. "Tell me, what is it with you people? Old jalopy on blocks in the yard, an old appliance as a flower container, flea-infested sofa on the front porch. I mean, is it some sort of poor white trash code you're adhering to?"

"Excuse me, mister. I'm white and, God knows I'm poor, but I'll have you know I am not trash, Mr. AnDEE LauraLARD."

The rain pelting the tin roof seemed to grow louder in measure with the sudden tension.

"No phone, huh?"

"No phone."

Johnny Ray stood at the far end of the porch and peeled off his white T-shirt. Holding on to the corner porch post, he swung his body out, allowing the rain to rinse his face and upper chest.

"Even the rain is hot," he said, spreading the water down to his stomach. "But I wouldn't mind the heat if we could just have a little breeze ever now and then."

The brighter light from that end of the porch silhouetted Johnny Ray's lean body. Drew noticed for the first time the deep curvature of the boy's lower back.

"How did you hurt your hand?" Drew asked, seeing the large flesh-toned Band-Aid when he sat back down on the sofa.

"I was helping Pa skin and gut a squirrel he shot. Knife slipped."

"You people eat squirrels?"

"Cook 'um down with rice and taters, onions, and they make fine eatin'."

"Sho'nough?"

"You teasing me?" He stretched his legs out on the sofa, leaning over the sofa arm to Drew. "You're gonna hurt my little feelings if you keep on."

"I'm bummed out. If this rain would just stop. Somehow it's making me feel kind of claustrophobic."

"Kind of what? Oh, I know, like you're locked in a closet?" He continued even though Drew appeared not to be listening. "Well, anyhow, rain just makes me feel all sleepy and limber, soft-boned, as if I could sink down into my featherbed like butter melting down into a hot biscuit."

Drew was listening though, and the image of the tanned blond boy stretched out on a fluffy white featherbed rubbed something too tender in his mind. Like finding soreness in a strained muscle; it hurts, but you can't stop your fingers from probing the spot again. He stood to shake it off.

Johnny Ray sat upright and leaned his shoulders back, stretching his arms high, bowing his stomach outward. "Oh my, that feels so good," he said, reaching higher. "I could stretch a mile if I didn't hafta walk back."

Drew blinked once and sighed, that tender spot rubbed again, when he saw Johnny Ray's lean rib bones and the hardening nipples held by the rounded breast flesh above his ribcage.

Drew's groin tightened, siphoning all strength from the rest of his body.

He sat beside Johnny Ray on the sofa as he continued talking about the rain, although now Drew was not listening.

Something about his presence and manner told him he could do anything he wanted without Johnny Ray protesting. But still, he wasn't sure he wanted to test his instinct, for if he was wrong there was a half drunk white trash father who might come to his son's aid with a double barrel shotgun, an ax, or a chain saw. Drew winced and snickered at the thought of dying in some Southern Gothic testosterone duel.

He shifted closer to Johnny Ray, concluding that he could easily outrun any middle-aged drunken bubba. Drew placed his arm on the back of the sofa and let his hand slide down the boy's shoulder, his fingertips deftly reaching the erect nipple. Johnny Ray didn't blink or alter the inflection in his voice when Drew lightly rolled the nipple between his forefinger and thumb.

Johnny Ray continued looking at the rain falling from the eaves of the house above the high azaleas. "In a few days all those little buds'll bloom out," Drew's other hand moved to the nearer nipple, "and make this ol'shack look like it don't belong nowhere near something so fine and pretty. Guess it's too cold in Connect . . . up north for azaleas, huh?"

"No, not really. My mom grows them in her greenhouse." Drew's hand dropped down, unsnapping and slowly unzipping Johnny Ray's shorts. "And somehow the gardener helps her force them to bloom so we always have them spread around the house at Christmas."

"You're kidding?" Johnny Ray asked, lifting his buttocks for Drew to slip his shorts down.

He pulled Johnny Ray's legs up on the sofa, spreading them. He held the boy's legs up in the air, inspecting his smooth white buttocks.

"Lord, wouldn't I love to see azaleas blooming here at Christmastime."

Drew leaned backward, jerking his running shorts off before rolling forward, straddling Johnny Ray's waist. "It's so cold in this old pile of kindling during wintertime, we almost freeze. So I know blooming azaleas wouldn't last."

Johnny Ray's eyes never left the azaleas, and Drew was glad.

"Oh, I don't know," Drew said, rubbing his erection across Johnny Ray's chest. "You'd just have to keep them warm."

"We used to have propane for heat, but they came and hauled the tank away when that old man in there didn't pay the bill."

"What's your heat source?" Drew asked, inching himself toward Johnny Ray's chin.

"Burning wood in that old fireplace. Cook over it too, but that chimney'll be gone with the first good hurricane wind like we had last season."

Without retreating, Drew reached down for his backpack, feeling for the zipper pouch that held his supply of condoms bought especially for spring break.

"What color are your mama's azaleas?" Johnny Ray asked as Drew placed a rubber on the back of the sofa. "Are they pinkish purple like these?"

"No," Drew said, placing the head of his dick on Johnny Ray's cheek to turn his face to him. "White. They're all white."

Drew placed himself on the boy's lips, supporting himself on the sofa arm behind Johnny Ray's head. After several deep lunges between the boy's lips he withdrew and rolled him over on his stomach.

"I'll bet those white azaleas are real pretty, like snow at Christmas." With his knees, Drew spread the boy's legs, shoving his hips forward to find the moist, warm depths he knew were between the whiteness of the tan-framed flesh beneath him.

"I've never seen snow," Johnny Ray said, still staring at the rain and azaleas.

Drew tried to go easy at first, but he couldn't help going too deep, too quickly. But Johnny Ray didn't flinch so Drew kept on; his hands anchored down on the boy's shoulder blades.

"You're crying?" Drew asked, seeing a tear roll down the inside corner of his eye onto the sofa. His hips stopped. "Are you?"

"I always cry when he does me."

"Jesus, you mean your old man?" He nodded yes. "Christ."

Drew lowered his face to Johnny Ray's. "Would it help, do you think," he asked, his hips slowly moving again, "if I kissed you?"

"Maybe," he said, turning his face around to Drew.

But Drew remembered that a kiss would make what he was doing real. After this had happened before, Drew knew he wasn't gay because he never kissed the guys. Without a kiss it was just another way of getting off, another way of masturbating, albeit more pleasurable than his hand.

Johnny Ray faced the azaleas again, seemingly unfazed by Drew's second thoughts. Drew was almost done anyway so he continued without restraint, closing his eyes to make the boy's tears not exist. In his mind he saw the white featherbed and the boy's brown frame beneath him. He pounded harder between the boy's ass cheeks and exploded into the hot whiteness of the image.

Drew opened his eyes and sweat fell from the tip of his nose onto the boy's back.

He rolled off Johnny Ray, resting his head on the back of the sofa. He closed his eyes, waiting for his breathing to slow. He thought of how he would revise this story for his friends, changing Johnny Ray to Johnnie Mae and bragging to the guys about getting some Georgia Peach pussy before he ever got to Fort Lauderdale.

Johnny Ray stood, pulling up his shorts. He gently lowered his T-shirt down over his chest as if it were a delicate veil. He leaned against a porch post, picked an azalea bud and peeled back the tight petals.

"Sometimes, you just hafta make things happen, don't you Drew?" He put the now open flower in his hair, above his ear, and smiled down at Drew with fresh, unsettling confidence.

Johnny Ray's cold blue eyes froze on Drew when the phone rang.

"You said you didn't have a phone," he said, sitting upright.

"I lied."

"Why?"

"I had to keep you here until Mr. Lonnie could got out here."

"Who is he?" Drew asked, standing.

"Mr. Lonnie Tankersley, the Sheriff."

Hairs prickled up Drew's arm and along the nape of his neck. He looked at Johnny Ray's chest, rising and falling rapidly.

He cried out, tears streaming down his flushed cheeks. "I called the sheriff when I saw you up yonder on the road. I hung up from tellin 'em and then ran out here to wave you down."

"Wait, now. Just what the hell's going on here?"

"I said to myself—"the phone rang for the fourth time—"I said Johnny Ray, ain't no reason why you hafta take blame for it. You been hurt enough. I'm a good Christian boy and I just figure God sent you to me, stranger outa nowhere, sent to bear this burden for me." They both listened when the phone stopped ringing.

"What burden?" Drew asked, looking down at the blood seeping through Johnny Ray's bandaged hand. "Where's your father?" He hid his injured hand behind him.

"He's lying in there on the floor just like I told you." He backed away when Drew stepped toward the front door.

Drew blinked rapidly, looking down at the floor before the door. "Okay, now I'm going to try to figure this out. So Johnny Ray, just tell me what is . . ."

"He's lying in there with a butcher knife clean through his heart." He held his head high. "And I put it there, right where I wanted it to be, just like I'd dreamed of doing since I was twelve, the first time it happened."

"Oh, shit," Drew reached for his backpack. "Oh, man. I'm getting my ass out of here."

"Fine . . . that's fine. It'd look better anyhow for him to catch you running. He should be along anytime now 'cause I called him soon as I saw you up on the road." He stepped back further. "I told the sheriff you killed my pa when he woke up and found you messing with me."

"Christ," Drew said, panting, holding his suddenly light head in his hands. "You didn't? You ignorant redneck faggot. You set me up."

He nodded yes and burst into tears again when he looked at his hand, fidgeting with the bandage. "I cut it when the knife slipped, guess I hit his breastbone."

"Oh, shit," Drew blinked, breathing heavily through his mouth. "Oh, man. Oh, God."

He knew he should grab his bag and run, but first he wanted to see the body. With his outer palms, so as not to leave fingerprints, he turned the doorknob until he heard the rusty lock loosen and click.

The arteries in his neck throbbed and his right leg began to shake uncontrollably. He shifted his weight to his left leg, kicking the door open with his unwieldy right. He gasped; throwing his arms up over his face as several pigeons flew out, their wings fanning his cheeks, brushing over the top of his head.

He turned to Johnny Ray, doubled over with laughter.

Drew looked inside at the stacks of bailed hay. A dozen or so pigeons flew up through the wide hole in the roof of the far side of the house where a kitchen chimney used to be. Wind had torn sheets of tin back to allow the birds their roost of exposed beams over the hay and stored farm equipment. A starving old mother birddog barked at Drew, eyeing him freely from where she stood on the back porch, for the back wall of the house had rotted and crumbled away.

"Shut up," Drew yelled, stomping his foot at the dog. "Get. Get away from here."

Johnny Ray continued to laugh hard as he pulled a large Saks Fifth Avenue canvas bag from behind the sofa.

Drew leaned back against the doorframe, open-mouthed, his mind working hard to sort out what had just happened to him.

"What? Tell me." The more he struggled for words the harder Johnny Ray laughed, holding his side, as he tried to pull things loose from the bag.

He held up a mobile phone, doubling over the sofa arm when Drew's eyes popped wide and his jaw dropped.

"Okay, there's not a body, you don't live here, and . . . " Johnny Ray was slipping on a pair of Italian leather sandals. "So who the hell are you?"

"John Paul Lastinger," he said, pulling a light brown suede vest up over his shoulders. "Just John Paul professionally."

"Tell me why . . . I mean, this is crazy."

"I'm an actor."

"You cried . . . "

"And a damned good one, huh?" He perched a pair of tortoise-shell sunglasses atop his head. "Regulation Hollywood issue shades, as if you need any more proof of my profession."

"Listen you queer sonofabitch," jabbing his forefinger through the air at him Drew yelled, "I'm getting really pissed. You'd better start talking."

"Okay, I am an actor." He sat on the sofa arm. "I work out of Atlanta mostly, but I got a small speaking role in a movie being shot in Orlando. I came down early to spend a few days visiting family, Uncle Johnny Ray, in Waycross. I was taking the back roads to I-95 when my car broke down. My convertible top wouldn't come up so I couldn't just sit there in the rain. I called Triple-A from the mobile and told them I was walking back to this shack I remembered passing."

"Your hand?"

"I pinched it trying to get the top up." He grinned. "Now that was genius, the way I worked that into my improvisation, wasn't it?"

"Improvisation? Why? Why did you do this?"

"Well, I truly had not planned for it to go this far, until I saw what a prick you are; the way you cut your eyes at me so condescendingly, assuming I was trash, or that poor equaled trash. Being only a generation away from a real Johnny Ray, sans the incest, I just couldn't help myself. I simply played to every stupid thing you said or did, just like in improv classes. My coach would be damned proud."

"Oh, I don't know. I think your 'Daisy Mae' was a little over the top."

"Well, sugar, your Connecticut Yankee fool was just about perfect."

Drew grabbed Johnny Ray's arm, yanking him back as he tried to pass by. "I ought to . . ."

"What?" Slowly, he turned his face to Drew. "You ought to what? Hit me? Slap me around a little bit? If you do, honey, just remember one thing . . . I can improvise to anything you try."

Seething through gritted teeth, he tightened his grip and jerked down on Johnny Ray's arm again.

"Careful . . . " He stared Drew down.

He released Johnny Ray and stepped backward. "You haven't done anything to me," Drew said softly.

Then he yelled, blinking through watery eyes, "I did you. I nailed you. I screwed your faggoty ass to that sofa."

"Oh, really? Did you? Well, Drew darling, I guess that is just a matter of . . . perception, isn't it? I mean, after all, you're the one here who seems to be sore and bleeding."

He pulled the canvas bag over his shoulder and stepped toward Drew. "Trust me, you arrogant little preppy shit, you didn't do a fucking thing to me that I didn't want you to do. It was my scene."

Before Drew's fist could reach his face, Johnny Ray had kneed him in the groin. "See, sweetie," he said, watching him double, fold, and fall to his knees, "I told you, I play off what my fellow actor gives me. And if you want to take this trite little scene further, I won't need any direction as to my motivation for kicking your pretty white teeth down your throat."

Drew pulled himself up onto the sofa edge. He sat quietly, crouched forward, rocking, and holding his crotch. John Paul lowered his sunglasses and pulled a cap from the Saks bag.

Johnny Ray's manner and attitude were completely gone, and now the last of him disappeared under an Atlanta Braves baseball cap. The ease of it left Drew with an eerie sense of loss.

"Oh, good," John Paul said, pulling the cap down further on his forehead. "I hear the wrecker."

The largest wrecker Drew had ever seen, bright red and shiny chrome, drove all the way up to the front steps. It was transporting a powder blue 1969 Mustang convertible.

"I would have given you a ride on down to Florida, if you'd been sweet, and maybe we could have improvised some more along the way, but as it is, well . . ."

"Why?" Drew asked meekly. "Just tell me . . . why?"

"Drew, I don't have time to explain life to you in a one-act play." He stooped, gently pulled Drew's hair back and kissed his forehead. "Poor baby, life is going to be rough for you if you don't learn some technique."

Standing on the bottom step, he held the bag over his head to block the rain. "Oh, by the way, you'd play better as an Andy than a Drew."

"What?"

"Bye-bye now."

John Paul Lastinger sat in the truck talking with the driver for some time. Drew feared he was telling the driver what he had done, or telling some version of the story to entertain the man. Finally they both laughed and the driver maneuvered the wrecker back from the house. John Paul waved and the driver blew the horn as they pulled away.

Drew was still sitting in the same position, staring unblinkingly, thinking, long after the sound of the wrecker had faded. He heard only the sound of the rain still pelting the tin roof, pigeons cooing, and blood throbbing through his hot wet ears.

Lying back on the sofa, Drew thought about how he might explain hitchhiking back to Connecticut without ever seeing Florida. But then he contemplated ways he might find John Paul in Orlando.

This is what loneliness feels like, he thought. He wished to be home. And Andy Lorillard wished he had kissed Johnny Ray Lastinger.

$\sim$$\mathfrak{C}$ 19   The Tattoo

Dayton Estes

June 22,1999

Dear Denny,

I am very seldom in Stanley County anymore, so if you want to contact me, you can write me at the above address.

I would very much like to hear from you, that you have a sponsor in prison and are working the steps. You gave me a great deal, the most precious thing you could, your body. But as much as I treasure the memories and the physical love you gave me, I would rather have had something more valuable, your heart and your love, and yourself free from drugs.

Enclosed is $15, not much, just enough to buy three joints, maybe. I wish you well, I will pray for you, and oftentimes I will think of you and that last Sunday night we spent together. And sometimes, even, I will think how much you have meant to me. I love you.

Alex

APRIL 1995

"What's going on?" Denny's voice greeted me cheerfully from my telephone receiver.

"Hi, Denny," I said. "Nothing really."

"How's about let's taking a little ride tonight?" Denny tended always to call at the most inconvenient times. It was almost 10 p.m. on Saturday evening, and I was just about to go to bed.

"Where to?" Though I didn't need to ask, I knew where—Charlotte, and I knew why—to get cocaine.

Denny had been out on bail for almost two months. I had paid his bail, $267. He had just learned he would most likely have to go to prison again because he was up against the "Habitual Felons Law," that is, under this law conviction of three or more felonies in North

Carolina results in a lengthy and mandatory prison term. Those charges against Denny, and more, were pending, and that is precisely what the District Attorney had intended to press for, a long sentence without parole. His trial was set for Monday.

"Alex, I need to go. This is the last time, I promise. I won't be asking you again," he laughed with gallows humor, "anytime soon." I didn't want to go and I did want to go. I got jonesy and began to tremble in anticipation. I knew he was going back to prison in a couple of days, and I was hoping he would and hoping he wouldn't be reincarcerated. I was afraid for him and for me on these "trips," but was myself as jonesy for sex, for him, as any drug addict would be upon seeing a drug dealer after a short bit of clean time. Just thinking about Denny after he would take that first blast was enough to get me aroused. "I can't have no sex with you unless I have the shit to help me. I ain't no queer."

"You gonna make love to me?" he would then ask on the way to getting tweaked, pronouncing each syllable carefully, as if reading an unfamiliar text with difficult words. And I knew what he was going to want to do unless he happened to think about a woman or women. If the thought of a woman he knew crossed his mind, however, or if we happened to pass by a trailer park or house where he knew some girl or woman lived who did dope, he would want to go there and get a piece of ass. The night would be wasted for me.

"You gonna make me feel good? You said you was the expert in sex." He would say this mockingly. And I wanted him so much. Trouble was, I loved the rascal. I had first met him at an AA meeting. He came in a little late, beautiful and cocky. His mother was full Cherokee, and he inherited from her his good looks, his sharp features, dark skin, very little body hair.

He and his buddy sat down. Dennis, I found out later, was his name, but he went by Denny. I couldn't take my eyes off him. His fingers kept moving playfully up and down his right thigh, fingering the ragged edge of his cut-off jeans, as he appeared to concentrate on every word the speaker said. I realized right then and there I never needed anybody else, nor ever wanted anybody else. Nine years later, I still feel that way, but a lot of water has flowed under the bridge since that sultry September night when we first met, or rather when I made it a priority item to get to know him.

"Turn left here." That signaled the end for me tonight. "I'll tell you when to stop," he ordered, and sucked again on the stem of the makeshift pipe, held the smoke. After hooking up, he had told me to stop at the nearest supermarket, in fact, the same one in which he had been arrested some months before for trying to cash a bad check. When he got clean in the local jail, a forced rehab, so to speak, he had asked me to go to the food market and see the manager and ask if anything could be done to rectify his "mishap." The day manager, not being the one on duty when he attempted to cash the check, was pleasantly naïve about such things, and I had left with a lot of goodwill, but no hope of success.

As a matter of fact, both Denny and I had been naïve about the whole matter, thinking that by paying off his forged checks, we could somehow or other erase the charges against him and thereby do away with the crimes he had committed. The week before, I had even called the District Attorney, "Call me Eric—"

"Mr. Heller, I was wondering—"

"Call me Eric!" A little confused, I complied with the demand in his voice.

"Uh . . . Eric," I stumbled, "is there anyway we can get the charges reduced for Dennis Priest? I'm his sponsor, and I've sort of been looking after him for a couple of years. I think he shows promise of—"

"Oh, yes, he's up on drug charges. Are you in NA?"

"No, I'm an alcoholic and active in Alcoholics Anonymous, but I have been his sponsor over a year. He has trouble with alcohol, too."

"Well, I would like to help you, but I make it a practice not to talk with family. Yes, I know you say you are his sponsor. . . . If I hadn't already signed the indictment . . . "

"Is there any way to get the charges reduced, Mr. Heller?"

"Call me Eric," automatic correction, the tone of voice indicated irritation. "No, as I said, I make it a practice of not changing my mind after I have put my name on a document. Now, if you had called yesterday. . . . No, I'm afraid the charges stand. You see I make it a practice . . . " he droned on.

Denny now dashed into the food store. Only a few cars were parked in the lot and the store remained open all night. He was gone about ten minutes, and I shuddered to think he might be repeating the petty crime. But finally he returned, tore a cheap metal pen apart so he could use the stem. He carefully stuffed the stem with plain steel wool which he had also purchased, placed a rock on the wire, and tamped it as gently as a seasoned pipe smoker, lit the rock with a cigarette lighter, a miniature flame thrower. What smoke there was swirled out the window, but I opened the sun-roof for good measure. I found that I liked the chemicallike aroma, "a mild, sweet plastic," I thought.

He was looking for a certain trailer where he claimed he had once visited a girl. He craned his neck out of the window of the car, "Here it is. Give her a rock, and she'll fuck. Drive in the driveway, yeah, on around to the back in front of the woods." I obeyed. He got out of the car and gently closed the door, went up to the door of the dark trailer and rapped on the door.

She was not to be found, but just then another girl's voice started calling to him softly from a dark pine grove next door. "Over here, over here. Please come here. What you got?"

"I'll be right back." His voice was slurred, and he was beginning to stutter from the effects of the coke. He disappeared into a house surrounded by the pine trees. I remained behind the wheel, tense and hoping that he would soon return, but despairing of being able to spend any time with him tonight. And frankly, I just wanted to go home. But I couldn't.

"He says for you to come in," a soft voice suddenly whispered through the right front window he had left partly open. The late winter night was cold and still, but I hadn't heard the girl leave the house and approach the car. "It's just me and my girlfriend inside." I got out and walked over to the door of the white frame house in the pines, entered through the kitchen into a sitting room. The small apartment seemed cold, but wasn't. A Kero-Sun heater had apparently run out of fuel and stood there darkly reminding me that it was cold and damp outside. The sparse furnishings indicated that the occupants were not fully settled into their new apartment. I later discovered that the two lovers were crack-heads and had begun to sell off their valuable antique furniture to buy dope. Apparently, at least one (if not both) of the girls had come from a rather well-to-do-family, judging from the heirlooms still unsold.

Denny said in a stage whisper, "They're two lesbians. I'm gonna get me a piece of ass from one of them, maybe both." The two girls were already so spaced out that they didn't hear, and even if they had, they wouldn't have cared.

"Let's go," I begged.

"In a minute. Give me ten minutes and we'll leave. Here, take this money," and he gave me $20, which Debbie, the larger one of the girls, had shelled out of her billfold. He cut off a small chip of coke and stuffed it into the makeshift pipe, lit it, and she greedily grabbed and began to suck on it, holding the precious smoke in her lungs as long as she could. She coughed and exhaled. "That was a little small, wasn't it?" she asked gently.

"You got what you paid for," he answered gruffly.

"It just seemed a little small," she said with resignation and stared out into space.

"I'll get that ass," Denny sneered, the lines in his drawn face were very obviously reflecting the severe strain he was under. His lips were now forming words with difficulty, "She'll give it to me in just a minute or two."

"Can I watch?" I asked half facetiously, half seriously. I had learned to ask and say things to him which I couldn't share with anybody else, and a denial from him would not have fazed me in the least. I wanted to see his reaction when he came with a woman. I knew how he was with me, how he quivered slightly. I saw, instead, what I didn't want to see.

"Sure," he grinned, obviously flattered. "First, give me two minutes in the bedroom alone with her." In the meantime, Sharon, the smaller girl, had changed places with Debbie who was now in the bedroom and was taking the hit, having counted out another $20, which he handed me when she wasn't looking, and which I stuck in my pocket. She was sucking on the stem of the makeshift pipe as the light went out and I closed the door. I sat down on the couch and petted a bulldog lying there. He was very friendly; his name was Kyle. I could see through the door into the kitchen. Sharon began to check the window, going from window to window, peeking through the blinds. She was attractive in her own way, not glamorous, not pretty by the usual standards, but comely, a word you might use for a young novice in a religious order. And given another age and another country, she might well have spent her life as a bride of Christ, rather than being married to crack cocaine.

"What are you looking for?" I asked.

"Oh, you get paranoid when you do that stuff," she said in a resigned tone. "Don't you smoke?"

"No, I had to stop eight years ago," I said, realizing only after I had answered that I had misunderstood the question, but I let it go, and answered accordingly, "I had cancer and I had to stop." It didn't matter what I said, anyway.

I must have been tripping also by this time, because I automatically went into the kitchen and closed the blind over the back door, began to peek out through the slats into the cold grove of pine trees. A security light at the back of the house shone ominously through the pines and made the place look eerie, like in a movie, when you know the murderer is somewhere out there, hiding in the dark, just beyond the seam of light. I began to get suspicious and afraid the place was staked out, a possibility, so far obvious to everyone, it seemed, but me. "This is stupid," I thought. Then a pang of fear slashed into my chest that the narc stake-out at the food market parking lot had gotten my tag number when I had been waiting for Denny to make the pick-up in McDonald's.

Since he was standing trial on Monday, our plan tonight had been to take him to his sister's apartment as I usually did, then leave and go to an AA meeting, return in an hour and a half, and pick him up. Both of us could truthfully say that he had been to visit his sister and her son for the stated time, if we should be asked by a parole officer. He said it would take only a minute or so to expedite things, make the purchase.

I was to wait while he darted into McDonald's. The *quick purchase* took almost a full hour, and even though paranoid, I correctly concluded he had not been busted in the process of making the purchase. He had already blasted in the men's room. In the meantime, however, while I waited outside for Denny to hook up, a white four-door Toyota Tercel kept circling around the parking lot. Taking license numbers! My car, a blue Paseo, was easily recognizable, and I began to fabricate a story as to why I was in the parking lot.

All the narcs knew my car. After all, I had sponsored a guy, a former student, and he had been paroled but failed to get off drugs, took me for a couple of hundred bucks, and after he got busted, probably spilled everything to the cops to get favors. His old man was also a detective. Although this kid was now sitting out the rest of his sentence, what had he told?

All these fears from skirting along the edges of acceptable behavior for a sponsor now came back to haunt me. Maybe the dealer had a flat, I thought frantically, and that's why Denny was so slow in returning. But what if he, in reality, had not had a flat, and that was just a delay to get Denny's connection, the one giving him the ride from out of town to Charlotte? Did I realize the dealer was actually in AA and that's why Denny was so secretive so as to protect me from possible violence, on the precept that "What I didn't know wouldn't hurt me." I knew no one else in this city, or at least no one who counted in such operations. I thought I didn't, but did I? And was that something that moved out there on the edge of the yard under the pines, just beyond the light? I was frantic. I had to get out of that house right now, but I wanted Denny to go, too.

I opened the door to the bedroom, turned on the small lamp, but the light didn't come on. Denny said to turn on the ceiling light because the bulb in the smaller lamp had just burned out. They both looked up and squinted in the bright overhead light. He was sitting opposite Debbie, both were naked. Sitting opposite her, he had his hand between her legs, gently stroking her clitoris with his thumb and first two fingers of his right hand. I also knew, firsthand, so to speak, how gently he could stroke. I wanted to sniff his fingers; I wanted to sniff him all over.

"Go down on me," he had to force out the consonants, squeezed the vowels, and took a hit. "Give me, you promised me," Debbie begged. He just pointed to his flaccid penis.

She obeyed the gesture. She had very large teats and the nipples were as huge as those you see displayed in the girlie magazines. She was somewhat overweight, but it was not particularly noticeable and not objectionable. Debbie took Denny's penis in her mouth.

"Suck it hard," he ordered which really sounded like a plea. "Don't stop," he cried desperately.

"What a waste!" I thought. Since she was a lesbian, she could not possibly enjoy his body, neither the macho-man smell, nor the smoothness of his Native American skin, not the cinnamon-peppery smell of his pubic hairs, the pungency of his penis. Being a girl, she would not know to run her tongue around the corona of the glans to make him tremble as he came. She would not carefully insert her finger into his anus, feeling the sphincter muscle boldly resist the intrusion at first, and then finally open up to accept the unaccustomed massage of the prostate, as gently and lovingly and delicately as he had stroked her clitoris. She could not vicariously enjoy at all his orgasm and the resulting slight quiver which he tried unsuccessfully to hide.

He was, after all, macho, part Cherokee, part mean (at least he thought so). That's why, he insisted, he had collected such an array of tattoos in the course of the years he had spent in prison. All of them were in color except for one black and white one with the names of his three children and the wife he had lost and the word "love" that he recently acquired when he was still in the medium security prison.

During this last period, I had visited him every week as his AA sponsor, had sent him money, and we had talked about God, the Twelve-Step Program, and I had wanted to get in his pants so awfully bad. He did his Fifth Step with me, such as it was, and I had no doubt but that everything he told me about his former life was true. Trouble was, his life was so boring that I didn't wonder that he had taken to using drugs.

I probably knew him better than anyone else, and as I often made a point of telling him, I loved him more than anyone else ever had, except perhaps his mother. And I think I am the only one who ever really got him off, but he never admitted that. He genuinely enjoyed sex, and once I had been with him, I knew I loved him and he, me. Though when the drugs had worn off, he would blame me relentlessly, as well as the drugs, for "forcing" him to do unnatural acts.

Outside the bedroom, Sharon continued to peek through the blinds, but now she had moved into the bathroom. She had picked up his clothes from where he had dropped them when he took them off, and I took them from her and checked to see if they were all there. I raised his shorts to my face. No Denny smell yet, freshly washed. I took everything back to the bedroom.

"Let's go," I pleaded again and turned to Debbie as he gathered up the paraphernalia. "You're very pretty," I said.

"I don't feel very pretty right now," she said sadly, standing there naked and staring straight ahead. "I feel dirty."

I wanted to hate him for what he was doing to these girls, but I couldn't. I hated what the drugs had done to them all. I wanted to fuck him, but I knew I wouldn't tonight. He was not now very beautiful; his face was tortured into the caricature of a human being, his eyes vacant, devoid of soul. I had seen that face before and I was again frightened by what might lurk within. He struggled to speak and finally forced out, "Let me dress and we're out of here." I handed him his clothes.

He dressed very slowly, first looking at each piece of clothing as if it were something foreign, a totally unfamiliar piece of clothing from another age and culture. He seemed to be trying to figure out what each piece was and how to put it on. After what seemed to be an eternity, we left, got into the car and drove away from the two lesbians, the white frame house, and the eerie dark pine grove with the bright cold security light.

"You gonna make love to me like you promised," he whined. "I thought you was the expert and you cain't even seem to get me off," he taunted.

"Come on, you got it back there," I barked, resentment showing in my voice, as I kept rubbing his left thigh between his legs. He was dead now, as I knew he would be the rest of the night. I handed him the money he had taken from the girls for the dope and had passed on to me for safekeeping. "Nah," he began to count the money, "she won't no good."

Suddenly: "Let's go back," and he wouldn't hear otherwise. We argued, I pleaded, he insisted, and I turned around and took him back to stay the night and try as he might "to bust a nut," as he termed it.

I went home, thought about Denny and jerked off. I must have still been tripping because I was still anxious, if not still bordering on paranoia, about the coke purchase and the unmarked car (in my mind the white Toyota Tercel had become an "unmarked" car, driven by a narc agent who had taken down my license number as an important buyer from outside Charlotte). I wanted to get rid of Denny; he was bad news, but I found myself powerless, my life unmanageable as the first step of the AA Steps so clearly states about addiction to alcohol. The guy really turned me on, and on top of that, I really liked him, more than that even, loved him. "God, take control of my life before I mess things up so bad that there is no way out," I prayed. "I turn it all over to you; I can't handle it." But I continued to feel uneasy. God eventually answered my prayer, but in a way I would never have expected and much later.

The next morning, Denny called a little before ten. His voice was still somewhat shaky; he was beginning to come down. I went to Charlotte to pick him up. First, he had to "pay" a man some money—$80, to be exact. He, or rather we, picked up another stash from a trailer in the black ghetto, so that he "could entertain Lorraine" that night. As he termed it again, he was planning "to bust a nut," his last night of freedom.

I knew he couldn't have an erection without the crack, and even with the dope he couldn't sustain one long enough to have sexual intercourse with anyone. He would do well to manage a jerk-off session with the hurry-up final act of a blow-job, maybe, but that would be about all he could sustain, and that would also take continual huffing and puffing on the rock, as well as expert finger-work to get him off. No woman was going to go to that length for him "to bust a nut." He always claimed to come twice with every date except for last night, and that was because he was a little "afraid of the dyke." That, of course, meant he was afraid she might have some disease, so he didn't fuck her. In reality, however, he couldn't.

I dropped him off at his trailer, a mile from my house. He was going to crash in anticipation of Lorraine's visit that evening, and Lorraine did indeed come as she had promised. She apparently smoked a couple of joints to prepare for sex and to get off. At least, that's what he claimed later that night, but as it also turned out, "She was not really in the mood for sex, the bitch, and wasted my time to boot, and so I told her to leave." So that evening he phoned about nine. "You still want to make love to me, like you said?"

I had been that route before, and, "Yes, I do." Again I got jonesy.

At his trailer I waited in the living room while he *prepared.*

Preparing meant something like getting undressed, rubbing himself with "grease," as he termed the skin lotion, and, by all means, the only thing that would let him relieve the horniness, start the crack coke, which would maliciously bring on the intense desire as well as zap his ability to carry through.

He was greased all over when I entered. He was beautiful with his thin lithe body and coal-black hair, but he looked like the laborer that he was. His legs were a little too long for his torso. His feet, already covered with globs of skin lotion, were heavily calloused. I gently rubbed the coconut lotion into his feet, made my way up his legs, his thighs, cupped his scrotum, and then I bathed his pubic hair in spittle. He liked wetness.

He shivered as I rubbed sensitive areas on his stomach and he cried out to be sucked. I took the flaccid penis into my mouth and vigorously ran my tongue around the glans and the tip of the urethra until he had a half-hard. Then I ran my fist up and down his soft slippery shaft, over the corona and the glans until he began to cry out, "Don't stop; don't stop; please, don't stop."

With the second and third fingers of my left hand, I delicately entered his anus. His sphincter provided no opposition to my friendly entry, but kept teasing and grabbing my fingers as he wiggled like a young girl, experiencing the joy of being finger-fucked for the first time. He grabbed his penis and I saw the ejaculate escape through his fingers as he jerked. "Take it; take it; swallow it," he pleaded. I obeyed and got a mouthful of coconut skin cream, instead.

He couldn't just relax, lie there for a while, touch, be touched, make love without sex and, finally, rest. The dope kept him going. He would get up, run to the door, peek out through the towel he had hanging over the small window, check all the shades to see whether or not somebody from outside was peeping in, and then he would return to the bed, desperate, trying in vain to masturbate his soft penis. He would want me to play with his ass and fuck him. He thought he would like that, but I couldn't have raised a hard in that melee anyway, he so intimidated me with his confused and insane movements and disjointed thoughts and paranoia.

Finally, I became equally as confused and insane and paranoid as he was. I got up and likewise began to check the windows, pulling back the shades a little to look outside, just as I had done at Debbie and Sharon's house. My only thought was to get out of there after two or three hours of his sucking on the pipe and my sucking on his dick.

And then suddenly, as if he just simply gave up, "Alex," he groaned, "suck me again."

And I did. By this time he was standing up again, sucking on the stem of the metal pencil he had used all night, taking one hit after the other. Smoke and the sweet smell of burning plastic and sex and coconut lotion filled the air.

Finally, after a long half hour, his body gave in and he came, not much, but a drop or so. I tasted the semen; it was acrid. He bent down to whisper in my ear, "Alex, stay with me tonight."

That was when I saw the tattoo on the inside of his left arm, minutely drawn by an amateur, not a prison professional. It read "Alex," and around it had been sketched a crude heart.

Apparently, he had done it himself while he was in prison this last time, but the tattoo indicated that I meant something to him, for I now shared a place with Julie, his ex-wife, his three children, and mother.

He made his final crash and I held him throughout the night. He couldn't do anything except let himself be held. He was the sweetest person I have ever known and the first and only person I have ever loved.

The next day, Monday, he appeared in court to be tried on the three felony charges. It wasn't necessary to prove the charges; they were clear and he didn't appeal. He was sentenced to seventy-two months in prison without possibility of parole.

August 15, 1999

Alex,

I need your help after I get out. I'm not saying handouts. I mean advice, guidance, and friendship. The love you've shown me has truly turned my thinking around 360 degrees. I never thought that a man's love could ever be as strong as the love you have given me these past four years.

The first few years I didn't quite know how to take you. Plus I was out to get as much as I could to support my habit. You showed me sides of myself I didn't know existed and I will always love you.

Denny

20   No Way!

Jeffrey Jasper

Brian was the only boy I knew who had a queen-sized bed.

"NO WAY!"

Mine, like every other boy's bed I had ever seen, was a twin. We used to prop up sheets and make a tent on his bed, talking late at night with flashlights on until his mom would softly tell us it was time to go to bed.

"We are in bed!"

"You know what I mean . . ."

Brian's mom actually knocked on his door and waited for a response before she would enter.

"NO WAY!"

Every boy I knew, including myself, had a mother who would just barge right in or even demand the door be left open. Brian also had a lock on his door; another luxury only the adults in my life enjoyed. And he was allowed to eat dinner in his room alone.

"COOL!"

He even had a stereo, not a small box—but a full stereo, in his room. The boy got everything he wanted. I envied Brian and spent as much time as I could with him.

At the time I was in 4-H, raising pigeons that I showed at the county fairs in our area. I had many different breeds and named each bird. They fascinated me and gave me a sense of pride. Their successes at shows made me glow. "Yes sir, that is my Trumpeter that won first place. No, sir, he isn't for sale."

If I wasn't a winner, I could at least help these pretty creatures become winners. They were so beautiful, especially when I let them fly free. It was such a thrill to watch them return to me.

Life then was waking up, feeding the pigeons, eating, getting ready for school, sticking my tongue out at my sister (who always responded with a raised middle finger), and waiting for Mom to drive me to school.

After school, I would be back outside with the pigeons, cleaning the old toolshed I had converted into a home for them, talking to each bird and dreaming of the day I would work at the San Diego Zoo. I would also be anxiously waiting for Brian to call.

"Your mom bought you what? NO WAY! I'll be right over!"

Brian was a year and a half older and one grade above me, so we never saw each other during classes. He was about a foot taller than me and had about thirty pounds of tight muscle that I wished I had on my scrawny frame. He seemed to me to be a real great guy, not just a "boy" like me. His hair was short, dark, and straight, with no part and his skin was clear and pale. He also had the bright blue eyes of an alpha male who went after whatever he wanted because nothing was denied him.

I, in comparison, was a case study in denial. I was skinny with wavy blond hair, tan skin, and hazel eyes. Who ever heard of hazel eyes? I remembered the first time someone told me my eyes were hazel. I hoped there was a cure. My mom had brown eyes and my dad had green eyes. I guess I fell right into the hereditary middle.

I felt so average; I wasn't tall enough or buff enough; or anything. Then some weirdo would come up and say, "You look exotic" and make me feel like a total freak. How embarrassing. I wanted to tell them, "I know. I have hazel eyes and my mom won't take me to the doctor for it, so could you please just shut up?"

Brian usually called me right after school. I would jump up on my bike and hang out at his house until dark. I always rode my bike back to my house thinking of how cool he was. I wished my mom belonged to a country club and drove a Mercedes and bought me and my friends season passes to Disney World.

On Fridays, I was allowed to stay overnight, but I had to wake up early enough to get back and take care of the birds the next morning. Brian didn't understand. He could sleep as late as he wanted.

One Friday, Brian's parents left to golf for the whole weekend. They were actually letting Brian stay by himself while they were gone.

"NO WAY!"

It was incomprehensible to me. We agreed that I would say absolutely nothing about this fact to my mom. It was our secret.

"Cool!"

What do two boys do when there are no parents around for them to avoid or tell them what to do? We watched TV, blasted the stereo, played Brian's new video game, and biked to Burger King with the money his mom left for food. Finally, we pitched a tent on his bed, turned out the lights and laughed and joked by flashlight, like we always did.

At one point, Brian's face lit up and became a giant smirk. He leaned toward me and whispered, "Wait right here. I have something to show you." He crawled out of the bed and went into another room. When he returned he was carrying a stack of magazines.

"NO WAY!" Brian had *Playboy*s!

Brian's dad apparently had a stash of porn and Brian's mom and dad had a thief. He displayed the loot with the subtlety of a pirate showing off purloined doubloons.

"Look at her tits! Did you see that one's pussy?"

Page after page of something I tried to avoid seeing at all costs was literally unfolded in front of me by a gleaming boy who was clearly headed for trouble.

I had never seen any nonfamily member naked before. And I had no desire to see them—even with their clothes on. But these women looked nothing like my family. My mom never yelled for me to bring her a rum and Coke, lying in a bathtub filled with rose petals. My sister's hair was always matted over her forehead when she dripped out of the pool. My grandma . . . well, I'll let Grandma rest in peace. The point is, these women didn't look real to me. These were like women on TV or in the movies or advertisements. These were bad women. And what we were doing was bad. Brian laughed at me when I told him so.

I don't recall what issue it was or even who was on the cover, but tucked into the back of one magazine, where less perceptive eyes might have missed it, was the turning point in my Florida boyhood: a naked man.

"NO WAY!"

Brian and I were riveted. Somehow all those ruby red lips and diamond-shaped mounds were forgotten as we feasted our eyes on this new, dazzling, and more forbidden jewel. It didn't hurt that he was handsome and hung like a horse.

We couldn't speak and where before the pages were flying, now the magazine stood telling still. After a few awkward moments, we thumbed through the rest and quietly hoped like hell that Mr. Hefner would bless us with another naked man. He did not. There were more Christis and Barbis and Debbies and even one Wanda, but no more dicks.

We quietly returned the booty to its rightful owner and were at a loss for what to do next. It was only eleven thirty and we wanted to stay up as late as possible since we could this one night. We decided to go swimming. The boy who had everything, of course, had a pool.

I was in jeans and a T-shirt, which was exactly what I had planned to wear the next day. Brian offered me a pair of trunks. He was much bigger than I was, at least a twenty-nine. They barely stayed on my bony hips. It was okay, though, because it was just us.

Shorts that barely stay on dry do not fit any snugger when they are drenched. While Brian could jump and lunge around and climb up the ladder to slide into the water, I was stuck wading slowly in the shallow end holding onto the trunks trying to cover up my little secret: I had a boner.

Ever the perceptive one, Brian noticed a weakness and decided to attack. I was usually fast, but tonight I had more than one handicap. He easily overtook me and held me down, then hoisted me up and caught my trunks at the side and yanked for all he was worth. Dash, Brian's Jack Russell, had nothing on Brian's tenacity. The boy would not let up. His pulling was starting to rip the shorts and cut into my side.

There comes a time in every young man's life when his dignity is worth more than a friendship. "STOP IT!" I demanded.

"Why? You don't want me to see your boner?"

I was horrified.

"Shut up and stop it! I'm going home!'

I furiously brought myself to the pool's edge and was getting out when Brian said "I'm sorry. Please don't go. Here . . ."

He jumped out of the pool and got me a towel and put on his puppy dog face. "Please don't be mad. I'm sorry, Chris."

I crept out of the pool and wrapped the towel around what was left of the trunks and did something regrettable: I started to cry. So much for dignity.

Brian sat next to me and put his big wet arms around me. He apologized and apologized and apologized, then quietly said, "Your hair curls nicely."

"WHAT! Shut up, Brian!"

"Really, Chris. I think it's kind of cool the way the hair under your belly button curls up."

"STOP IT!" I couldn't believe he would make fun of me like that.

"No, I mean it. It's like that guy's in the magazine. Mine is dark and straight, like on my head, but yours is light and curly. I like it."

I looked up from my silly head-on-knees crying position and over at his crotch.

He smiled and pulled his shorts down far enough to reasonably demonstrate his observation. Then he started touching the little bit of hair I had down there.

NO WAY! I couldn't move.

"See, it's nice and it's soft, too."

"Let me see yours again," I said.

"Okay. But let's go inside under the tent." We both got up and dried off a bit and went to his room and changed into our briefs and grabbed the flashlights.

"I'm sorry I hurt you, Chris."

"It's OK. I was just embarrassed and you wouldn't quit."

"I know. I'm sorry. Friends—right?" His smirk was a mile wide.

"Friends," I responded.

"Cool!"

We smiled and looked at the tents that had grown under the tent we had created on his bed. Each of us had a big bulge in our little white briefs.

"Yours is big." he said.

"So is yours."

"Not as big as yours," he exclaimed with his focus directed between my legs. "Let's see."

Of course, Brian made the first move, but then he was accustomed to getting whatever he wanted. Tonight he wanted me. Who was I to deny him? Off came the briefs and out popped destiny. We stood side by side to compare, then we went face to face. His was a little longer and mine was a little thicker. We decide to call it even and smiled at each other.

How Brian had any idea of how to proceed, I don't know. But I thank him to this day for leaning forward and putting his mouth over my dick.

"WOW! NO WAY!"

It was incredible. And I wanted to try it too. He willingly obliged. After that we sixty-nined, but had to stop because it made us laugh too hard to "sixty-nine." He sucked on my balls, but it tickled so much that he had to quit.

Then, he told me to turn off my flashlight and in the dark asked me "What do you want to do to me?"

The question was lost on someone who only a few minutes ago had discovered oral sex and then only because it was being performed on him. "I don't know. Do you want me to suck on yours again?" I meekly offered.

"Sure, but isn't there anything else you want to do that we haven't tried yet?"

"Um . . . no, I don't think so." I responded, a bit confused.

"Nothing?"

"Brian, I haven't done any of this before. I'll do whatever you want me to."

I could hear him moving around on the bed and then heard him say "Come here. Get on top of me."

I truly had no idea what was going to happen or what was expected of me. I moved toward his voice and could tell that Brian was now lying on his stomach and his legs were spread far apart.

NO WAY! Brian was a whore!

I got on top of him. He spit on his hand and rubbed it over my dick. "That feels good," I told him.

"Just wait," he replied.

"What?"

He didn't answer, he just positioned my spit-lubed dick between his cheeks and told me to press it into him.

"OW!" He yelled.

"What? Are you okay?" I just knew I was doing this all wrong.

"Yeah, I'm fine. Keep going in."

"Okay . . ." I said, still worrying that I didn't know how to do what he wanted me to. He said "OW!" quite a few times but always insisted that I not stop.

After a few minutes he said, "Start pumping into me" and the "OW's" were replaced by a rapid succession of "oh yeah!"s Brian started to buck back into me faster than I was pumping into him.

"NO WAY!"

Even face down in bed, spread-eagled, getting humped, Brian had to have it his way. No wonder he liked Burger King so much. We stayed up late that night. After our first blows, we were so excited we did it again. Each orgasm made me wonder why people didn't do this all the time. Why was anyone watching TV or jogging when they could be doing this? And why—OH WHY—didn't anyone tell me about this sooner?

After the fourth time, Brian told me to stop because it hurt.

"What! Really?" I couldn't believe what I was hearing.

"Yeah. I'm going to go to the bathroom. He walked off and after what seemed an eternity, climbed back into the bed saying, "Let's go to sleep."

I was so disappointed. I didn't want to go to sleep, but I managed to somehow.

I woke up the next morning a new person. I also woke up with Brian's mouth on my dick. The little boy who got everything he wanted was now taking what he wanted and not even asking.

I looked at the clock and realized I was running late. My mom was going to be mad and the birds were going to be hungry. While Brian blew me, I reflected on the night before. It was a night of many firsts. I couldn't possibly comprehend everything that had happened or begin to understand its relevance at that moment. I was unusually contemplative . . . and then I shot into his mouth.

He smiled and said, "My turn!"

I smiled back and said, "I have to go."

"NO WAY!"

Our friendship had become so close that now Brian was taking on my vocabulary.

It was a beautiful, sunny Florida day when I biked home realizing that I had something very valuable to the little boy who had everything—something his mom couldn't just buy him. That afternoon I became aware of an asset I never knew I had and it made me feel kind of proud and, for the first time, a little more confident.

I didn't bother waiting for Brian to call me that afternoon.

"You want to do what? NO WAY, Chris! I'll wait right here!"

❧ 21

Pueraria lobata

Carlos Dews

As he walked beside the dark residential street toward the man's house, Dewey continued to obsess over what he risked, how much he had to lose, how embarrassed he would be, how difficult this would be to explain. That is, if he were caught. Although nothing he had on him was illegal, he was parked on a public street, and was walking down a public sidewalk, when Dewey took that first step onto the cushion of the man's spring lawn, he knew he crossed a line—an invisible barrier that separated him from the life he led every day, the life others knew, and what he felt he must do now.

Dewey's rudimentary attempts at self-analysis back when he was an adolescent led him to the mistaken conclusion that he had discovered the cause of his homosexuality. Despite the fact that Dewey related this theory now as a joke to his faculty colleagues at dinner parties and had gotten great anecdotal mileage out of it for the past fifteen years, it still saddened him when he paused and realized that he had once been in search of an explanation for his own desire for other boys and men. The self-loathing so apparent in the desire for an external explanation—and perhaps then absolution—also made Dewey angry at the unaccepting world and family through which that boy—himself—had had to find his way.

As pathetic as it sounds, Dewey believed from the age of eleven until age seventeen that the cause for his homosexuality was the almost daily potent cocktail of preventative medicines his mother forced upon him: liquid Geritol vitamins, Correctol (the women's laxative), Fletcher's Castoria, Flintstones chewable vitamins, and pink Bayer's baby aspirin. This vitamin formula was concocted for the aged and around it there was always a hint of sexual restoration conflicting with the cartoon character children's vitamins; the pink pill laxatives with a sugary coating he shared with his mother juxtaposed with the foul tasting one given to him by the tablespoon and which evoked the image of an evil doctor Fletcher laughing madly in a dark factory, imagining the effect his potion had on the children forced to swallow it day after day.

Dewey thought that these medicines, lacking a motive for their contradictory, or at least unrelated symptoms and cures, had settled somewhere deep inside him and conspired to cause his homosexuality.

Dewey put the canvas bag under the edge of an azalea bush in a dark corner of Rocco's lawn, near the picket gate to the backyard. He began with the seeds—having planned each detail for weeks in advance he figured that by planting the seeds first, the roots second, and finally the cuttings that he would not risk stepping on the cuttings during his work. In fact he thought the subsequent passes over the yard and garden would, if anything, help pack the soil further over the seeds and newly buried roots.

This was not Dewey's first obsession, not by twenty years at least. There was the high school football coach, with whom Dewey had a tortured two-year, albeit fantasy, involvement. The closest he ever came to expressing his passion for the coach was a single-page letter. He pleaded for the coach's help in overcoming his attraction—of course Dewey secretly hoped that the coach would return his feelings and not want to absolve him of his desire. After typing the letter, Dewey burned the ribbon and threw the practically new typewriter off a bridge into the muddy river that ran just outside his small East Texas hometown. A few days later, in the middle of the night, Dewey left the letter in the coach's aluminum mailbox at the end of his country driveway. He called the coach at the high school fieldhouse two days later, just as the letter had promised, only to hear the coach say "No way," then hang up.

Then there was the man who owned a gym near the apartment Dewey rented as an undergraduate in Austin, Texas. Dewey called the gym and pretended to be a photographer from Dallas who had been contracted by *Playgirl* magazine to photograph men nominated by their co-workers and girlfriends as the sexiest small business owners in the United States. Through this guise, Dewey was able to have five hour-long conversations with the man before the bodybuilder finally decided that he would not agree to be photographed in the nude and asked Dewey not to call again.

After all his years of therapy and analysis, Jungian and Freudian, and countless additional hours of introspection, there were only three moments from his life that Dewey felt were in any way related to his mission on this night. Dewey was certain of the reality of the first of these defining moments that proved so crucial to his understanding of himself. From the smell of Dial deodorant soap lingering in the humid bathroom air to the sound and feel of the green and white cloth tape measure, he did not remember every detail, but a few remain painfully and confusingly clear. It happened when he was almost five years old, during the summer of 1968. His mother, busy preparing dinner after spending the day picking black-eyed peas in the heat of the East Texas sun, asked his father to make sure Dewey had a bath.

Dewey does not remember if the tape measure happened to be in the bathroom or if his father brought it in on purpose. Regardless of how it found its way there, Dewey remembers stepping out of the bathtub, awkward at being naked in front of his father who was standing at the lavatory with a towel around his waist. Dewey does not recall how his father approached the subject. He does remember his father asking him to sit on the seat of the toilet and he does remember his father parting the towel, flicking his hand to unroll the tape measure, placing the metal tab at the end of the tape measure against his body at the root of his dick, and while holding the tape against his body and his dick in one hand, extending the tape along the top of his dick to its tip. Making sure that Dewey could see the bold black numbers against the green measure, indicating the length of his shaft, his father then wrapped the tape around his dick, halfway between the purplish head and the cock's bushy root, to measure its circumference. With a wide grin on his face, he then gave the tape to Dewey. He knew what he was supposed to do. When Dewey was done with his own embarrassed fumbling attempt at measuring—for after all his numbers were unimportant, the point was clearly made—his daddy tried to assure him that someday, Dewey would grow to his father's impressive size.

Finally, his father dismissed him from the bathroom with a wink and a suggestion that they not share what had just happened with Dewey's mother. It would be their secret. Dewey realized only later the significance of this moment. Dewey knew this was only one of many lessons intended to teach him how to be a man of his father's type. A man who, like his father, like his grandfather, and like his father before him, defined his relationship to the world through his sexual facility and natural endowments. Talents and abilities no one, except for Father Time, could take away from them and for which no education or training was necessary. These men felt that what came naturally to them—sexual prowess—was their gift from God and that to decline this calling would leave them without life.

He removed the Ziploc bag filled with the seeds he ordered from an eccentric lady in central Georgia. He used a tool he had fashioned from half a toilet plunger handle and sharpened to a point to make small holes—one for each seed, approximately two inches deep—he had marked his tool with a piece of electrical tape to gauge the depth. He planted seeds approximately one foot apart—per the instructions he received with the seeds—across the lawn, around the edges of the beds of shrubs, throughout the yard and vegetable gardens, around the small outbuildings in Rocco's lawn, and especially near all vertical surfaces—hoping to maximize the plant's propensity for climbing.

This time all it took was a photograph in the newspaper. Dewey recognized it at the time too. He cut out the photo of the man and wrote next to it in his journal, "the beginning of an obsession—7/17/96." In the photo a dark-haired man, who wore only a pair of black nylon shorts and an armature of well-developed muscle, was demonstrating a piece of exercise equipment. A local inventor, hoping to make a fortune by selling it during the Atlanta Olympics, had given one of his machines to a gym to drum up business. The caption under the photo read "Rocco Tomba works out Tuesday on the Torso Flex Exerciser at Pensacola's Los Campeones Fitness Center. The workout machine will be on display at a pavilion near the Olympic Games beginning Friday."

After planting the seeds, Dewey retraced his route through the garden, planting the roots, and then the cuttings. He used a small sharp trowel to make slits in the dirt into which he dropped the two-inch pieces of root. He was reminded of the potatoes he was forced to help his daddy plant in their garden when he was a boy—his father's voice saying "be sure the eyes are up, the eyes are up" echoed in his ears still. He was especially careful in planting the cuttings; he did not want to leave any telltale signs that he had been there; to maximize the effect of what he was doing. He wanted it to appear natural. As he planted, he fantasized about what he imagined the vine would do. Like Jack and the beanstalk he wished that the vine might miraculously grow overnight to cover every square inch of Rocco's prized garden.

Dewey knew Rocco's telephone number and address within fifteen minutes of seeing the photo and reading the caption. He called the number and asked for Rocco when a man with a thick Southern accent answered the telephone. Dewey was surprised by the incongruity of the name and the voice. The name Rocco Tomba with the voice of some Bubba Johnson. He thought he must have reached the wrong party but his imagination immediately solved the problem. He imagined an Italian father and U.S. mother—a child born out of unorthodox passion—a military flyer on a UN passport here to train as a top gun during the Vietnam era. Like this, everything Dewey knew or felt about this Rocco could be divided into two categories—those things Dewey knew to be true—the mundane facts of Rocco's life—and those that called upon Dewey's powerful imagination. Dewey knew that Rocco lived in a nice older neighborhood near the center of town (Dewey's imagination explained the house as an inherited family home). Dewey knew that Rocco's lawn and garden were meticulously maintained and that Rocco did all the work himself. Dewey knew that Rocco owned a business selling militaria—caps, shirts, license plate covers, key chains, beer steins, all with the insignia of the branches of the U.S. military (Dewey's imagination conjured images of Rocco having sex with the military men who came into his shop). He knew Rocco traveled to air shows around the country pulling a trailer of his stock behind his pickup (Dewey fantasized about what happened in all those motel rooms along the way and wondered how

Rocco managed to maintain his lawn while traveling). And Rocco worked out at a gym called Los Campeones (Dewey fantasized about showers and locker rooms).

Suspended in the twilight between memory and dream, the second of Dewey's defining moments was the most unclear. It happened, or he dreamed it, when he was twelve years old. His grandmother was in a hospital in Houston, dying of cancer. His mother had traveled the three hours by car to be with her mother during her final hours. Dewey does not remember where his two older sisters were; perhaps they were there at home with Dewey and his father. The first night his mother was in Houston would be the first Dewey would be without his mother since her hysterectomy surgery, when Dewey was four years old. Dewey would sleep in his parents' king-sized bed with his father while his mother was away. This was not an unusual arrangement.

Dewey had slept with his parents for as long as he could remember. Since he was "getting too old for that" bedtime had become a struggle for the entire family. Dewey would be put to bed in his own bed only to cry and interrupt the early sleep of his parents and two sisters with a final "goodnight" followed soon after by another and another. The fact that Dewey still slept with his parents at age twelve was his family's current deepest, darkest secret. Dewey knew that the nightly threats by his parents to tell his teachers and classmates that he slept with them would not be carried out. This revelation would not just embarrass Dewey but would bring shame to the entire family.

So Dewey looked forward to bedtime that first night. He knew he would miss his mother but he looked forward to the peace of going to bed without the expected struggle. He would sleep securely that night.

Dewey knew his father's penis was large. Not only because of the experience of measuring and comparison from years before but because he had had on occasion seen it. And then there were the jokes Dewey's daddy exchanged with his male friends—Dewey remembered one clearly. While driving down the East Texas sand roads of his childhood—going to buy cattle feed in town or to retrieve a lost hound dog—Dewey, his father, and one of his father's male friend would on occasion have to stop in the road to "take a piss" as they called it. It was almost expected for Dewey's father, as he stood next to the bed of his pickup, back by one of the rear tires, to pretend to have difficulty getting his cock back in his pants after pissing. He would put his hands around an imaginary cock the size of a fire hose and slam his hands against the bed of the truck while saying, "I'll be done in a minute, as soon as I can get this big meat shook off and put back in my pants."

During this night without his mother in the bed, Dewey woke after what felt like hours of sleep. It was still dark outside. He was sleeping on his left side facing his mother's window—or at least the window on her side of the bed. He felt his father's warm hairy chest and stomach against his back. His father's right arm was draped over Dewey's body and rested in front of Dewey. This was not an unusual position. Dewey usually slept between his parents and often went to sleep within his father's embrace.

Dewey always made a point to describe this sense of comfort—in his parents' bed—to all of his therapists. As he woke up, Dewey realized that his father's erect penis was between his own legs. The cock was as hard as a section of pipe and protruded through Dewey's thighs, halfway between his knees and his own crotch. This had never happened before. Dewey wondered if his father was mistaking him for his absent mother. Was Dewey's father also awake? Dewey did not know what to do. At this point in his thought process, Dewey realized his own arousal. Was this wrong? Dewey does not recall, now as an adult, what eventually happened or even if this moment occurred. Was it simply a fleeting dream? Or was it real and Dewey simply drifted back to sleep without waking his father or acknowledging what had happened?

The most lasting impression of this night for Dewey, the one he told about to all his therapists and analysts, was of the intense sense of arousal combined with equally intense feelings of comfort and uncertainty. All orgasms Dewey since experienced, all his erotic experience since, all desire, was only an approximation of this moment. An unattainable ideal was born.

Dewey continued to sleep with his parents until Christmas vacation of 1976—the Christmas of his new stereo and his Dolly Parton eight-track—when, with a friend during a sleepover, he experienced his first orgasm. The secret joy he discovered with this friend was finally strong enough to break the spell of his parents' bed. And although the guilt-ridden pleasure he found with his teen-age friends and with himself never provided the ultimate sense of security he had found with his parents, and although this new pleasure never approached the intensity he experienced that night alone in bed with his father, Dewey accepted the inevitability of his new maturity and the quest that had begun when he left behind his parents' bed.

Rocco's yard and garden bespoke a studied masculinity, perhaps a defensive type to counter the easily mounted charge of femininity associated with decorative gardening. Yet Rocco's masculine gardening was not of the same character as that of suburban husbands who toil for the sake of appearance only or because their wives goad them into the work. No. Rocco felt a bodily connection to the earth. He cultivated his small part of the earth for the same reasons he did not shave on the weekends and did not use deodorant unless there was a social necessity—he thought of his virility as of the earth. Of course, all of this was from Dewey's imagination. Dewey spent considerable time attempting to understand Rocco. When he was not able to discern fact, Dewey gladly, easily, provided imaginary detail. He felt the truth was most compelling—as long as it supported his fantasy—but was more than willing to turn a blind eye to anything that contradicted his desire.

Dewey tried many times to understand why he sometimes responded with such strength to certain men, always athletic, most often bodybuilders. Dewey even traced his interest in psychology to his quest for understanding of this desire and felt that all his colleagues had similar, secret, reasons for their careers. Arrest was the best word Dewey could conjure to describe the gut-wrenching feeling he had when he saw someone who provoked such a powerful response—arrest, arrested development, cardiac arrest, arrest warrant. Dewey could never settle on whether he wanted to have such men, in every sense of the word, or to be one of them. He did know that this arresting response was made up of the most tortured, rapturous, ecstatic, and hate-filled emotions possible. When he experienced this response, Dewey felt he was held in a grip of his own devising, but from which he could not escape.

He knew it had nothing to do with the actual person inside the beautiful skin and behind the rock-hard muscles. He knew, also, how superficial his response was. Had he not in many of his classes admonished his students to see the humanity within each of their clients? He had even participated in marches in graduate school against pornography and its obvious objectification of women. Dewey knew, however, that his response to the man went much deeper than Rocco's appearance. His response must be traced inward, into Dewey himself.

It seemed such an appropriate discovery when Dewey realized, while watching the PBS documentary *The Amazing Story of Kudzu,* that this one plant could bridge the gap between his past and present, his place then and his place now. Dewey pursued information on kudzu with the same zeal he sought the same for Rocco. Bearing the scientific name *Pueraria lobata,* kudzu was brought to the United States by the Japanese government as a demonstration plant for the 1876 Centennial Exposition in Philadelphia. The vine with large leaves, long racemes, late-blooming reddish purple flowers, and flat, hairy seed pods can grow up to sixty feet in a single season. The huge root of the kudzu vine can grow to the size of a human body.

Dewey knew that the third piece of the puzzle of his psyche was a dream. During his first year at the University of Texas, Dewey began seeing a woman therapist—a lesbian hippie earth mother type—and early in his work with her he arrived at her office to tell of a dream he had the night before. It began with the point of view of the eyes of an adult surveying the landscape from high above the center of a vast flat valley—like the salt flats used for high-speed automobile record attempts—the point of view from above zooming in like a film shot from a camera mounted on a boom. Observable across the expanses of the valley—evenly spaced twenty paces or so apart—were small clutches of people. Upon closer inspection—and as his point of view drifted downward to land on one gathering in particular—Dewey realized that the clutches of people were made up of family groups—at least a mother, a father, and a child in each group. He recognized his own parents in one group as his point of view shifted again. He was no longer observing from above. He saw his parents looking down on him. His parents were on their knees on either side of him, looking down, and at first seemed to be comforting him. Dewey then realized that his child-self was naked—an unsoiled cotton diaper gaped on the ground near his mother's bent knees. He tried to make sense of the scene and thought that perhaps they hovered over him to shield him from the sun. Dewey knew at this point that he was looking out from his own eighteen-month-old eyes. He tipped his head down toward his feet in an attempt to figure out his situation. Then he saw the fire and the stick. With horror that shocked him out of his narrow view and propelled his consciousness upward and out of the child, Dewey realized that the parents—his parents—had impaled their son—him—on a spit; had lit a small fire beneath him and were admonishing him to keep still lest he make it more painful than it had to be and make it more difficult for them. Dewey's impression from the dream was perfectly clear: his parents were compelled to do what they had done—they didn't have any choice in the matter—were resigned to their task, were attempting to convince him of its inevitability, and were expected to provide both comfort and discipline. The final image of the dream that Dewey recalled to his therapist was seeing his mother, her pained face and trembling hand, spanking his bare child bottom just above where the stick had been inserted, sternly instructing him not to squirm. Dewey's point of view quickly withdrew from the scene as if it were a bird in flight. Dewey does not recall what his therapist said about the dream but he does remember an overwhelming sense of anger followed by an equal dose of pity toward his parents. A few years after having this dream he tried to capture it in a poem—largely unsuccessful he recalls. He only remembers the first line: "I dreamed of a Dali-esque landscape."

In the 1920s, Florida nursery operators Charles and Lillie Pleas of Chipley, Florida, sold the plant from their Glen Arden Nursery to customers all over the United States. A historical marker in downtown Chipley still proclaims "Kudzu Developed Here." Used for alcohol withdrawal support and as a natural support for obsessive-compulsive disorder, the large amount of isoflavones in kudzu aid in improving the blood flow through coronary arteries as well.

Dewey's confusion over whether he wanted to be Rocco or to have him was especially troubling to him. If he worked on his body to take on the appearance of Rocco, he knew he could not change himself on the inside. He has worked on the inside for years to no avail. The outside, in fact, was the easy part. The inside was the problem. Dewey knew himself too well and knew that it was impossible for him to be like Rocco. He hated himself too much to change for the better. This is where he saw his own connection to Jeffrey Dahmer.

Dewey always felt a strange identification with Dahmer. He felt that they could understand each other. He even cried when he heard that Dahmer had been killed in prison; and although Dewey admitted how physically attractive he found Dahmer, and nothing scared him more than imagining himself as one of Dahmer's victims; he could easily understand Dahmer's motivation.

He remembers mentioning this empathy for Dahmer to his students in class. They were discussing Franz Kafka's "The Hunger Artist,"—Dewey always read short stories with his psychology students, remembering what Freud said about getting his ideas from the poets. Dewey made the remark to his students before he realized how it might be misinterpreted. Perhaps he had revealed too much to them. The class was discussing the psychological aspects of eating—internalization, consumption, subsummation, annihilation, incorporation. He suggested to his students that Dahmer's fear of rejection and abandonment had led to his desire to become one with his victims— to consume them. Dewey felt his connection to Dahmer was through their shared confusion between having and becoming. Dewey's students groaned when he punned in his analysis of Dahmer's motivation—"You are what you eat." Unfortunately he took it one step further reminding his students of the sick joke: "Did you hear what Jeffrey Dahmer said to Lorena Bobbitt?" . . . "You gonna eat that?"

Dewey's imagination failed him when he tried to imagine a sexual encounter with Rocco. His mind rushed ahead. He could manage a few vivid images but not a complete narrative—he failed to fix an image of the man's body in his mind—like the fleeting images of the face of a long-dead relative. Dewey's inability was not due to lack of experience, he had had sex with bodybuilders, having paid for it—but found those experiences disappointing; the imagined muscle was harder than that in reality. This lack of satisfaction or inability to ignore this idée fix is what Dewey used to explain to himself how he found himself this night lurking in this man's lawn.

Dewey grew up hearing about kudzu. It was both beautiful and hated. As child he did not understand why it was hated. It seemed so lush, so beautiful, exotic, aggressive, and unrelenting. The idea of a plant being removed from its natural habitat only to become uncontrollable elsewhere. The out of control, out of place nature of kudzu attracted Dewey most. Like kudzu, Dewey felt out of place in the South yet remained there and appeared to thrive.

Dewey was surprised to see on his watch that three hours had passed since he started his work and was reminded once again of his father and how difficult it would have been for his father to have gotten three hours of gardening or yard work out of him when he was a boy.

In Dewey's years of therapy, he had learned much about his own psyche. Unfortunately, as he often told his own psychology students, insight does not necessarily ensure a change in behavior. One of his college professors told Dewey that he had never met another person with Dewey's "access to his primary process"—as the professor put it. This was back before Dewey learned the disappointing lesson he now insisted on passing on to his students. This was perhaps the reason that so many people were ultimately disillusioned by traditional talking cures—as Freud had called psychoanalysis. Perhaps it was best to remain ignorant of the source and complexity of one's neuroses, if a full understanding of them did not guarantee relief. Dewey often longed for a selective lobotomy.

Dewey did not choose this plant lightly—it had to work, literally growing to cover all—quickly and inexplicably, and had to work as a symbol—the literal was not rich enough for Dewey. The plant had to have additional significance, metaphorical import. He wanted Freud to be proud. Since he knew the impossibility of fulfilling his desire toward the man, Dewey hoped to capture the man's attention, to force him to experience an obsession. Dewey's obsession was the acquisition of the unattainable while Rocco's would be the elimination of the invasive. Dewey wanted to make sure to make the kudzu attack appear natural, an out-of-nowhere response, like a biblical plague. The seeds he bought, the cuttings he grew in his own backyard greenhouse, the roots he harvested from a few of the many kudzu-covered spots in the country outside Pensacola.

Dewey has traced with many therapists the trajectory of his psyche. From his childhood in East Texas during the 1960s with an emotionally abusive father and a therefore abused mother, to his much too early sexual awakening, a view of a full moon seen through a screened window on a summer's night and a dream that followed of a shoebox of penises under his bed, to his first sexual experiences with older cousins; then flight away from East Texas to college and internal Texas exile in Austin, with its depressing nights in deafening clubs dancing to the Eurythmics and Madonna; to his years in Minneapolis completing his doctorate at the University of Minnesota, home of that much-lauded diagnostic tool which Dewey used weekly, the Minnesota Multiphasic Personality Inventory; then his return to the South with a PhD to teach psychology classes to students too similar to his adolescent self for his comfort, and whom he felt were beneath him for never having escaped northward, all in a town too similar to his hometown for him to find peace. And although he is settling down now that he has passed his thirty-seventh birthday and considers himself more mature and in control—all it takes is a Marine jogging along the side of the highway, the silhouette of a man of the right shape, or a photograph in the newspaper to send Dewey racing back across time to his past and a place he thought he had escaped.

He gathered up the sharpened plunger handle, the trowel, the empty seed and cutting bags, and the empty water bottles that he had used to soak each cutting after he had tamped down the earth around it. He stood in the darkest corner of the lawn, under the nighttime shade of an ancient live oak, and inspected Rocco's domain. Would this be enough?

Dewey imagined Rocco returning from this long trip only to find his entire house, lawn, and garden covered, engulfed, in vine. Dewey longed for the Rocco's first thoughts to be—What did I do to cause this? What did I do wrong? What did I do to deserve this? Malicious intent on the part of another must remain outside the man's consideration. He wanted the botanical inevitability to overwhelm Rocco. He wanted Rocco to ask himself what he had done to deserve such fate; Dewey wanted Rocco's Catholic background—another unconfirmed speculation on Dewey's part—to provide the answers to Rocco's questions about the weed. Dewey wanted Rocco to feel responsible for the growing vine—to question himself about fertilizer use, the source of his soil amendments and mulch. The weed had to come from somewhere. Dewey wanted him to try to figure it out—wanted Rocco to turn inward and sound the depths of his soul finally coming to a devastating final conclusion about himself. The particulars of this conclusion did not matter to Dewey, only the effect mattered—devastation through introspection—without even knowing the source of his frustration. Rocco would never think of someone doing this to him. It was an unseen hand reaching up from the man's past to prick his attention toward introspection.

Dewey returned to his car and heard the thunk of his car doors automatically unlock—a reassuring sound of completion. He had avoided detection. He had not been caught and would not have to use the excuse he had prepared in advance—that he was a friend of Rocco and was planting daffodil bulbs in his yard as a birthday surprise.

He wanted to promise himself not to do this again, that this would be the end of it. His point was made. He had allowed himself this gesture as a gift to himself—a giving in to an impulse that at times felt stronger than his desire to live. He put the keys in the ignition, felt the vibration of the engine start and was surprised by the chill of the blast of air-conditioning as it hit his sweaty chest. For now, he took this decisive action on the cusp between self-aware self-assertion and an out-of-control return to what he thought to be a distant immature past.

22   Everybody Loves the Musée d'Orsay

Marshall Moore

Three hours into Mom's first visit to Malaysia, she was already scratching her fingernails across the blackboard in my head. She had called from London two weeks before, telling me she'd bought a ticket to Kuala Lumpur and would I mind a visit. Somehow she'd asked in the tone of voice that lacked a question mark, and I hadn't put up much resistance. Too strange, the idea of this woman who until retirement had not ventured farther from North Carolina than one or two trips to Maryland and DC. Having untangled herself from the workforce, she had gone to the U.K. to research family history.

I should have flown up to meet her somewhere, I thought. If she wanted to see me that badly. Haven't been to England lately. Or France. That's close. What was I thinking?

"You just can't get good iced tea outside of the South." My mother's face wrinkled in a moue of disapproval. She sipped the drink I ordered for her again, then shook her head and pushed it away just far enough to show she'd stick with her ice water, thank you very much.

"I believed that until I visited Malaysia the first time," I said. "Iced lemon tea—I mean, it's not the Luzianne we grew up drinking, but it's really quite refreshing."

Iced lemon tea is a Southeast Asian beverage: part limeade (although it's called lemon, go figure), part brewed black tea. Not too tart, not too sweet, perfect for the torrid, suffocating weather here next to the equator. Which, when you think about it, is not much different from those swampy summers on the North Carolina coastal plain.

A handsome Chinese waiter brought our appetizers. He caught my eye and offered the subtlest smile as he placed the platter of spring rolls on the carved wooden table between my mother and me. As

Mom leaned forward to peer at the spring rolls as if she expected them to be writhing on their plate, I sent a look the waiter's way: Parents! His smile widened by a millimeter or two—hadn't I seen him out dancing at Liquid?—and he moved on to the next table, to attend to the patrons there. I let my eyes linger on the rear view as he walked away.

"The crust on these things looks like foreskin," my mother said.

"Mom, this is one of the best Thai restaurants in Kuala Lumpur," I said. "I feel confident the crust isn't made of anything inappropriate." Deep breath, Quentin. "They're too hot to eat right now. Give them a few minutes to cool or you'll wish you hadn't."

Mom's had a favorite story about me, and she dragged it out for company whenever she had the chance: When I was a baby, I was too pretty to be a girl. In grocery stores and other public places, she often felt called upon to pull down my diaper to prove my sex. Isn't that funny? As if I ought to laugh along with her and her mortified audience, which of course I never did. And she used to have a picture of me as a little boy, maybe three years of age, naked in a wading pool. She kept it in her wallet until I was eleven.

The restaurant, Chakri Palace, anchored a series of exorbitant-by-local-standards Asian eateries along the top floor of the shopping mall at the base of the Twin Towers. (Mom made awed sounds and craned her neck to look up, as we parked.) The décor, a sort of international Tasteful Thai I'd seen in restaurants on four continents, smoothed my frayed edges. Deep purples and greens, wooden screens, orchids everywhere. I had chosen this place to make a nice first impression. The penis-like appetizers seemed to have stolen my thunder.

Mom's plane from London landed early this morning. She was going to be here a week. I hadn't seen her in two years. Shudder to think.

I took the day off from work, no easy task, to meet her at the airport and get her checked into her rooms. I had thought after a month in the U.K., Mom would have been used to driving on the left side of the road, but she wasn't. On the way into KL from the airport, she clutched the Oh-Jesus bar on the A-pillar and stomped an imaginary brake several times. She emitted dramatic gasps whenever someone cut me off or I had to swerve. This being Southeast Asia, that happened every three or four minutes.

"And I thought traffic in Raleigh had gotten bad! Jesus!"

She came in on a red-eye, she has jet lag, and that does tend to diminish one's social skills, I reminded myself. Go easy on her.

I had booked her rooms at a guest house at the edge of Bangsar, a fashionable district with enough bars, cafés, clubs, and funky shops to make the local expats believe they weren't really so far from Soho after all. The guest house itself was a sprawling old colonial memsahib skirted with broad verandas, featured ceiling fans in every room, and old but charming pewter fixtures. It looked Old South enough to make Mom feel right at home, or so I thought when I arranged for her to stay there.

"Looks like this place your father took me to in New Orleans, right after we got married," Mom said, depositing her purse on the bed. "Don't try to explain how the phone works or anything. I'm too damn tired. Just take me somewhere for lunch, and then let me come back here for a nap. I'll be fine in time for dinner, I promise."

"Do you like it?"

She looked around, dubious. I think she was waiting for a cockroach to scurry across the floor. "Yes," she said at last. "It looks like the plantation house in *Indochine,* only smaller."

She had seen a Catherine Deneuve film, with subtitles. The last film I could remember her going to the cinema to see was *Dirty Dancing* or possibly one of the more recent *Star Wars* sequels. It was going to be a weekend of surprises.

"Honey, what's that little sticker on the ceiling?" she asked, pointing up at a discreet red arrow in one corner of the room.

"It points to Mecca, for Muslim guests," I answered. "You're in a Muslim country now." I waved my fingers in an Ooh, aah gesture and hoped she'd smile.

"As long as I don't get caned," she said. "Where are you taking me for lunch?

Our entrees arrived: prawns with asparagus, a mild chicken curry, and a stir-fried vegetable dish. I waited for Mom to serve herself— she took tinier portions than I remembered her liking—then experienced a moment of cultural schizophrenia as I tried to decide whether to eat like a generic Westerner, a Southerner, or an Asian.

"Well, you've said several times how Kuala Lumpur [she pronounced it queue-walla-lumper] doesn't really have tourist destinations, and the National Gallery here doesn't have works by anybody I'd recognize, so I thought I'd just spend the time with you. It'll be so nice to catch up. I've gotten so much work done in England, you just wouldn't believe it. The people there are so nice. And to think— we're related to them, something like six hundred years back!"

It had begun. Mom, true to form, launched into an extended ramble about the genealogical research project that had taken her to Britain. Without charts in front of me, nothing she said made a glimmer of sense. Think of the begats in the Bible. And she wouldn't slow up, nor leave me room to get a word in edgewise, until my eardrums looked like the homecoming queen's hymen the day after the prom. I dumped a spoonful of the curry over my bowl of steamed rice and, as I was going to spear some potato with my chopsticks . . .

"Aren't you going to use your plate?"

I sagged with relief. Something other than ancestral babble was rolling out of her mouth. "It's funny," I said. "People here serve themselves a little bit of this over their rice, then a little bit of that. They keep going back to the serving bowls and platters rather than dumping everything across a big plate. It's kind of nice."

As a Westerner, I was raised to fill my plate, then to clean it. Serving myself from a communal bowl with my own utensils would have been considered uncouth at Mom's table. Germs! She had brought me up on a meat-and-potatoes diet, pork chops and lima beans, casseroles wide and deep enough to do the backstroke in, and she kept after me to eat second helpings. "You're a growing boy!" "You're on the track team, so you need something that'll stick to your ribs!" "Have another glass of milk!" When I didn't gain weight or fill out, she shoveled more food onto my plate. "Dive in! You've got a hiney like two biscuits on a china plate!"

"But isn't it . . ." The question hung unasked. She collected herself. "Never mind." After looking around the restaurant, she asked, "Will everybody, you know, notice, if I eat the regular way?"

"You'll be fine," I assured her. "I've found that the people here are very reserved, but very accommodating. You'll enjoy yourself."

She answered with an immense yawn. "Gee," she said. "That's good to know." Another yawn. I felt for her. "I believe I'm going to fall asleep in your car on the way back to my little hotel!"

* * *

Two structures dominate the Kuala Lumpur skyline: the Petronas Towers, also known as the Twin Towers, which are the world's tallest buildings, and the KL Tower, a combination broadcasting tower/ highrise restaurant/ tourist trap along the lines of the Space Needle in Seattle and the CN Tower in Toronto.

The queues to get into the Twin Towers are formidable. Or rather, the queues for the forty-sixth-floor observation deck are formidable; the only people privileged to see the view from on high are, I assume, the petrochemical zillionaires who built the place. Show up an hour before one of the two daily tours and you still won't get in. Waiting out in that jungle-metropolis weather for God knows how long the day after a gruesome flight from London would have been torture for Mom. I couldn't put her through that. The KL Tower is a more accessible spot. You can get in. You can park. You zoom up the escalator to an observation deck almost 600 meters above ground, swallowing to equalize the pressure in your ears as you would in a plane after take-off, and marvel at what of the surrounding cityscape you can actually see through the haze.

"I don't think I've ever been this high up outside of an airplane," Mom said, staring out a window that faced south. "Except this one time on our honeymoon, when we were in Hawaii, we went up the side of this mountain in a Jeep. I think it was higher than this. We were in the clouds."

She stared off into space. My father left her for another woman fifteen years before, but I don't believe Mom had ever gotten her head around the idea.

"What do you think of the view?" I asked.

We strolled around the observation deck to look at the Twin Towers. From here, they resembled two immense silver ears of corn planted in the earth. Behind us, a bookend pair of strapping blond guys murmured in German. Brothers? Lovers? Friends? Some combination of the above? I couldn't tell. Mom squinted at the top of the Towers, gauging how tall they were relative to our position, then asked how much the admission charge was in U.S. dollars.

"At the bureau de change [she pronounced it with a hard American CH and long A], I just said I wanted to convert a hundred English pounds to Malaysian money, and I got all these little colorful bank notes back. I never even thought to look at the exchange rate first! Isn't that funny?"

"The exchange rate is fixed at 3.8 on the dollar. Has been for years. A ringgit is worth a smidge more than an American quarter."

"So we paid a couple of bucks to get in and see this." Mom looked smug for having done the math in her head. When I nodded, she asked, "You don't really care about my research, do you?"

Four or five responses drowned each other out. As I stood, jaw opening to form one word and then a different one, unconsciously backing up to let the German wonder twins have a better view of the Towers, because even in a horrid family drama moment straight out of a Tennessee Williams short story I cannot help but be polite, Mom went on to say, "I can see your eyes glaze over every time I bring it up. It's your own family, too, Quentin. Isn't that important to you?"

How to explain that I loved my family but if I wanted or needed them nearby I wouldn't live in Malaysia? On the other side of the planet? So some queer magazine or other has proclaimed Durham one of the most livable U.S. cities for gay men and lesbians. Break out the Moët. North Carolina has come a long way, then. I still don't want to live there.

"You started this project—what was it—five years ago? Yes? And since then, how many times have we had this conversation?" The idea that bystanders might hear this made my skin crawl. English is one of Malaysia's official languages. "I don't know either. I'm glad you're doing this, I appreciate it, I encourage it, and I'm grateful you want to share it with me, but it's not something I want to take up. And without the big picture, when I hear that John Henry Bumblefuck begat five children by a German émigré princess named Brunhilde van Thunderwald, it's just not useful information."

I stopped cold. The Germans were watching us, not the skyline. Mom was looking at me with a sideways smile, Mona Lisa of the Magnolias. She had gotten exactly what she wanted. She had poked a hole in my composure.

"Great view," she said, walking toward the elevator. "It's like this building was put here to give those two bigger ones [she flipped a hand behind her without looking back] the finger. Can we go now? I'm ready to do some shopping."

* * *

Kuala Lumpur's streets are anything but logical. To get an idea what I mean, imagine someone dropped Atlanta and it broke. (Atlanta's roadways are not orderly to begin with.) I drove preoccupied through KL's spaghetti-tangle infrastructure to Bintang Walk, choosing that district over several others on the assumption, perhaps naïve, that nobody in her right mind could possibly badmouth the place. We ended up passing the U.K. and French embassies. Lost. I had to turn around in another embassy parking lot—Italy, I think—and double back. Lost. Great. Something else for her arsenal, to be dropped into a conversation with a third party later in the visit, apropos of nothing, to elicit a giggle at my expense.

Bintang Walk, to continue the Atlanta analogy, is KL's Buckhead, only more so, and with nastier summer weather. Chic shops, unique restaurants, fashionable people, and humidity. I chose Lot 10, my favorite of the malls in the area, as a starting point. The façade of the mall itself is an incandescent shade of lime green. Isetan, Japan's answer to Macy's, is the anchor store. Dôme, which bills itself as having "The World's Finest Coffees," tempts you with liquid refreshments mostly too hot for the local climate. At least until you walk inside and the layer of sweat you're filmed with breeds squawking flocks of goose bumps. The second that first blast of air-conditioning buffets you, hypothermia threatens, and about a gallon of coffee seems like a very good idea. Essential oils from The Body Shop waft out of a storefront and cleanse your sinuses, soothe your stresses, and open your pores as you pass by, just as they do at malls in every other civilized country on the planet.

"Oh my Lord," Mom says.

The architecture at Lot 10 has an organic science fiction look, as if designed by HR Giger or lifted from the set of *Alien*. I spasmed with self-doubt: I should have chosen Star Hill Centre, down the street, which looks more like something you'd see in Raleigh than a *Star Trek* episode. I love Lot 10 but some people prefer a kinder, gentler retail ambience.

"You'll feel better inside Isetan," I said.

The shoe department had the tonic effect I had hoped for: Mom did the math, squealed when she saw what she could get for her tourist dollar (as diffracted through the British pound and the Malaysian ringgit), and soon had two salesclerks, a boy and a girl, neither more than twenty, scurrying to bring her one pair of shoes after another. I had almost relaxed when Mom looked up in the middle of trying on a pair of low-heeled black pumps, seemed to realize I had caught her enjoying herself, and dropped her face into a pout. Christ. Mom sent the salesgirl back for a size I knew she couldn't wear, and I decided I'd had enough for now. A brief trip upstairs to the men's department resulted in the purchase of a pair of trainers I'd been eyeing, and when I came back, Mom stood at the checkout counter with eight boxes of shoes stacked into two four-story towers. My heart missed a beat from shock.

I grew up in clothes from the Salvation Army. Why spend the money when you're going to outgrow them anyway, was her stock response when I asked why she bought herself nice things and me crap. Who was this woman impersonating my mother?

"Retirement's agreeing with you," I told her.

"I just can't believe the exchange rate here! It's all so cheap! When I was in England, good heavens, everything there costs a hat-arm and an overcoat when you go from American dollars to pounds, and it's just unbelievable, what people pay for things! When you see a value like this, you just have to go for it!" She turned to the blushing girl who was ringing her up. "Isn't that right? Goodness, listen to me, I sound like such a tourist. OK, get me out of here at once before I buy anything else."

I tried that, but we couldn't escape the gravitational pull of British India (think Eddie Bauer with jodhpurs), where she cooed over the inventory before settling on a pair of linen blouses and a lightweight dress.

"I went shopping in Scotland," she said as she surrendered a Visa card to make her purchases. "When I was up there checking out the family castle. One of them, anyway. You know there's another one down in Devonshire. Of course nobody lives in them any longer, but it's so exciting to think of that as our roots! I stayed in Glasgow a couple of days, just doing the town up, and I wanted to go shopping but I was spending pounds, and I just didn't have the heart—it was all so expensive!" To the checkout girl, she said, "Hold on, I've decided on something else. Hold that thought."

Mom dashed over to a nearby rack and grabbed a blouse like one she was already buying, only in a different color—blue this time, not green.

I didn't say a word.

At Tang's, in Star Hill Centre, Mom picked out a few dresses she liked. Even at a favorable exchange rate, these were not inexpensive items. I was not used to seeing her burn up money so freely, and made a mental note to find the right moment to swallow the lump in my throat and ask what had happened to her income. Some of her research had led to a modest history of eastern North Carolina being published, and I thought she had realized a small profit from that, but the way she spent money raised questions. As long as I could remember, she'd been a paragon of thrift.

"Scotland was lovely, and the castle was just amazing," she said, out of the blue, returning to the subject she had dropped when we left British India. She handed me one of the garment bags containing two dresses to carry, then the other when I gestured to let me carry more. "I wanted to spend more time there, but I had to get back to England."

"I've never made it to Scotland. David and I have talked about a holiday in the U.K. but we've just never gotten around to it. We're probably going to buy a house in Melbourne, so our last couple of trips have been down there."

"Well, I hope you don't mind that I'm talking about my family history project again, since it doesn't mean anything to you. I wouldn't want to put your nose out of joint," Mom said. She walked toward Dôme and asked if I felt like treating her to a cup of the finest coffee in the world. *Invasion of the Body Snatchers* had come true, and an affluent pod person had replaced my mother. The likeness was good, the guilt-trip routine couldn't be beat, and she still completely lacked tact and timing, but who was this woman and what did she want? I followed her into the café and suppressed a random death-wish as she yoo-hooed a waiter like a Biloxi debutante.

* * *

From the lavatory I called David on my mobile.

"You can opt out," I told him after I said I love you and he said I love you too and I said I love you more and he said I love you more than that and I said Oh bite me and he said Later. "She's on the warpath, and it's all this covert passive-aggressive shit she's done all my life, and I'm going fucking nuts but unfortunately she's my mother and I do love her."

"Of course you do, darling. That's what she's for. I'll meet you at Balakong, just like we planned."

"You don't have to," I told him. "I can tell her you're stuck working on a last-minute proposal for a bazillion-ringgit project, and your job's on the line if you don't give 110 percent on this . . ."

"Don't," he said. "I'll be there. If she's being difficult, I can handle her. I'm Chinese, remember? We had difficult mothers and methods of dealing with them thousands of years before the Europeans landed in America. I'll be fine."

"You never cease to amaze me," I said. "Just don't say you weren't warned."

* * *

"Son, you're just not with it today, are you? Did you make another wrong turn?" Mom looked out the car window in obvious apprehension at the warehouses around us. "I thought we were going to a nice restaurant for dinner. We must be lost. This doesn't look like the restaurant district."

"You're right. It's the pothole district," I said, as the car jolted through one I hadn't noticed, for looking at her.

"It's a little out of the way, but it's there, believe me. This place is like that. Malaysia, I mean. Things aren't always quite where you'd expect them to be, but it all works anyway."

"Well." She looked around. "I guess I should shut up and let you do the driving, shouldn't I? You do live here, after all."

"Imagine that," I said.

When I pulled into a parking spot beside Balakong, I saw David at a table talking with our favorite waiter, a Chinese (of course—the restaurant was run by a Chinese family) guy of my own height, with shoulder-length hair and an exquisite face. We knew he was gay but had never seen him out. From the intensity of David's facial expression and the animation of his gestures, I could tell they were discussing the menu. David is an unrepentant food snob. He has strong opinions on the various cuisines of Malaysia and how they should be prepared. I'm sure the wait staff at the restaurants we frequent either love him or want to dip his satay in cyanide. I killed the engine and set the parking brake.

"Quentin, this restaurant doesn't look . . . I mean, it doesn't have walls." A quaver had crept into Mom's voice. She sounded old.

"Lots of restaurants here don't," I told her, climbing the low steps surrounding the restaurant to take a seat next to David at the table.

The waiter, Gershwin, smiled and said hello in English, and returned to the kitchen. Mom lagged several paces behind, and took her seat with a huff. Apprehension radiated out of her like factory exhaust.

To a Westerner visiting this part of Asia for the first time, this style of restaurant may seem questionable: built into the corner of a building, there are only two walls, at the interior. Instead of having an outer two walls, which would otherwise form a corner of the building, the restaurant is open to the outside. Ceiling fans circulate air and tile floors keep the place reasonably clean and cool. The chairs are often the cheap molded plastic kind one might buy at Wal-Mart and park in front of one's double-wide, along with a glow-in-the-dark bird bath. What the Westerner who can't get past appearances fails to realize is that food here is a source of intense pride to both the kitchen staff and the patrons. Malaysians of whatever ethnicity take their food seriously.

After introductions, I tried to explain some of this to Mom. She didn't seem to want to hear it.

"Where's the ladies' room?" she asked. David pointed the way.

"Poor thing," he said.

"Don't get me started," I told him. "What have you ordered?"

"You'll love it," he replied. "I hope she will. Gershwin said the steamed fish is not to be missed. He also said the eel is good but I decided to give that a pass. I doubt your mother would be happy if I ordered eels. There's a prawn dish—you said she likes seafood—and paper chicken."

"Did you order the shark's fin soup?"

He nodded. One of Balakong's specialties is a shark's fin soup made with tofu instead of Jaws. It tastes like the real thing and you don't have to be Bill Gates to afford it.

"Let's not tell her it's tofu," I suggested. "I think shark is inside her comfort zone, and she can brag to her girlfriends when she gets home about how she ate shark in Malaysia."

"Can't you get it in the States?"

I nodded. "Yes. That's the point. Oh, here she comes, and she doesn't look happy."

"The toilets here aren't the best part of the restaurant." Mom took a seat. She looked a bit pale.

Before she could speak, Gershwin returned with our pot of tea and a bowl of teacups in steaming-hot water. He set these on the table, then took the cups out of the water, shook them off, and poured tea for the three of us. He then filled the customary extra cup, which he set before an empty chair.

"It's a tradition here," David explained, following Mom's gaze and anticipating her question. "I don't know who the extra cup is supposed to be for, but we do it anyway."

You'd have thought he'd said the teacups had been brought out in a bowl of goat urine, and I felt my patience slipping. I wanted to ask her, If you wanted everything to be exactly like North Carolina, then why did you come? But I had sense enough to keep my mouth shut. My goals for the weekend: for Mom to have a pleasant visit, to see fascinating and lovely things, and to meet David and his family; and for myself, to keep her at arm's length, even when she was as close as the passenger's seat of my car. I'm batting about 500 so far, at best, I thought. If that.

Mom sipped her tea and offered up a tiny smile that vanished the second she caught me looking. The same thing happened with the food. First the soup: Mom ate as if she had just crawled starving out of the Sahara, blowing on spoonful after spoonful to cool it, then slurping the stuff down. She caught David and me exchanging a victorious look—She likes it!—and soured right away.

"What are these gristly things?" she asked, pointing with a chopstick.

"Tofu," David said. "There's some tofu in the soup, too."

"Not the shark? I thought it was cartilage."

Oops. "The shark is the tender part," I said.

The chicken provided more of a challenge: she didn't know what to make of the presentation, bits of meat in a rich, dark sauce, all wrapped in packets of baking paper, and tied with string. Impossible to eat without making a mess. She tried. I always tried, too. No matter what you did, the sauce spattered, your fingers got slimed, and you had to remind yourself "this is fun" while you struggled to take your first bite of the stuff.

Kind of galling, to be reminded of my own first visits here. I watched Mom to see whether I had done a better job with this stuff before I knew what I was doing. She gave up on that dish, then asked in obvious relief when the prawns came, "You look like you've lost weight, Quentin. This must be why!" A titter. "The food's so complicated!"

She sobered up. A sip of tea, then, "So, David, how did you and Quentin meet? He's so cagey on that subject."

"On the Internet," David replied. "Several years ago, we subscribed to the same newsgroup. I was still in grad school in Australia. He thought something I posted was funny, and he sent me an e-mail to say so."

"We were like pen pals for about nine months," I added. "Then I flew over here to visit."

"Well, that's sweet," Mom said. To David, "I thought it might be something like that, or a personals ad, or something. I'm sure Quentin would rather I didn't say this, but why not—you're family now." Her eyes sparkled, and she smiled my way. This was probably how it felt to realize you were one or two seconds away from being hit by a speeding bus. "He's always been such a loner, and I just—well, he's been through two or three failed relationships, really bad ones, and I know by the time he hit thirty he must have been wondering if he'd ever meet someone special. I think it's been very lonely for him. I just hope this works out for you both. You seem like a nice young man."

David's cultural advantage of becoming inscrutable to Westerners came in handy just then. I knew him well enough to recognize the millimeter narrowing of his eyes, but he didn't miss a beat: "I'm sure Quentin is very fortunate to have such a concerned mother. I think it's wonderful. Would you like more prawns now? I can tell you like them. I can order more if you're still hungry."

Under the table, he moved his leg until his left foot touched my right one. I studied Mom as she watched David resume eating. When she turned and saw me looking, I gave her a smile even as her own face slid back into a well-practiced pout.

Had another realization, just then: She's lying.

* * *

After dinner, in a strangled sort of voice, I suggested picking up dessert at our favorite coffee shop in Bangsar—Alexis. I'd already be in the neighborhood, dropping Mom off, and not a moment too soon.

"I am awfully tired," Mom said, exaggerating a yawn.

"I know how you love that tiramisu," I reminded David.

"Meet you at home, then," he said.

He came into my arms and kissed my face and ears and mouth and neck."Don't even say a word," he said.

Behind his back, I jiggled the box containing his tiramisu so he'd feel my arms move. "Let me light the candles. I'll be right back."

In the kitchen, I mixed a tall gin and tonic. The swirling ice drew me in like a hypnotist's crystal pendant. David surprised me: I felt something behind me, started, then looked down to see two olive-tan arms wrapping themselves around my waist.

"I'm not sure how well gin mixes with tiramisu," I cautioned him, turning to follow him into the bathroom.

He was deliciously naked.

"I don't care. Come get into the tub with me."

He had transformed the bathroom into a candle-lit shrine. Flowers in the sink, a stick of champa incense burning, my favorite Enya CD adding sonic perfume to the air. "You have your choice of three bath ballistics," he said, referring to the fizzy, scented spheres we bought at Lush, down in Singapore. When dropped into bathwater, they zoomed around the tub as they dissolved, dispersing scent and providing great entertainment at the same time.

"Your call," I told him, not standing on ceremony but climbing in and taking another deep swallow of gin. He unwrapped and chucked a blue one into the water.

"You know I'm trying," I said. "I mean, she makes me nuts, and you know she makes me nuts, but I'm trying to make this an enjoyable trip, and she's pulling out every passive-aggressive sabotage technique she knows."

"Darling, you can't let it cause you stress. She'll be leaving in five days. You don't have to spend every waking minute with her." He stroked my hair. "I do have one question, though. Does she always divulge such personal things about you to people she has just met?"

I nodded. "Cross my heart."

"Proof that we don't change with age, we just become more completely ourselves," David said, kissing the back of my neck.

"So you see what I mean, now, yes?" I liked what he was doing with his hands.

"Of course I do, darling. No matter what you do for her, she always wants more. You've said it yourself: she doesn't know where she ends and you begin. Fortunately you do know. Now can we talk about other things?"

"Like what?"

"I don't know. Kiss me and one of us will think of something."

* * *

I called Mom at the guest house the next morning and proposed a road trip down to Malacca, a small city rich with history, about an hour and a half south of Kuala Lumpur. Malacca is the city where Europeans first colonized what is now Malaysia. Dutch and Portuguese settlers landed there centuries ago and built tidy churches and squares. In the old section of town, any number of cute shops, galleries, and restaurants vie for the contents of your wallet. Majestic temples and mosques coexist side-by-side. Mom listened for a few minutes before heaving a sigh, announcing she had horrific diarrhea, and asking if I'd be offended if we just stayed in KL and had some tea.

"Do you want me to bring over some medicine? You can buy Lomotil over the counter here. It's fantastic stuff," I offered. "If you're hungry, I'll pick up an order of chicken rice on the way. It's tasty, but it's very mild and kind to your system."

"No," she said. "I've taken something already, and the concierge told me about a place nearby that delivers. He ordered me some soup, and when it came, there was this nice bouquet of flowers on the tray with it! Such a sweetie, and I only had to tip him the equivalent of fifty cents! Can you believe that?"

"Welcome to Malaysia. Why don't I come over around lunchtime, then, to give you more time to rest?"

"Sure, honey. Anyway, I think I need to go spend some more time on the throne. I am just torn up!" With that, she hung up.

* * *

Mom waited to assault me with guilt until after the film I took her to see that afternoon. She chugged enough medicine to feel confident leaving her hotel room. We saw a German techno-adventure-comedy at a new cinema in Bangsar. Mom laughed in the right places but I could tell something was wrong. I assumed the problem was intestinal in nature.

"I don't think you want me here," she said at a café afterward, as we sipped hot tea. I instantly felt miserable on two levels: exasperated that she kept going round in circles like this, but also guilty as charged because up to a point she was right. Like America itself, my parents are easier to appreciate from a distance.

"I wanted you to have a nice time," I told her. "I was hoping you'd see why I like living here."

"But you're so . . . I just don't know. Distant. You act like having a relationship with me is the last thing on earth you want. I know it's been two years since we've seen each other, but I don't understand where you're coming from. Am I such a burden?" Without giving me time to answer, she plunged ahead, like she worried I might say Yes. "OK, then I'll just tell you why I'm really here. I do want you to consider a move back to North Carolina."

All the blood drained out of my head.

"Just hear me out," she insisted. "I don't know how much I told you about the part-time job I took to supplement my income, after I retired from the state. It's a network marketing company—they're based in Dallas—and they specialize in utilities. Power, gas, Internet, paging, long distance. If you sign up through them, you can save ten or fifteen percent compared to what you normally pay. If you become a representative, well, the earning potential is unlimited. I'm going to become a Regional Sales Coordinator in two months, and my income—why, I bet I make more than you do! How do you think I could afford this trip?"

"I assumed your book had sold well," I said. Christ, my accent was coming back. The blood hadn't returned to my head yet, and in a minute my brain was going to collapse like a failed soufflé.

"It did OK," she said. "But not well enough to turn me into a world traveler. Son, I'm getting older, and sooner or later I'm going to need care. I don't like to think about that eventuality, but I can't avoid it either. Have you thought about that much? What you're going to do when I'm—"

I interrupted, "You're not there yet."

"Sooner or later you're going to have to give up this globe-trotting lifestyle of yours and come home," she said.

"What's home?" I asked. "Where's that? The States? North Carolina? Which city? Or do you mean your house? Do you think my life is only a temporary detour, and I'm supposed to end up living with you again someday? That's how it sounds."

"You're not married," she said. "You don't have kids. Isn't that what homosexual bachelors do in the end? Move home to take care of their mothers?"

"I can't even count the number of ways that's offensive," I said. This discussion was going downhill fast, and I was going to have to escort her back to her hotel soon. I couldn't look at her much longer if she kept this up. "You've met David," I said. "I'm not going anywhere without him, and he's not going anywhere without me."

"Well, I'm not saying he has to stay behind," Mom started.

I interrupted her. "It's not for you to say where he goes or doesn't go. And we're not going to keep having this conversation. You obviously don't have a clue how insulting it is."

"You're all I've got left," she said. "Your sister hasn't talked to me in ten years. I don't even know where she lives. I'm getting old all by myself. I need you."

"Insulting me and treating my relationship—my entire life—as if it's all just a passing phase is not the way to win me over," I told her, reeling. "I think we need to pay the check now. If you want to go back to your hotel, I'll take you. You're welcome to have dinner with David's family tonight, because they were looking forward to meeting you, but give some thought to what you've said and why I'm upset about it."

"I'll take a cab back," she said. "They're cheap. You've said so yourself."

"I'll hail one for you."

When she was gone, I ordered a glass of Shiraz from the bar and sipped it staring out the window at pedestrians and passing cars.

* * *

On my first trip to Malaysia, David took me to dinner at Tamarind Hill, an extravagant Thai restaurant nestled in the heart of the city. If you didn't know it was there, you'd never find it by accident: you leave the main road, turn up a gravel side road that looks like it's going to end up in a parking lot next to a disused building, follow the path, and end up in front of another of the sprawling colonial houses the British left behind. This one serves what David and I consider the best Thai food in Kuala Lumpur.

We were seven for dinner: David, his sister and parents, his grandmother (visiting from Sabah), Mom, and me. David and I had brought along three bottles of a South African Chardonnay. We finished the first two, pleasantly enough, over appetizers.

David's father and sister speak excellent English. His mother knows enough to get by, but she's not ready for James Joyce. His grandmother knows a few words, but the older she gets, the less she speaks anything but Cantonese.

Mom had been pleasant all evening, smiling at everyone, speaking with exaggerated care (I caught David's sister's eyes glazing over once), not drinking too much. Maybe she really had reconsidered her approach.

Of course I was wrong. The horror show began when our waiter brought out my favorite dish, pandan chicken, bite-sized pieces of white meat tied in fragrant pandan leaves.

"I was telling Quentin that I think he has lost some weight since he's been here. Not that he had any to spare. The cuisine is so different from what we eat in America!"

"They don't have Thai food in America?" David's sister asked.

"Oh, that's not what I meant. I mean, it's very good." She untied a strip of pandan leaf, took a bite of the chicken, and made a rapturous face. "Delicious, but it's such a change for him. You know he has a sensitive stomach, and—"

"And that's not what we all came to dinner to hear about, now, is it?" I laughed. Actually the Chinese tend to be more sanguine about the squishier facts of life than we Americans, but this wasn't where the conversation needed to go. "So why don't you tell us about England and Scotland instead? I think it's great that you're traveling overseas, after all this time."

David and I had a telepathic moment just then. I knew he was thinking "Bravo."

"England and Scotland." For the first time I realized that Mom was not sober. Her slushy pronunciation of Scotland gave her away. She had probably taken some Lomotil, which is an opiate, before dinner. That, plus dehydration, plus a couple of glasses of wine . . . "England and Scotland are beautiful."

Smiles all around. I didn't think anyone else had caught on yet.

"I went to London last year for a convention," David's father said. "Unfortunately, I was too busy to see much. But I enjoyed the trip. Long plane flight."

"My ancestors left England three hundred years ago," Mom announced. "They are descended from the British Royal Family, and there's a castle in the south of England that has been in my family ever since."

David's sister, in particular, looked surprised by this news. She murmured a quick explanation in Cantonese, for her mother and grandmother's benefit. They gave a very similar mother-daughter start, looked at each other, and began a side conversation of their own.

"They're very impressed," David's sister said. "That's very interesting."

"Quentin doesn't seem to think so," Mom said, selecting another bite of pandan chicken from the serving platter. "Quentin would rather I didn't talk about my family history at all, because it's not important to him. His family isn't important to him, and he demonstrates it by moving to a remote [she looked around], practically third-world country, and breaking off ties with practically all of us—"

"Mom, that's enough," I told her.

If a trapdoor could be made to open up beneath one of us, I wouldn't have been able to choose who should drop into the oubliette beneath, Mom or me. Until that night I didn't believe anyone could be as mortified without keeling over dead.

"Do you feel well?" David asked. "I think you need to get to bed."

"Yes lah," David's mother said, addressing the group for the first time. "Hot tea. Maybe doctor."

"I don't need a doctor, I need for my son to stop living with a man and come back to his senses and come back to his family!" Mom shouted.

Heads turned.

I rose. "Please accept my apologies," I said to them all. "She's a little sick from her travels, and I think I should take her home—"

"That's for goddamn sure," Mom said. "Home. Christ, how can you people stand it? Our sons are living together."

David's mother looked stricken. His father bowed his head, but not before I noticed a flash of anger. She knew; he didn't. Not officially, at least. These things were not spoken of. I didn't like the arrangement, nor did David, but when you butt heads with 5,000 years of

Chinese culture, you're not going to win the battle: his parents, while educated, were also ashamed. Deeply ashamed. We were moving to Australia because in the long term, if we wanted there to be a long term, we had no choice.

His grandmother got in one question before I got Mom to her feet to propel her toward my car: "Gay?"

David turned so pale he looked almost white.

* * *

Mom had been gone a week and I hadn't heard from her. Didn't expect to, either. At least not until she got back to the States, after she concluded her stay in England, and perhaps not then.

"I think you need to change your ticket," I told her in the car that night, leaving Tamarind Hill. David sat in the back, shell-shocked. "Whatever you were trying to accomplish tonight, it blew up in your face. You're not welcome here."

"I didn't mean . . ." She sounded indignant, and I was past patience with her, past apologizing, past making excuses, past trying.

"Save it. You know perfectly well what you meant. Now do you want to call British Airways? I can do it from my mobile, right now. In fact, why don't I?"

I put her on a plane the next day. The only seat left was in first class, the telephone sales agent told me. I sacrificed a staggering number of frequent-flier miles to change the ticket.

David and I were on a flight to Melbourne, house-hunting. Our real estate agent had called, promising exciting leads in South Yarra, St. Kilda, and Port Melbourne, three of our favorite suburbs.

"Promise me there won't be more visits like that," David said.

He looked gaunt after a week of family upheaval. His parents would barely speak to him. His grandmother refused to tell anyone else in the family, thank God, but she made it clear she wanted nothing further to do with me, since this whole gay thing was obviously my fault, an affliction I brought from the States and infected David with, corrupting his Asian values, blah blah blah. Only his sister showed any sign of humanity.

I had been nauseated all week myself. Malaysia isn't Denmark. You don't just casually out Chinese guys to their families and assume there will be no repercussions. Hell, you can't even assume they'll be safe. She had to have known that. All week, I had been coming back to the same question: Did she plan it, or was it an accident? And in the end, which was scarier, and did it matter?

David and I had a long talk and decided Australia couldn't wait.

"The next time I see her, if there's a next time, it'll be somewhere safe," I said. "Letting her visit Malaysia was one of the worst ideas anybody ever had. I should never have allowed it. Hell, I can't say I like the idea of bringing her to Melbourne. Not after this. The length of the flight, alone, would require her to spend a couple of weeks, just to get over the jet lag, and I'm not up to it. I'm just not."

"What will you do, then? She's not going away."

"You're right, but when I can't put it off any longer, and believe me I'm going to stall as long as possible, then we'll meet in London or something. We can take the train down to Paris, through the Chunnel. She'll dig that. Check out the tourist stuff there—the Eiffel Tower, Versailles, those places. Everybody loves the Musée d'Orsay." I reflected. "The Louvre. Whatever. As long as I can keep her at a safe distance, I'll be fine."

"You're not going to leave me and move back to North Carolina, then?"

I took his hand. "When hell freezes over," I said.

ABOUT THE EDITOR

Jay Quinn is the Senior Editor of Southern Tier Editions, an imprint of The Haworth Press, Inc. He is the editor of the first volume of the *Rebel Yell* anthologies as well as the author of *The Mentor,* a memoir, and a novel, *Metes and Bounds.* A native of coastal North Carolina, he now lives in South Florida with his partner of nearly ten years and their two huge Doberman/Lab-mix dogs.

CONTRIBUTORS

Joe Frank Buckner has been published in *The Savannah Literary Journal, Southern Exposure,* and the Alyson Publications anthology, *Bar Stories.* A native of Statesboro, Georgia, Joe Frank lives on a Gulf Coast Florida island with his spouse of nearly twenty years, and their Basset hound, Scout. He is currently at work on a novel and a short story collection.

Jameson Currier is the author of a collection of short stories, *Dancing on the Moon,* and a novel, *Where the Rainbow Ends.* A native of Marietta, Georgia, he attended Emory University and currently resides in Manhattan.

Carlos Dews is originally from Texas, now living in Pensacola, where he teaches at the University of West Florida. He is joint editor (with Carolyn Leste Law) of *This Fine Place So Far from Home* and also *Out in the South.* He is also the editor of Carson McCullers' unfinished autobiography.

Dale Edgerton a long-time resident of Durham, North Carolina, now lives in Athens, Georgia. After many years of being a reader, he has completed his first novel. This is his first published work.

D. (Dayton) Estes is a North Carolinian. He taught German and German literature and philology for twenty-eight years at Pfeiffer College in Misenheimer, North Carolina, has published in his own field, and is now writing gay fiction. He is retired and lives at Oak Island, North Carolina.

P. J. Gray was born and raised on the sandy white shores of northwest Florida and can trace his paternal ancestry to the areas of central Alabama and northern Florida. A graduate of Columbia College, Chicago, he is Managing Editor of *Pride Magazine* and a freelance writer. He currently resides in Chicago, Illinois.

Greg Herren is the editor of the *Lambda Book Report.* A certified personal trainer, he also writes a monthly fitness column for *Southern Voice* newspaper in Atlanta. He has written for publications such as

Genre, LA Frontiers, The Washington Blade, XY, Instinct, Harvard Gay and Lesbian Review, and *Unzipped Monthly,* among others. His first novel, *Murder in the Rue Dauphine,* will be published in January 2002. He is currently editing an anthology and working on his second novel.

Jeffrey Jasper was born in San Juan, Puerto Rico. He attended school in California and Florida, ending his education at the University of Tampa. He currently lives, works, and writes in Miami. His book reviews regularly appear in *The Lambda Book Report.* This is his fiction debut.

Robin Lippincott was born and raised in central Florida, and is now currently living and working in Boston. A Yaddo alumnus, he is the author of three books—*The Real, True Angel,* a collection of short stories, and the novels *Mr. Dalloway,* and *Our Arcadia.* He is currently at work on a new novel.

Thomas L. Long is an associate professor of English at Thomas Nelson Community College and editor of *Harrington Gay Men's Fiction Quarterly.* His fiction has been published in *Blithe House Quarterly* and in *Rebel Yell 1.*

Durrell Mackey was born in Martinez, California. He has lived in Memphis intermittently and now makes his home in the San Francisco Bay area. *Unfinished Business* is his first published story. He is currently at work on a novel, *The Song of a Manchild.*

Jeff Mann grew up in southwest Virginia and southern West Virginia. Currently he teaches Appalachian Studies and creative writing at Virginia Tech. He has published in *The Laurel Review, Antietam Review, Poet Lore, Appalachian Heritage, The Hampden-Sydney Poetry Review, Spoon River Poetry Review,* and *Prairie Schooner.* His collection *Bliss* won the 1997 Stonewall Chapbook Competition. *Mountain Fireflies* won the 1999 Poetic Matrix Chapbook Series, and *Flint Shards from Sussex* won the First Annual Gival Press Chapbook Competition. His collection of essays, *Edge,* is currently making the rounds for editorial review.

Eugene M. McAvoy was raised in Tulsa, Oklahoma, and is currently an instructor of English at Old Dominion University (ODU) in Norfolk, Virginia. He is now working on his first novel, *All That Becomes a Man.* His nonfiction works have appeared in *UpBeat* and *Homecoming* magazines, and his poetry in *Our Own Community Press,*

PoeTalk, and *The Ebbing Tide.* This is his first fiction credit, though another will appear shortly in *The Harrington Gay Men's Fiction Quarterly.* Eugene lives with Marc, his partner of ten years, in Portsmouth, Virginia.

Kelly McQuain, a West Virginia native now living in Philadelphia, is the only writer to win *The Philadelphia City Paper Writing Award* in both poetry and fiction. His stories have appeared in *The Philadelphia Inquirer Magazine, Harrington Gay Men's Fiction Quarterly, The James White Review, Kansas Quarterly/Arkansas Review, The Sycamore Review, Men on Men 2000,* and *Best American Erotica 1999.* His poetry and nonfiction have appeared in *American Writing, Obsessed: A Flesh and the Word Collection, Lambda Book Report,* and *Journal of Gay, Lesbian, and Bisexual Studies.*

Marshall Moore, a North Carolina native, now lives in the San Francisco Bay Area. His work has appeared or is forthcoming in various journals and anthologies, among them *The Ghost of Carmen Miranda, Of the Flesh: Dangerous New Fiction, Space, and Time, Harrington Gay Men's Fiction Quarterly,* and *Suspect Thoughts.* His first novel, *The Concrete Sky,* is inching toward publication.

Felice Picano has written twenty books, including his recent novel, *Onyx,* from which an excerpt appears in this anthology. Despite originally coming from New York and currently living in California, in this editor's opinion, he has created some of the most perceptive and resonating portraits of Southern gay men in a variety of his works. Ever challenging, ever changing, Felice Picano is a modern master of literary fiction and a hero to many.

George Singer has been a playwright with an MFA from the Iowa Playwrights' workshop. His plays have been performed in London, Washington, DC, San Francisco, and New York. He also wrote the screenplay for a short film, *Assassination,* which won second place in the International Lesbian and Gay Film Festival in San Francisco. His short story *The Preacher's Son* was included in *Rebel Yell 1.*

John Michael Trumbo is a fiction writer and associate creative director for an advertising agency in Alexandria, Virginia. His work has appeared in *Christopher Street* as well as *Rebel Yell 1.* He has also been featured in *Harrington Gay Men's Fiction Quarterly.*

Martin Wilson was born in Tuscaloosa, Alabama, and was educated at Vanderbilt University and the University of Florida. In 1997, he won a *Transatlantic Review* award from the Henfield Foundation. His short stories have appeared in *Virgin Fiction 2* and *Pieces: A Collection of New Voices*. His book reviews are published regularly in the *Austin Chronicle* and the *Lambda Book Report*. He currently lives in Austin, Texas.

Gerard Wozek won the Second Annual Gival Press Poetry Prize for his book *Dervish*. His short fiction has appeared in numerous journals and anthologies, including *Harrington Gay Men's Fiction Quarterly* and *Erotic Travel Tales*. His poetry videos have been viewed around the world and his most recent effort, *Elemental Reels,* will showcase at *Planet Out*'s online Web site cinema. He teaches creative writing at Robert Morris College in Chicago.

Christopher Wynn is a native Texan who is often accused of not sounding Southern enough. He currently lives in New York City. He is a popular commentator for National Public Radio's *Weekend Edition* and a contributing editor and writer for *HERO Magazine*. Wynn's essays and articles also appear in publications ranging from the *Dallas Morning News* to the *Las Vegas Review Journal*.